Sources of
THE MAKING OF THE WEST

PEOPLES AND CULTURES

A CONCISE HISTORY

Volume II: Since 1340

Sources of
THE MAKING OF THE WEST

PEOPLES AND CULTURES

A CONCISE HISTORY

Second Edition

Volume II: Since 1340

KATHARINE J. LUALDI
University of Southern Maine

BEDFORD/ST. MARTIN'S   Boston   ◆   New York

For Bedford/St. Martin's

Publisher for History: Mary V. Dougherty
Executive Editor: Katherine Meisenheimer
Director of Development for History: Jane Knetzger
Developmental Editor: Sara Wise
Senior Production Supervisor: Dennis J. Conroy
Executive Marketing Manager: Jenna Bookin Barry
Project Management: DeMasi Design and Publishing Services
Text Design: Wanda Kossak
Cover Design: Billy Boardman
Cover Art: Boris M. Kustodiev, *Shrovetide, 1919.* Courtesy of Smithsonian Institute
    Traveling Exhibition Service. The Brodsky Museum, St. Petersburg.
Composition: LinMark Design
Printing and Binding: RR Donnelley & Sons Company

President: Joan E. Feinberg
Editorial Director: Denise B. Wydra
Director of Marketing: Karen Melton Soeltz
Director of Editing, Design, and Production: Marcia Cohen
Manager, Publishing Services: Emily Berleth

Library of Congress Control Number: 2006923856

Manufactured in the United States of America.

2 1 0 9 8
f e

For information, write: Bedford/St. Martin's, 75 Arlington Street, Boston, MA 02116
(617-399-4000)

ISBN-10: 0-312-41694-6
ISBN-13: 978-0-312-41694-2

Acknowledgments
Acknowledgments and copyrights are continued at the back of the book on pages 245–48, which constitute an extension of the copyright page.

It is a violation of the law to reproduce these selections by any means whatsoever without the written permission of the copyright holder.

Preface

COMPILED SPECIFICALLY TO accompany *The Making of the West: Peoples and Cultures, A Concise History,* second edition, *Sources of The Making of the West* is intended to help instructors bring the history of Western civilization to life for their students. This collection—newly expanded to five documents per chapter—is organized to parallel the chapters in *The Making of the West,* and thereby offer instructors varied opportunities to ignite a dialogue in the classroom between the past and present. With this goal in mind, I have added a broad range of new sources, both written and visual, to complement the thematic and chronological framework of the textbook. The intellectual, emotional, and visual landscapes of people living at the time enrich facts and chronology, revealing that the study of history is not fixed, but is an ongoing process of evaluation and interpretation.

The criteria governing the selection of sources reflect historians' changing understanding of Western civilization. Although the collection includes traditional political sources, these views are broadened by less conventional documents illuminating not only social and cultural life but also Europe's increasing interconnectedness with the world beyond its borders. The voices of women and minorities were also granted a special place in the selection process because of their crucial and often underappreciated role in shaping the course of Western history both from within and outside the corridors of power. In Volume II, Chapter 16, for instance, students can hear the collective voice of the National Assembly as it launched the French Revolution (Document 2) alongside that of female political activist Olympe de Gouges (Document 3).

Of course asking the right questions and finding the right answers lie at the heart of "doing" history. For this reason, this edition of *Sources of The Making of the West* begins with a new introduction on how to interpret written and visual primary sources that leads students step by step through the process of historical analysis. It opens with a brief overview of what this process entails, followed by an extended discussion of the process at work in the analysis of a source drawn specifically from this collection. I adopted this integrated approach for the introduction to help students move easily from abstract concepts to concrete examples. As a result, the introduction does not rely on telling students what to do but rather on showing them how to do it for themselves based on the raw data of history.

The inclusion of visual primary sources in this second edition adds an exciting new dimension to students' ability to see and interpret the past. These documents visually enrich traditional written documents while challenging students to read the past in new ways. Along with training their minds to analyze texts for meaning, students will learn to view images and their spatial arrangement as an equally valuable window into the past. Examples range from a Roman blueprint (Chapter 5), to a photograph of young victims of the Vietnam War (Chapter 23), to a political cartoon (Chapter 24). Throughout the collection, I chose written and nonwritten sources that work well together to elucidate important events and opinions of a specific historical era.

Each source was also selected based on its accessibility and appeal to students. When necessary, I have carefully edited documents—without impairing the documents' overall sense and tone—to speak to specific themes. I have also included documents of varying lengths to increase their utility for both short class exercises and outside writing assignments.

To assist students with their journey into the past, I have revised the chapter summaries to situate the sources within their broader historical context and address their relationship to one another. An explanatory headnote accompanies each source to provide fundamental background information on the author or artist and the source while highlighting its significance. Revised and expanded discussion questions help students examine key points and issues in greater depth. Finally, each chapter concludes with new comparative questions intended to encourage students to see both the harmony and discordance among the sources. Although these editorial features intentionally strengthen the coherence of each chapter as a unit, they also allow instructors to choose sources and questions that best suit their specific goals and methods.

Acknowledgments

Many people deserve thanks for helping to bring this second edition to fruition. First among them are the authors of *The Making of the West,* Lynn Hunt, Thomas Martin, Barbara Rosenwein, R. Po-chia Hsia, and Bonnie Smith. Many thanks as well to the instructors who provided valuable insights and suggestions when I revised the second edition of *Sources of The Making of the West:* Alexandra Cuffel, University of Massachusetts; Patricia Franz, John Jay College; James Jaffe, University of Wisconsin–Whitewater; Kathleen Kamerick, University of Iowa; Michael Kulikowski, University of Tennessee, Knoxville; Eileen Lyon, State University of New York at Fredonia; Michael Maher, St. Louis University; Shannon McSheffrey, Concordia University; Joelle Neulander, The Citadel; Justin Pettegrew, Loyola University Chicago; Jeff Plaks, University of Central Oklahoma; and Dakota Hamilton, Humboldt State University. I would also like to thank Larissa Juliet Taylor at Colby College and also Christine Pennypacker, who was my undergraduate research assistant at Colby College while I was a visiting professor there, for their help and encouragement. I also owe a huge debt of gratitude to Ashley Waddell for her invaluable assistance in selecting and editing many of the excellent new sources included in Volume II, and to Jilana Ordman for reviewing the selections so carefully and providing helpful suggestions.

Introduction: Working with Historical Sources

THE LONG HISTORY of Western civilization encompasses a broad range of places and cultures. Textbooks provide an essential chronological and thematic framework for understanding the formation of the West as a cultural and geographical entity. Yet the process of historical inquiry extends beyond textbook narratives into the thoughts, words, images, and experiences of people living at the time. Primary sources expose this world so that you can observe, analyze, and interpret the past as it unfolds before you. History is thus not a static collection of facts and dates. Rather, it is an ongoing attempt to make sense of the past and its relationship to the present through the lens of both written and visual primary sources.

Sources of The Making of the West, A Concise History, second edition, provides this lens for you, with a wide range of engaging documents—from an Egyptian chronicle to a political cartoon to firsthand accounts of student revolts. When combined, the sources reflect historians' growing appreciation of the need to examine Western civilization from different conceptual angles—political, social, cultural, economic—and geographic viewpoints. The composite picture that emerges reveals a variety of historical experiences that shaped each era both from within and outside of Europe's borders. Furthermore, the documents here demonstrate that the most historically significant of these experiences are not always those of people in formal positions of power. Men and women from all walks of life have influenced the course of Western history.

The written and visual sources in this reader were selected with an eye toward their ability not only to capture the multifaceted dimensions of the past but also to ignite your intellectual curiosity. Each document is a unique product of human endeavor and as such is often colored by the personal concerns, biases, and objectives of the author or the artist. Among the most exciting challenges facing you is to sift through such nuances for what they reveal about the source and its links to the broader historical context.

INTERPRETING WRITTEN SOURCES

Understanding a written document and its connection to larger historical issues depends on knowing which questions to ask and how to find the right answers. The first step in this process of discovery is to identify who wrote the source and when and where it was written. This basic information will allow you to situate the document and its author within a specific geographical and chronological context. With this basic groundwork laid, you should then consider the document's type and its intended audience. The answers to these questions will guide you to a deeper level of analysis: What are the main points of the document? What does it reveal about the society in which the document was created? As you work through each question, you will progress from identifying basic facts contained directly within the document to inferring their broader meanings. Thus, at its very heart, the study of primary sources centers on the interplay between "facts" and "interpretation." To help you engage in this interplay, let's examine an actual historical document. Read it carefully, keeping the questions just outlined at the front of your mind. In this way, you will gain insight into this particular text while training yourself how to interpret written primary sources in general.

1
Henry IV
Edict of Nantes
1598

The promulgation of the Edict of Nantes in 1598 by King Henry IV (r. 1589–1610) marked the end of the French Wars of Religion by recognizing French Protestants as a legally protected religious minority. Drawing largely on earlier edicts of pacification, the Edict of Nantes was composed of ninety-two general articles, fifty-six secret articles, and two royal warrants. The two series of articles represented the edict proper and were registered by the highest courts of law in the realm (parlements). *The following excerpts from the general articles reveal the triumph of political concerns over religious conformity on the one hand, and the limitations of religious tolerance in early modern France on the other.*

Henry, By the Grace of God, King of *France,* and *Navarre,* To all Present, and to Come, greeteth. Among the infinite Mercies that God hath pleased to bestow upon us, that most Signal and Remarkable is, his having given us Power and Strength not to yield to the dreadful Troubles, Confusions, and Disorders, which were found at our coming to this Kingdom, divided into so many Parties and Factions, that the most Legitimate was almost the least, enabling us with Constancy in such manner to oppose the Storm, as in the end to surmount it, reducing this Estate to Peace and Rest. . . . For the general difference among our good Subjects, and the particular evils of the soundest parts of the State, we judged might be easily cured, after the Principal cause (the continuation of the Civil Wars) was taken away, in which we have, by the blessing of God, well and happily succeeded, all Hostility and Wars through the Kingdom being now ceased, and we hope he will also prosper us in our other affairs, which remain to be composed, and that by this means we shall arrive at the establishment of a good Peace, with tranquility and rest. . . . Amongst our said affairs . . . one of the principal hath been, the many complaints we received from divers of our Provinces and Catholick Cities, for that

From English text of "The Edict" as in Edmund Everard, *The Great Pressures and Grievances of the Protestants in France,* London, 1681, appendix 4 in Roland Mousnier, *The Assassination of Henry IV,* trans. Joan Spencer (London: Faber and Faber, 1973), 316–25, 333, 343, 347.

the exercise of the Catholick Religion was not universally re-established, as is provided by Edicts or Statutes heretofore made for the Pacification of the Troubles
arising from Religion; as also the Supplications and Remonstrances which have
been made to us by our Subjects of the reformed Religion, as well upon the execution of what hath been granted by the said former Laws, as that they desire to have
some addition for the exercise of their Religion, the liberty of their Consciences
and the security of their Persons and Fortunes; presuming to have just reasons for
desiring some inlargement of Articles, as not being without great apprehensions,
because their Ruine hath been the principal pretext and original foundation of the
late Wars, Troubles, and Commotions. Now not to burden us with too much business at once, as also that the fury of War was not compatible with the establishment of Laws, how good soever they might be, we have hitherto deferred from
time to time giving remedy herein. But now that it hath pleased God to give us a
beginning of enjoying some Rest, we think we cannot imploy our self better, than
to apply to that which may tend to the glory and service of his holy name, and to
provide that he may be adored and prayed unto by all our Subjects: and if it hath
not yet pleased him to permit it to be in one and the same form of Religion, that it
may at the least be with one and the same intention, and with such rules that may
prevent amongst them all troubles and tumults. . . . For this cause . . . we have
upon the whole judged it necessary to give to all our said Subjects one general
Law, Clear, Pure, and Absolute, by which they shall be regulated in all differences
which have heretofore risen among them, or may hereafter rise, wherewith the
one and other may be contented, being framed according as the time requires: and
having had no other regard in this deliberation than solely the Zeal we have to the
service of God, praying that he would henceforward render to all our subjects a
durable and Established peace. . . . We have by this Edict or Statute perpetual and
irrevocable said, declared, and ordained, saying, declaring, and ordaining;

That the memory of all things passed on the one part and the other, since the
beginning of the month of *March,* 1585. Until our coming to the Crown, and also
during the other precedent troubles, and the occasion of the same, shall remain
extinguished and suppressed, as things that had never been. . . .

We prohibit to all our Subjects of what State and Condition soever they be, to
renew the memory thereof, to attaque, resent, injure, or provoke one the other by
reproaches for what is past, under any pretext or cause whatsoever, by disputing,
contesting, quarrelling, reviling, or offending by factious words; but to contain
themselves, and live peaceably together as Brethren, Friends, and fellow-Citizens,
upon penalty for acting to the contrary, to be punished for breakers of Peace, and
disturbers of the public quiet.

We ordain, that the Catholick Religion shall be restored and re-established in
all places, and quarters of this Kingdom and Countrey under our obedience, and
where the exercise of the same hath been intermitted, to be there again, peaceably
and freely exercised without any trouble or impediment. . . .

And not to leave any occasion of trouble and difference among our Subjects,
we have permitted and do permit to those of the Reformed Religion, to live and
dwell in all the Cities and places of this our Kingdom and Countreys under our

obedience, without being inquired after, vexed, molested, or compelled to do any thing in Religion, contrary to their Conscience....

We permit also to those of the said Religion to hold, and continue the Exercise of the same in all the Cities and Places under our obedience, where it hath by them been Established and made public by many and divers times, in the Year 1586, and in 1597, until the end of the Month of *August*....

In like manner the said Exercise may be Established, and re-established in all the Cities and Places where it hath been established, or ought to be by the Statute of Pacification, made in the Year 1577....

As also not to exercise the said Religion in our Court, nor in our Territories and Countries beyond the Mountains, nor in our City of *Paris,* nor within five Leagues of the said City....

We prohibit all Preachers, Readers, and others who speak in public, to use any words, discourse, or propositions tending to excite the People to Sedition; and we enjoin them to contain and comport themselves modestly, and to say nothing which shall not be for the instruction and edification of the Auditors, and maintaining the peace and tranquillity established by us in our said Kingdom....

They [French Protestants] shall also be obliged to keep and observe the Festivals of the Catholick Church, and shall not on the same dayes work, sell, or keep open shop, nor likewise the Artisans shall not work out of their shops, in their chambers or houses privately on the said Festivals, and other dayes forbidden, of any trade, the noise whereof may be heard without by those that pass by, or by the Neighbors....

We ordain, that there shall not be made any difference or distinction upon the account of the said Religion, in receiving Scholars to be instructed in the Universities, Colledges, or Schools, nor of the sick or poor into Hospitals, sick houses or public Almshouses....

We Will and Ordain, that all those of the Reformed Religion, and others who have followed their party, of what State, Quality or Condition soever they be, shall be obliged and constrained by all due and reasonable wayes, and under the penalties contained in the said Edict or Statute relating thereunto, to pay tythes to the Curates, and other Ecclesiasticks, and to all others to whom they shall appertain....

To the end to re-unite so much the better the minds and good will of our Subjects, as is our intention, and to take away all complaints for the future; We declare all those who make or shall make profession of the said Reformed Religion, to be capable of holding and exercising all Estates, Dignities, Offices, and public charges whatsoever....

We declare all Sentences, Judgments, Procedures, Seisures, Sales, and Decrees made and given against those of the Reformed Religion, as well living as dead, from the death of the deceased King *Henry* the Second our most honored Lord and Father in Law, upon the occasion of the said Religion, Tumults and Troubles since happening, as also the execution of the same Judgments and Decrees, from henceforward cancelled, revoked, and annulled....

Those also of the said Religion shall depart and desist henceforward from all Practices, Negotiations, and Intelligences, as well within as without our Kingdom;

and the said Assemblies and Councels established within the Provinces, shall read-ily separate, and also all the Leagues and Associations made or to be made under what pretext soever, to the prejudice of our present Edict, shall be cancelled and annulled, . . . prohibiting most expresly to all our Subjects to make henceforwards any Assesments or Leavy's of Money, Fortifications, Enrolments of men, Congre-gations and Assemblies of other than such as are permitted by our present Edict, and without Arms. . . .

We give in command to the People of our said Courts of Parliaments, Cham-bers of our Courts, and Courts of our Aids, Bayliffs, Chief-Justices, Provosts and other our Justices and Officers to whom it appertains, and to their Leivetenants, that they cause to be read, published, and Registred this present Edict and Ordi-nance in their Courts and Jurisdictions, and the same keep punctually, and the con-tents of the same to cause to be injoyned and used fully and peaceably to all those to whom it shall belong, ceasing and making to cease all troubles and obstructions to the contrary, for such is our pleasure: and in witness hereof we have signed these presents with our own hand; and to the end to make it a thing firm and stable for ever, we have caused to put and indorse our Seal to the same. Given at *Nantes* in the Month of *April* in the year of Grace 1598. and of our Reign the ninth

Signed

HENRY

■ Who wrote this document, when and where?

The "doing" of history depends on historical records, the existence of which in turn depends on the individuals who composed them at a particular time and place with a specific goal in mind. Therefore before you can begin to understand a document and its significance, you need to determine who wrote it and when and where it was written. Although many documents will not answer these questions directly, whereupon you will have to look elsewhere for clues, here the internal ev-idence is clear. The author is Henry IV, king of France and Navarre, who issued the document in the French town of Nantes in 1598. This information will help shape your interpretation, for, as you may have already guessed, the language of docu-ments often reflects their authors' social and/or political status. One of the most obvious examples in this document of Henry IV's status is his use of the first-person plural when referring to himself, a grammatical choice that accentuated his royal stature.

■ What type of document is this?

Because all genres have their own defining characteristics, identifying the type of document at hand is vital to elucidating its meaning. In this source, you do not have to look far for an answer. Henry IV describes the document as an "edict," "statute," and "ordinance." These designations reveal the public and official nature of the document, echoing their use in society today. Think of the statute of limita-tions governing the prosecution of certain crimes or city ordinances prohibiting public nudity. Even if you do not know exactly what an edict, statute, or ordinance meant in late sixteenth-century terms, the document itself points the way: "we

[Henry IV] have upon the whole judged it necessary to give to all our said Subjects one general Law, Clear, Pure, and Absolute. . . ." Now you know that the document is a body of law issued by King Henry IV in 1598, which helps to explain its formality as well as the predominance of legal language.

■ Who is the intended audience of the document?

The type or genre of a source often goes hand in hand with the intended audience. For instance, popular songs in the vernacular are designed to reach people across the socioeconomic spectrum whereas papal bulls written in Latin are directed to a tiny, educated, and predominantly male elite. Moreover, an author often crafts the style and content of a source to appeal to a particular audience and to enhance the effectiveness of his or her message. Henry IV begins by addressing "all Present," which, when combined with the edict's formality and legal language, suggests his audience is some form of political and/or legal body. The final paragraph supports this conclusion. Here Henry IV commands the "People of our said Courts" to register and implement the edict.

Reading between the lines, you can detect a mixture of power and dependency in Henry IV's tone. Look carefully at his verb choices: *prohibit, ordain, will, declare, command.* Each of these verbs casts Henry IV as the leader and his audience as his followers. This strategy was essential because without the courts' compliance, an edict would be nothing but empty words. Imagine for a moment that Henry IV was not the king of France but rather a soldier writing a letter to his wife or a merchant preparing a contract. In either case, the language chosen would have been changed to suit the audience. Thus, identifying the relationship between author and audience can help you to understand both what the document does and does not say.

■ What are the main points of this document?

All primary sources contain stories — whether in numbers, words, and/or images. Before you can begin to analyze their meanings, you need to have a good command of a document's main points. For this reason, while reading you should mark words, phrases, and passages that strike you as particularly important to create visual and mental markers that will help you navigate the document. Don't worry about mastering all of the details; you can work through them later once you have sketched out the basic content. The preamble of this source makes your job somewhat easier because it explains why the edict was issued in the first place: to replace the "dreadful Troubles, Confusions, and Disorders" in France with "one general Law, Clear, Pure, and Absolute, by which they [our said subjects] shall be regulated in all differences which have heretofore risen among them. . . ." But what differences specifically? Even with no knowledge of the circumstances surrounding the formulation of the edict, you would notice the numerous references to "the Catholick Religion," "the reformed Religion," and "the said religion." With this in mind, read the preamble again.

Here we learn that Henry IV had received complaints and supplications from French Catholics and Protestants ("those of the reformed Religion") regarding the exercise of their respective religions. Furthermore, as the text continues, since "it hath pleased God to give us a beginning of enjoying some Rest, we think we cannot imploy our self better, than to apply to that which may tend to the glory and service of his holy name . . . and if it hath not yet pleased him to permit it [France] to be in one and the same form of Religion, that it may at the least be with one and the same intention, and with such rules that may prevent amongst them [our subjects] all troubles and tumults. . . ." Now the details of the document fall into place. Each of the articles addresses specific "rules" governing the legal rights and obligations of French Catholics and Protestants, ranging from where they could worship to where they could work.

■ Why was this document written?

The simplicity of this question masks the complexity of the possible answers. Historical records are never created in a vacuum; they were produced for a reason, whether public or private, pragmatic or fanciful. Sometimes a source will state outright why it was created, as is the case with the Edict of Nantes. Yet with or without such direct cues, you should look for less obvious signs of the author's intent and strategies for success, as reflected in word choice, for example, or by the way in which a point is communicated. As we have already seen, Henry IV relied on the written word to convey information and, at the same time, to express his "power" and "strength." The legalistic and formal nature of the edict aided him in this effort. Yet, as Henry IV knew all too well, the gap between law and action could be large, indeed. Thus Henry IV compiled the edict not simply to tell people what to do but to persuade them to do it by delineating the terms of religious coexistence point by point and presenting them as the best safeguard against the return of religious war.

■ What does this document reveal about the particular society and period in question?

This question strikes at the heart of historical analysis and interpretation. Whether intentionally or not, every source opens a window onto its author and time period. Often your view through this window will be obscured, but it is important, and fascinating, to look as closely as possible. Perhaps the most striking thing about the Edict of Nantes is what it reveals about the role of religion in society at the time. Our contemporary notion of the separation of church and state had no place in the world of Henry IV and his subjects. As he proclaims in the opening lines, he was king "[b]y the Grace of God" who had given him "Power" and "Strength." Furthermore, you might stop to consider why religious differences were the subject of royal legislation in the first place. Note Henry IV's statement that "if it hath not yet pleased him to permit it [France] to be in one and the same form of Religion, that it may at the least be with one and the same intention. . . ." What does this suggest about sixteenth-century attitudes toward religious difference and tolerance? You cannot answer this question simply by reading the document in black-and-white terms; you need to look beyond the words and between the lines to draw out the document's broader meanings.

INTERPRETING VISUAL SOURCES

Historians do not rely on written records alone to reconstruct the past; they also turn to nonwritten sources, which are equally varied and rich. Historians have reconstructed the material dimensions of everyday life in centuries long past by drawing on archeological evidence, for example; still others have used church sculpture to explore popular religious beliefs. This book includes a range of pictorial representations to enliven your view of history while enhancing your interpretive skills. Interpreting a visual document is very much like interpreting a nonvisual one. You begin with a set of questions similar to the ones you have already applied to the Edict of Nantes, and move from there to a more complex level of interpretation. With this goal in mind, start by identifying the artist or creator, what type of image it is, and when and where it was produced. Because many pictorial representations provide little explicit guidance in this respect, the headnotes accompanying each image will help you to piece together this basic information. You can then consider who the intended viewers were, and what message the image is trying to convey. Since artists use images, color, and space to communicate with their audience, you must train your eyes to look for visual rather than verbal cues. Here it is important to evaluate all of the features of a particular image as well as the relationship among them. In doing so, you can better understand the image on its own terms as well as the ways in which it speaks to the broader historical context.

CONCLUSION

Through your analysis of historical sources, you will not only learn details about the world in which the sources were created but also become an active contributor to our understanding of these details' broader significance. Written documents and pictorial representations don't just "tell" historians what happened; they require them to step into their own imaginations as they strive to reconstitute the past. In this regard, historians' approach is exactly that described here: They determine the basics of the source — who created it and when and where — as a springboard for increasingly complex levels of analysis. Each level builds on the other, just like rungs on a ladder. If you take the time to climb each rung in sequence, you will be able to master the content of a source and to use it to bring history to life. The written and visual primary documents included in this second edition of Sources of The Making of the West, A Concise History will allow you to participate firsthand in the process of historical inquiry by exploring the people, places, and sights of the past, and how they shaped their world and continue to shape ours today.

Contents

11

Crisis and Renaissance, 1340–1500

CURRENTS OF BOTH CRISIS and renewal swept through medieval society in the years 1340–1500. On the one hand, throughout the fourteenth century Europeans faced a myriad of challenges, from pestilence to war to rebellions. On the other, the city-states of the northern Italian peninsula helped to spark a period of great creativity that historians often refer to as the Renaissance, which reached its peak in the 1400s. The documents in this chapter capture these twin themes, beginning with contemporary accounts of the catastrophic effects of the Black Death and the search for scapegoats, though many people viewed the plague as divine punishment. In its wake, the nobility sought to keep the people "in their place," adding restrictions and taxes that led to rebellions across Europe, including the English Peasants' Revolt of 1381, described in Document 2. At the same time, however, men of the upper classes in Italy defined themselves self-consciously as living in new times. For such men and a few women, this was a time of rebirth, distinct from what they viewed as the barbarism of a millennium and closer to the values and styles of antiquity. It was defined by the *studia humanitatis* (roughly, the liberal arts), from which the nineteenth-century term *humanism* derived. The third document illustrates the application and possibilities of humanism, while the fourth document demonstrates that the realities of Italian life often did match the ideals. The final source, by a Portuguese chronicler, details the quest for new lands and knowledge, which was an outward, geographical expression of the intellectual and cultural discoveries of the Renaissance.

1.
The Black Death
Fourteenth Century

Few events in history have had such a shattering impact on every aspect of society as the plague, which reached Europe in 1347. The Black Death decimated a society

From Rosemary Horrox, ed. and trans., *The Black Death* (Manchester: Manchester University Press, 1994), 16–21, 23, 207, 208, 219–22.

already weakened by a demographic crisis, famines, and climatic disasters. It is esti-
mated that one-third of Europe's population died in the first wave of plague, which
was followed by repeated outbreaks. Some cities may have lost over half their people
in 1347–1348 alone. Though the devastation was social, psychological, economic, po-
litical, and even artistic, many historians believe that in the long term the plague led
to significant changes and even improvements in Western life. The following docu-
ments describe the arrival of the plague in various places and responses to it, includ-
ing searches for its cause and people on whom to fix blame. The plague ultimately pre-
cipitated much of the crisis that characterized the fourteenth century.

From Gabriele de' Mussis (d. 1356), a Lawyer in Piacenza

In 1346, in the countries of the East, countless numbers of Tartars and Saracens
were struck down by a mysterious illness which brought sudden death. . . . An
eastern settlement under the rule of the Tartars called Tana, which lay to the north
of Constantinople and was much frequented by Italian merchants, was totally
abandoned after an incident there which led to its being besieged and attacked by
hordes of Tartars who gathered in a short space of time. The Christian merchants,
who had been driven out by force, were so terrified of the power of the Tartars
that, to save themselves and their belongings, they fled in an armed ship to Caffa,
a settlement in the same part of the world which had been founded long ago by
the Genoese.

Oh God! See how the heathen Tartar races, pouring together from all sides,
suddenly invested the city of Caffa and besieged the trapped Christians there for
almost three years. There, hemmed in by an immense army, they could hardly
draw breath, although food could be shipped in, which offered them some hope.
But behold, the whole army was affected by a disease which overran the Tartars
and killed thousands upon thousands every day. It was as though arrows were
raining down from heaven to strike and crush the Tartars' arrogance. All medical
advice and attention was useless; the Tartars died as soon as the signs of disease
appeared on their bodies: swellings in the armpit or groin caused by coagulating
humors, followed by a putrid fever.

The dying Tartars, stunned and stupefied by the immensity of the disaster
brought about by the disease, and realizing that they had no hope of escape, lost
interest in the siege. But they ordered corpses to be placed in catapults and lobbed
into the city in the hope that the intolerable stench would kill everyone inside.
What seemed like mountains of dead were thrown into the city, and the Christians
could not hide or flee or escape from them, although they dumped as many of the
bodies as they could in the sea. And soon the rotting corpses tainted the air and
poisoned the water supply, and the stench was so overwhelming that hardly one in
several thousand was in a position to flee the remains of the Tartar army. Moreover, one infected man could carry the poison to others, and infect people and
places with the disease by look alone. No one knew, or could discover, a means of
defense.

Thus almost everyone who had been in the East, or in the regions to the south and north, fell victim to sudden death after contracting this pestilential disease, as if struck by a lethal arrow which raised a tumor on their bodies. The scale of the mortality and the form which it took persuaded those who lived, weeping and lamenting, through the bitter events of 1346 to 1348—the Chinese, Indians, Persians, Medes, Kurds, Armenians, Cilicians, Georgians, Mesopotamians, Nubians, Ethiopians, Turks, Egyptians, Arabs, Saracens and Greeks (for almost all the East has been affected) that the last judgment had come. . . .

As it happened, among those who escaped from Caffa by boat were a few sailors who had been infected with the poisonous disease. Some boats were bound for Genoa, others went to Venice and to other Christian areas. When the sailors reached these places and mixed with the people there, it was as if they had brought evil spirits with them: every city, every settlement, every place was poisoned by the contagious pestilence. . . .

Scarcely one in seven of the Genoese survived. In Venice, where an inquiry was held into the mortality, it was found that more than 70% of the people had died, and that within a short period 20 out of 24 excellent physicians had died. The rest of Italy, Sicily and Apulia and the neighboring regions maintain that they have been virtually emptied of inhabitants. The people of Florence, Pisa and Lucca, finding themselves bereft of their fellow residents, emphasize their losses. The Roman Curia at Avignon, the provinces on both sides of the Rhône, Spain, France, and the Empire cry up their griefs and disasters—all of which makes it extraordinarily difficult for me to give an accurate picture.

By contrast, what befell the Saracens can be established from trustworthy accounts. In the city of Babylon alone (the heart of the Sultan's power), 480,000 of his subjects are said to have been carried off by the disease in less than three months in 1348—and this is known from the Sultan's register which records the names of the dead, because he receives a gold bezant for each person buried. . . .

I am overwhelmed, I can't go on. Everywhere one turns there is death and bitterness to be described. The hand of the Almighty strikes repeatedly, to greater and greater effect. The terrible judgment gains power as time goes by.

FROM HERMAN GIGAS, A FRANCISCAN FRIAR IN GERMANY, WHOSE ACCOUNT GOES UNTIL 1349

In 1347 there was such a great pestilence and mortality throughout almost the whole world that in the opinion of well-informed men scarcely a tenth of mankind survived. The victims did not linger long, but died on the second or third day. . . . Some say that it was brought about by the corruption of the air; others that the Jews planned to wipe out all the Christians with poison and had poisoned wells and springs everywhere. And many Jews confessed as much under torture: that they had bred spiders and toads in pots and pans, and had obtained poison from overseas; and that not every Jew knew about this, only the more powerful ones, so that it would not be betrayed. . . . [M]en say that bags full of poison were found in many wells and springs.

FROM HEINRICH TRUCHESS, A FORMER PAPAL CHAPLAIN AND CANON OF CONSTANCE

The persecution of the Jews began in November 1348, and the first outbreak in Germany was at Sölden, where all the Jews were burnt on the strength of a rumor that they had poisoned wells and rivers, as was afterwards confirmed by their own confessions and also by the confessions of Christians whom they had corrupted.... Within the revolution of one year, that is from All Saints [1 November] 1348 until Michaelmas [29 September] 1349 all the Jews between Cologne and Austria were burnt and killed for this crime, young men and maidens and the old along with the rest. And blessed be God who confounded the ungodly who were plotting the extinction of his church.

FROM THE COUNCILLORS OF COLOGNE TO CONRAD VON WINTERTHUR TO THE BÜRGERMEISTER AND COUNCILLORS OF STRASSBURG ON 12 JANUARY 1349

Very dear friends, all sorts of rumors are now flying about against Judaism and the Jews prompted by this unexpected and unparalleled mortality of Christians, which, alas, has raged in various parts of the world and is still woefully active in several places. Throughout our city, as in yours, many-winged Fame clamors that this mortality was initially caused, and is still being spread, by the poisonings of springs and wells, and that the Jews must have dropped poisonous substances into them. When it came to our knowledge that serious charges had been made against the Jews in several small towns and villages on the basis of this mortality, we sent numerous letters to you and to other cities and towns to uncover the truth behind these rumors, and set a thorough investigation in train....

    If a massacre of the Jews were to be allowed in the major cities (something which we are determined to prevent in our city, if we can, as long as the Jews are found to be innocent of these or similar actions) it could lead to the sort of outrages and disturbances which would whip up a popular revolt among the common people—and such revolts have in the past brought cities to misery and desolation. In any case we are still of the opinion that this mortality and its attendant circumstances are caused by divine vengeance and nothing else. Accordingly we intend to forbid any harassment of the Jews in our city because of these flying rumors, but to defend them faithfully and keep them safe, as our predecessors did—and we are convinced that you ought to do the same.

PAPAL BULL *SICUT JUDEIS* OF CLEMENT VI ISSUED IN JULY 1348

Recently, however, it has been brought to our attention by public fame—or more accurately, infamy—that numerous Christians are blaming the plague with which God, provoked by their sins, has afflicted the Christian people, on poisonings carried out by the Jews at the instigation of the devil, and that out of their own hot-headedness they have impiously slain many Jews, making no exception for age or sex; and that the Jews have been falsely accused of such outrageous behavior. . . . [I]t cannot be true that the Jews, by such a heinous crime, are the cause or occasion of the plague, because throughout many parts of the world the same plague, by the hidden judgment of God, has afflicted and afflicts the Jews themselves and many other races who have never lived alongside them.

We order you by apostolic writing that each of you upon whom this charge has been laid, should straitly command those subject to you, both clerical and lay . . . not to dare (on their own authority or out of hot-headedness) to capture, strike, wound or kill any Jews or expel them from their service on these grounds; and you should demand obedience under pain of excommunication.

■ Discussion Questions

1. What explanations are offered for the onset of plague? What is the understanding of the disease process?

2. What do the accounts by Mussis and the bull of Pope Clement VI have in common? How did different groups of people react to the plague?

3. Why might the city councillors or the pope have attempted to protect the Jews? Why was such protection of no avail in many places? Why might some Jews have confessed?

2.
Thomas Walsingham
Peasant Rebels in London
1381

Thomas Walsingham (d. 1422) was the Benedictine author of six chronicles, including a portion of the famous "St. Alban's Chronicle." Although little is known of his life, his description of the Peasants' Revolt is a riveting and, by the standards of the time, reliable account of events early in the reign of King Richard II (r. 1377–1399). The revolt, one of the largest of its kind, was a response to noble demands on a population experiencing declining incomes as a result of the Black Death, the costs of war with France, and the realm's poor administration. The poll tax imposed on adult males in 1380 sparked a rebellion, led by Wat Tyler (d. 1381) and preacher John Ball, of townsmen and peasants in southeastern England. The larger causes can be found in the final breakdown of serfdom—a breakdown vigorously opposed by a nobility in decline and supported by a peasantry with new opportunities brought about by the scarcity of laborers.

From Thomas Walsingham, "Historia Anglicana I," in R. B. Dobson, *The Peasants' Revolt of 1381*, 2d ed. (London: Macmillan, 1983), 169–76, 178–81.

On the next day [Corpus Christi] the rebels went in and out of London and talked with the simple commons of the city about the acquiring of liberty and the seizure of the traitors, especially the duke of Lancaster whom they hated most of all; and in a short time easily persuaded all the poorer citizens to support them in their conspiracy. And when, later that day, the sun had climbed higher and grown warm and the rebels had tasted various wines and expensive drinks at will and so had become less drunk than mad (for the great men and common people of London had left all their cellars open to the rebels), they began to debate at length about the traitors with the more simple men of the city. Among other things they assembled and set out for the Savoy, the residence of the duke of Lancaster, unrivaled in splendor and nobility within England, which they then set to the flames. . . . This news so delighted the common people of London that, thinking it particularly shameful for others to harm and injure the duke before themselves, they immediately ran there like madmen, set fire to the place on all sides and so destroyed it. In order that the whole community of the realm should know that they were not motivated by avarice, they made a proclamation that no one should retain for his own use any object found there under penalty of execution. Instead they broke the gold and silver vessels, of which there were many at the Savoy, into pieces with their axes and threw them into the Thames or the sewers. They tore the golden cloths and silk hangings to pieces and crushed them underfoot; they ground up rings and other jewels inlaid with precious stones in small mortars, so that they could never be used again. . . .

After these malicious deeds, the rebels destroyed the place called the "Temple Bar" (in which the more noble apprentices of the law lived) because of their anger . . . and there many muniments which the lawyers were keeping in custody were consumed by fire. Even more insanely they set fire to the noble house of the Hospital of St. John at Clerkenwell so that it burnt continuously for the next seven days. . . .

For who would ever have believed that such rustics, and most inferior ones at that, would dare (not in crowds but individually) to enter the chamber of the king and of his mother with their filthy sticks; and undeterred by any of the soldiers, to stroke and lay their uncouth and sordid hands on the beards of several most noble knights. Moreover, they conversed familiarly with the soldiers asking them to be faithful to the ribalds and friendly in the future. . . . [They] gained access singly and in groups to the rooms in the Tower, they arrogantly lay and sat on the king's bed while joking; and several asked the king's mother to kiss them. . . . The rebels, who had formerly belonged to the most lowly condition of serf, went in and out like lords; and swineherds set themselves above soldiers. . . .

When the archbishop finally heard the rebels coming, he said to his men with great fortitude: "Let us go with confidence, for it is better to die when it can no longer help to live. At no previous time of my life could I have died in such security of conscience." A little later the executioners entered crying, "Where is that traitor to the kingdom? Where the despoiler of the common people?" . . . [They] dragged the archbishop along the passages by his arms and hood to their fellows once outside the gates on Tower Hill. . . . Words could not be heard among their horrible shrieks but rather their throats sounded with the bleating of sheep, or, to be more accurate, with the devilish voices of peacocks. . . .

Scarcely could the archbishop finish [his] speech before the rebels broke out with the horrible shout that they feared neither an interdict nor the Pope; all that remained for him, as a man false to the community and treasonable to the realm was to submit his neck to the executioners' swords. The archbishop now realized that his death was imminent and inevitable. . . . He was first struck severely but not fatally in the neck. He put his hand to the wound and said: "Ah! Ah! this is the hand of God." As he did not move his hand from the place of sorrow the second blow cut off the top of his fingers as well as severing part of the arteries. But the archbishop still did not die, and only on the eighth blow, wretchedly wounded in the neck and on the head, did he complete what we believe is worthy to be called his martyrdom. . . .

Nor did they show any reverence to any holy places but killed those whom they hated even if they were within churches and in sanctuary. I have heard from a trustworthy witness that thirty Flemings were violently dragged out of the church of the Austin Friars in London and executed in the open street. . . .

On the next day, Saturday 15 June (the feasts of Saints Vitus and Modestus), behold, the men of Kent showed themselves no less persistent in their wicked actions than on the previous day: they continued to kill men and to burn and destroy houses. The king sent messengers to the Kentishmen telling them that their fellows had left to live in peace henceforward and promising that he would give them too a similar form of peace if they would accept it. The rebels' greatest leader was called "Walter Helier" or "Tylere" (for such names had been given to him because of his trade), a cunning man endowed with much sense if he had decided to apply his intelligence to good purposes. . . .

On this the king, although a boy and of tender age, took courage and ordered the mayor of London to arrest Tyler. The mayor, a man of incomparable spirit and bravery, arrested Tyler without question and struck him a blow on the head which hurt him badly. Tyler was soon surrounded by the other servants of the king and pierced by sword thrusts in several parts of his body. His death, as he fell from his horse to the ground, was the first incident to restore to the English knighthood their almost extinct hope that they could resist the commons. . . .

But the king, with marvelous presence of mind and courage for so young a man, spurred his horse towards the commons and rode around them, saying, "What is this, my men? What are you doing? Surely you do not wish to fire on your own king? Do not attack me and do not regret the death of that traitor and ruffian. For I will be your king, your captain and your leader. Follow me into the field where you can have all the things you would like to ask for." . . .

The commons were allowed to spend the night under the open sky. However the king ordered that the written and sealed charter which they had requested should be handed to them in order to avoid more trouble at that time. He knew that Essex was not yet pacified nor Kent settled; and the commons and rustics of both counties were ready to rebel if he failed to satisfy them quickly. . . .

Once they had this charter, the commons returned to their homes. But still the earlier evils by no means ceased.

■ Discussion Questions

1. How does Thomas Walsingham's class and position affect his recording of events? How does he describe the different classes of society?

2. What does the account suggest about economic and political conditions in late fourteenth-century England?

3. How did the rebels choose their targets, both human and material? What were they seeking? Against what were they protesting?

4. What was the rebels' attitude toward religious authority? What might explain their actions in this regard?

3.
Giovanni Pico della Mirandola
Oration on the Dignity of Man
1496

The work of Giovanni Pico della Mirandola (1463–1494), a Neoplatonic thinker and Dominican friar, epitomizes in many ways the philosophical beliefs of humanism. The Oration on the Dignity of Man, *part of a series of nine hundred theses written when Pico was twenty-three, is in many ways a manifesto of the Renaissance. Steeped in both the Aristotelian and Platonic traditions, Pico knew Latin, Greek, Hebrew, and Italian. He was also deeply interested in Hebrew mysticism, pre-Socratic thought, and occult knowledge attributed at the time to a supposed ancient god/teacher, Hermes Trismegistus. The discovery of truth from many different sources is known as syncretism. Not surprisingly, some of Pico's ideas were deemed heretical by Pope Innocent VIII (r. 1484–1492). Although Pico was arrested, he lived under the protection of Lorenzo de' Medici (1449–1492) until he died at the age of thirty-one. The* Oration, *first published in 1496, revolves around the concept of free will—the human ability to choose, for good or ill.*

I have read in the ancient annals of the Arabians, most reverend Fathers, that when asked what on the world's stage could be considered most admirable, Abdala the Saracen answered that there is nothing more admirable to be seen than man. In agreement with this opinion is the saying of Hermes Trismegistus: "What a great miracle, O Asclepius, is man!"

When I had thought over the meaning of these maxims, the many reasons for the excellence of man advanced by many men failed to satisfy me. . . .

At last, it seems to me that I have understood why man is the most fortunate living thing worthy of all admiration and precisely what rank is his lot in the

From Julia Conaway Bondanella and Mark Musa, eds., *The Italian Renaissance Reader* (New York: Meridian, 1987), 180–83.

universal chain of being, a rank to be envied not only by the brutes but even by the stars and by minds beyond this world. It is a matter past faith and extraordinary! ...

God the Father, the supreme Architect, had already built this cosmic home which we behold, this most majestic temple of divinity, in accordance with the laws of a mysterious wisdom. He had adorned the region above the heavens with intelligences, had quickened the celestial spheres with eternal souls and had filled the vile and filthy parts of the lower world with a multitude of animals of every kind. But when the work was completed, the Maker kept wishing that there were someone who could examine the plan of so great an enterprise, who could love its beauty, who could admire its vastness. On that account, when everything was completed, as Moses and Timaeus both testify, He finally took thought of creating man. However, not a single archetype remained from which he might fashion this new creature, not a single treasure remained which he might bestow upon this new son, and not a single seat remained in the whole world in which the contemplator of the universe might sit. All now was complete; all things had been assigned to the highest, the middle, and the lowest orders. But it was not in the nature of the Father's power to fail in this final creative effort, as though exhausted; nor was it in the nature of His wisdom to waver in such a crucial matter through lack of counsel; and it was not in the nature of His Beneficent Love that he who was destined to praise God's divine generosity in regard to others should be forced to condemn it in regard to himself. At last, the Supreme Artisan ordained that the creature to whom He could give nothing properly his own should share in whatever He had assigned individually to the other creatures. He therefore accepted man as a work of indeterminate nature, and placing him in the center of the world, addressed him thus:

"O Adam, we have given you neither a place nor a form nor any ability exclusively your own, so that according to your wishes and your judgment, you may have and possess whatever place, form, or abilities you desire. The nature of all other beings is limited and constrained in accordance with the laws prescribed by us. Constrained by no limits, in accordance with your own free will, in whose hands we have placed you, you shall independently determine the bounds of your own nature. We have placed you at the world's center, from where you may more easily observe whatever is in the world. We have made you neither celestial nor terrestrial, neither mortal nor immortal, so that with honor and freedom of choice, as though the maker and molder of yourself, you may fashion yourself in whatever form you prefer. You shall have the power to degenerate into the inferior forms of life which are brutish; you shall have the power, through your soul's judgment, to rise to the superior orders which are divine." ...

In man alone, at the moment of his creation, the Father placed the seeds of all kinds and the germs of every way of life. Whatever seeds each man cultivates will mature and bear their own fruit in him; if vegetative, he will be like a plant; if sensitive, he will become a brute; if rational, he will become a celestial being; if intellectual, he will be an angel and the son of God. ...

Who would not admire this our chameleon? Or who could admire any other being more greatly than man? Asclepius the Athenian justly says that man was symbolized in the mysteries by the figure of Proteus because of his ability to change his character and transform his nature. This is the origin of those metamorphoses or transformations celebrated among the Hebrews and the Pythagoreans. For the occult theology of the Hebrews sometimes transforms the holy Enoch into an angel of divinity and sometimes transforms other people into other divinities. The Pythagoreans transform impious men into beasts and, if Empedocles is to be believed, even into plants. Echoing this, Mohammed often had this saying on his lips: "He who deviates from divine law becomes a beast," and he was right in saying so. For it is not the bark that makes the beast of burden but its irrational and sensitive soul; neither is it the spherical form which makes the heavens, but their undeviating order; nor is it the freedom from a body which makes the angel but its spiritual intelligence. . . .

Are there any who will not admire man? In the sacred Mosaic and Christian writings, man, not without reason, is sometimes described by the name of "all flesh" and sometimes by that of "every creature," since man molds, fashions, and transforms himself according to the form of all flesh and the character of every creature. For this reason, the Persian Evantes, in describing Chaldean theology, writes that man does not have an inborn and fixed image of himself but many which are external and foreign to him; whence comes the Chaldean saying: "Man is a being of varied, manifold, and inconstant nature."

But why do we reiterate all these things? To the end that from the moment we are born we are born into the condition of being able to become whatever we choose.

■ **Discussion Questions**

1. What, according to Pico, are man's abilities? Why were these abilities and possibilities given to him?

2. What kinds of sources does Pico use to support his ideas? What is their importance as part of his philosophy?

3. Why might the words and ideas Pico used to describe God and how God went about the process of creation have been considered dangerous?

4. What makes this document a "statement" of Renaissance thought?

4.

Bernardino of Siena
An Italian Preacher: Sins against Nature
1380–1444

At the same time that the great orators, civic humanists, and artists of the Renaissance were attempting to distance themselves from the perceived "barbarity" of earlier times,

From Franco Mormando, *The Preacher's Demons: Bernardino of Siena and the Social Underworld of Early Renaissance Italy* (Chicago and London: University of Chicago Press, 1999), 119–20, 124, 128, 130, 138, 139, 147–48, 152.

religion continued to play an enormous role in everyday life. The famous preacher Bernardino of Siena (1380–1444) exemplifies the continuing great importance of religion during this period. One of the most popular preachers of his day, Bernardino was an itinerant Franciscan, canonized only six years after his death. He preached throughout northern Italy and was active in efforts to unify the Roman and Greek churches at the Council of Florence in 1439. His greatest fame, however, came as a preacher of moral reform. Besides discussing the typical subjects one might find in sermons, Bernardino devotes special attention to "problems" he finds in his day, especially sodomy, sorcery, vanity, and the Jews. These excerpts are from several sermons.

Oooo! Have I heard stories. . . . Aooo! Once I was in a certain place where some man had taken as his wife a beautiful young woman. They lived together for six years, and she was still a virgin. That is, she had been with him in all those years in a state of most grave sin against nature. Oh, what disorder, oh, what grievous shame! Ooo, ooo, ooo! Do you know what this poor little thing was reduced to? She was all wasted, pale, pasty, sallow. She begged me for the love of God to help her if I could in any way. She said she had been to the bishop about this matter and even to the mayor; but they answered her that they needed proof of what she was charging. O what ignorance is this to need proof and witnesses for these kinds of things! I'll tell you what is needed: a bonfire, a bonfire. . . .

O ladies, make sure you don't send your sons [where there are sodomites]; send instead your daughters, because there's no danger for them if you send them among such people. They will not be contaminated by anything; and even if they were seized and violated, at least there wouldn't be as much danger and as much sin as there would be [if your sons were violated]. If there is no other way, I would permit it as the lesser evil. . . .

Don't you see that you are showing yourself to be against God, who said to the man and the woman, our first mother and father: "*Crescite et multiplicamini, et replete terram?* Increase and multiply, and fill the earth?" O sodomite of the Devil, what are you doing? It's as if you're saying to God: "I want to spite you; I don't want anyone to be born." . . .

And what do you say? "Oh, it's completely harmless, no one's going to get hurt, he's just a boy, after all." If he were a girl, perhaps you wouldn't be doing this, because she could get herself pregnant this way. And since he can't get pregnant, you're happy and offer up your "flatcake" to the "queen of heaven." And you just keep on doing such things so much that you are provoking the wrath of God; and God, seeing this and all the other vices, is threatening you and says: "My wrath will come down over your head." Do you know what he will do? He will send you wars, plagues, and famines in order to punish the sodomites, so much so that you won't be left with either livestock, or farms or gardens or money or even your very population. In all these ways, God will show his wrath. . . .

They aren't even dry behind the ears and they're already contaminated and sodomites! Just look at them, fathers and mothers, it's astounding: At such a tender age and they're already contaminated by sodomy! . . .

I've heard about those [boys] who paint themselves up and go around bragging about their sodomizers and make it into a profession and incite others to do likewise. . . .

[T]hese types are never satisfied. Oh, woman, take note, if he's trapped in this vice, you'll never be able to satisfy him! He always complains about everything you do, always. When he comes home, he comes in turmoil, with a head full of frenzy, and nothing does he care for the judgment of God or honor in this world. He's always cranky and agitated, he's afraid—he's afraid of falling out of favor with his wicked little boy. . . . He obeys the boy like a servant and does everything he can to grant his wishes. . . .

[In Venice] I saw three things happening together. I saw [the sodomite] placed at the stake, and tied all the way up. [I saw] a keg of pitch, brushwood, and fire, and an executor who set him on fire, and a lot of people, all around, watching. The sodomite felt the smoke and the fire, and he burned to death; the executioner felt only the smoke, and whoever was standing around watching saw nothing but smoke and fire. What this stands for is that: in hell the sodomites will burn with smoke and fire [while] their torturers down there will get the smoke. . . . Those who stand watching [represent] the blessed spirits in paradise who see the punishment of the sodomites and rejoice over it because they see the justice of God shining forth from it.

■ Discussion Questions

1. Why might Bernardino have directed many of his comments to women? How would you compare his views of men and women?

2. Bernardino refers to the "population" at a number of points. To whom is he referring? Why might this have been a concern?

3. How does Bernardino exhibit an increasing repression of sexuality?

5.

Gomes Eanes de Zurara
Chronicle of the Discovery of Guinea
c. 1453

While Italian Renaissance thinkers were rediscovering the ancient past, the fall of Constantinople in 1453 to the Turks, blocking access to trade in the East, led to the so-called Age of Discovery or Exploration. As intellectual horizons expanded, so did geographical ones, sometimes with disastrous consequences for native peoples. In his Discovery of Guinea, official chronicler Zurara (c. 1410–1474) continued the work

From George Kish, ed., *A Source Book in Geography* (Cambridge and London: Harvard University Press, 1978), 295–97.

of his predecessors in writing histories of the kings of Portugal. Recognized as one of the first historiographers to provide an account of the initial exploration of the western coast of Africa, Zurara relied on earlier chroniclers as well as oral reports from Portuguese sailors and soldiers from 1433 to 1448. His chronicle offers information about Prince Henry the Navigator (1394–1460) whose circle at the port of Lagos in southern Portugal comprised astronomers, geographers, and navigators. Henry's desire to find a route to the East led to important advances in technology and geographical knowledge, and ultimately led to the Portuguese slave trade. In the following excerpt, Zurara describes early encounters and descriptions of the people of Guinea and a critique of those who had feared exploration.

HOW THOSE CARAVELS ARRIVED AT THE RIVER OF NILE, AND OF THE GUINEAS THAT THEY TOOK

Now these caravels having passed by the land of Sahara, as hath been said, came in sight of the two palm trees that Dinis Diaz[1] had met with before, by which they understood that they were at the beginning of the land of the Negroes. And at this sight they were glad indeed, and would have landed at once, but they found the sea so rough upon that coast that by no manner of means could they accomplish their purpose. And some of those who were present said afterwards that it was clear from the smell that came off the land how good must be the fruits of that country, for it was so delicious that from the point they reached, though they were on the sea, it seemed to them that they stood in some gracious fruit garden ordained for the sole end of their delight. And if our men showed on their side a great desire of gaining the land, no less did the natives of it show their eagerness to receive them into it; but of the reception they offered I do not care to speak, for according to the signs they made to our men from the first, they did not intend to abandon the beach without very great loss to one side or the other. Now the people of this green land are wholly black, and hence this is called Land of the Negroes, or Land of Guinea. . . . They understood right well that they were close to the river of Nile. . . .

It is well that we should here leave these matters at rest for a space and treat of the limits of those lands through the which our people journeyed in the labors of which we have spoken, in order that you may have an understanding of the delusion in which our forefathers ever lived who were affrighted to pass that Cape for fear of those things of which we have told in the beginning of this book; and also that you may see how great praise our Prince deserveth, by bringing their doubts before the presence not only of us who are now living, but also of all others who will be born in the time to come. And because one of the things which they alleged

---

[1]Dinis Diaz had "discovered" Cape Verde, fifteen hundred miles down the African coast, in 1445.

to be a hindrance to the passage into these lands consisted of the very strong currents that were there, on account of which it was impossible for any ship to navigate those seas, you now have a clear knowledge of their former error in that you have seen vessels come and go as free from danger as in any part of the other seas. They further alleged that the lands were all sandy and without any inhabitants, and true it is that in the matter of the sands they were not altogether deceived, but these were not so great as they thought; while as to the inhabitants, you have clearly seen the contrary to be the fact, since you witness the dwellers in those parts each day before your eyes, although their inhabited places are chiefly villages and very few towns. For from the Cape of Bojador to the kingdom of Tunis there will not be in the whole, what with towns and places fortified for defense, as many as fifty. They were no less at fault as regards the depth of the sea, for they had it marked on their charts that the shores were so shallow that at the distance of a league from the land there was only a fathom of water; but this was found not to be so, for the ships have had and have sufficient depth for their management, except for certain shoals; and thus dwellings were made that exist on certain sandbanks, as you will find now in the navigating charts which the Infant caused to be prepared.

In the land of the Negroes there is no walled place save that which they call Oadem, nor are there any settlements except some by the water's edge, of straw houses, the which were emptied of their dwellers by those that went there in the ships of this land. True it is that the whole land is generally peopled, but their mode of living is only in tents and carts, such as we use here when our princes do happen to go on a warlike march, and those who were captured there gave testimony of this, and also John Fernandez, of whom we have already spoken, related much concerning the same. All their principal study and toil is in guarding their flocks, to wit, cows and sheep and goats and camels, and they change their camp almost every day, for the longest they can rest in one spot will be eight days. And some of their chief men possess tame mares, of which they breed horses, though very few.

Their food consisteth for the great part of milk, and sometimes a little meat and the seeds of wild herbs that they gather in those mountains. . . . And those that live by the sea shore eat nothing save fish, and all for the most part without either bread or anything else, except the water that they drink, and they generally eat their fish raw and dried. Their clothing consisteth of a skin vest and breeches of the same, but some of the more honorable wear bournouses; and some preeminent men, who are almost above all the others, have good garments. . . .

The women wear bournouses which are like mantles, with the which they only cover their faces, and by that they think they have covered all their shame, for they leave their bodies quite naked. "For sure," saith he who compiled this history, "this is one of the things by the which one may discern their great bestiality, for if they had some particle of reason they would follow nature, and cover those parts only which by its shewing ought to be covered. . . . And the wives of the most honorable men wear rings of gold in their nostrils and ears, as well as other jewels.

■ Discussion Questions

1. How do the Portuguese first describe the land of Guinea?

2. Although Zurara does not go into detail, how do the native peoples react to the Portuguese? Why might account for their reactions?

3. How does Zurara describe the men and women of Guinea? What characteristics does he single out in an attempt to convince his readers of the native peoples' inferiority?

4. How might this source have been seen as a work of political propaganda for increasingly strong states?

■ Comparative Questions _____

1. What connections can you draw between the plague and the peasant rebellions that swept over Europe during the decades after 1347?

2. Compare the visions of both the human being and the state as described by Pico della Mirandola with those of Bernardino of Siena. In what ways do they differ? How might you account for this difference?

3. One of historian Jacob Burckhardt's chapters in *The Civilization of the Renaissance* is entitled "The Discovery of Man and the World." Based on the documents in this chapter and your understanding of the period, what is "new" about the Renaissance? What could be considered a continuation of medieval ideas?

4. Pico della Mirandola wrote nearly fifty years after Zurara. How might Pico's references to a wide range of sources, many non-Christian, have been affected by Europeans' expanding knowledge of other parts of the world?

12

Struggles over Beliefs, 1500–1648

T HE SIXTEENTH THROUGH the mid-seventeenth centuries were a time of turmoil and change for people from all walks of life, as the following documents illustrate. Despite the ending of the Great Schism in 1417, serious damage had been done to the authority of the Catholic Church. Many within the church tried to institute reforms, but change was slow in coming. Increasing numbers of laymen and women turned to individual avenues of devotion, including an evangelicalism that was given new life with the advent of the printing press. The problems of the church, joined with the spirit and methods of the Renaissance, ushered in a period known as the Reformation, which forever shattered European religious unity. With the possibility of religious choice came violence, fueled by both ecclesiastical and lay leaders' belief that political and social stability depended on religious conformity. As the violence escalated, however, some people argued successfully that peace could come only if state interests took precedence over religious ones. Europeans' views of the earth and heavens also changed because of the rise of new scientific methods and topics of inquiry. At the same time, the lure of traditional beliefs remained strong within communities struggling to make sense of the upheavals occurring around them.

1.
Martin Luther
Freedom of a Christian
1520

German monk Martin Luther's attempt to reform the Catholic Church from within developed into a new branch of Christianity known as Protestantism. After his excommunication by Pope Leo X in 1520, Luther published several treatises that attacked church authority, clerical celibacy, and the sacraments while elucidating his

---

From Martin Luther, *Christian Liberty,* ed. Harold J. Grimm (Philadelphia: Fortress Press, 1957), 6–10.

evangelical theology. He set forth the guiding principles of his beliefs with particular clarity in Freedom of a Christian. *Although originally written in Latin and addressed to the pope, the tract was soon translated into German and widely circulated among Luther's ever-growing number of followers. In the excerpt that follows, Luther defined what became a central tenet of the reform movement: faith in Christ and his promise of salvation is all that a Christian needs to be saved from sin.*

Many people have considered Christian faith an easy thing, and not a few have given it a place among the virtues. They do this because they have not experienced it and have never tasted the great strength there is in faith. It is impossible to write well about it or to understand what has been written about it unless one has at one time or another experienced the courage which faith gives a man when trials oppress him. But he who has had even a faint taste of it can never write, speak, meditate, or hear enough concerning it. It is a living "spring of water welling up to eternal life," as Christ calls it in John 4 [:14].

As for me, although I have no wealth of faith to boast of and know how scant my supply is, I nevertheless hope that I have attained to a little faith, even though I have been assailed by great and various temptations; and I hope that I can discuss it, if not more elegantly, certainly more to the point, than those literalists and subtile disputants have previously done, who have not even understood what they have written. . . .

First, let us consider the inner man to see how a righteous, free, and pious Christian, that is, a spiritual, new, and inner man, becomes what he is. It is evident that no external thing has any influence in producing Christian righteousness or freedom . . . It does not help the soul if the body is adorned with the sacred robes of priests or dwells in sacred places or is occupied with sacred duties or prays, fasts, abstains from certain kinds of food, or does any work that can be done by the body and in the body. . . .

One thing, and only one thing, is necessary for Christian life, righteousness, and freedom. That one thing is the most holy Word of God, the gospel of Christ, as Christ says, John 11 [:25], "I am the resurrection and the life; he who believes in me, though he die, yet shall he live"; and John 8 [:36], "So if the Son makes you free, you will be free indeed"; and Matt. 4 [:4], "Man shall not live by bread alone, but by every word that proceeds from the mouth of God." Let us then consider it certain and firmly established that the soul can do without anything except the Word of God and that where the Word of God is missing there is no help at all for the soul. If it has the Word of God it is rich and lacks nothing since it is the Word of life, truth, light, peace, righteousness, salvation, joy, liberty, wisdom, power, grace, glory, and of every incalculable blessing. . . .

You may ask, "What then is the Word of God, and how shall it be used, since there are so many words of God?" I answer: The Apostle explains this in Romans 1. The Word is the gospel of God concerning his Son, who was made flesh, suffered, rose from the dead, and was glorified through the Spirit who sanctifies. To preach Christ means to feed the soul, make it righteous, set it free, and save it, provided it believes the preaching. Faith alone is the saving and efficacious use of the Word of God . . . Therefore it is clear that, as the soul needs only the Word of God for its life and righteousness, so it is justified by faith alone and not any works . . .

When you have learned this you will know that you need Christ, who suffered and rose again for you so that, if you believe in him, you may through this faith become a new man in so far as your sins are forgiven and you are justified by the merits of another, namely, of Christ alone. . . .

■ Discussion Questions

1. According to Luther, what is faith and where does it come from?

2. How can an individual Christian become a "new man" through such faith?

3. By defining faith alone as essential to salvation, in what ways does Luther undermine basic Catholic teachings?

4. What authority does Luther draw upon to defend his point of view? What does this reveal about the basis of his theology?

2.
St. Ignatius of Loyola
A New Kind of Catholicism
1546, 1549, 1553

The interests of Ignatius of Loyola (1491–1556), born of a Spanish noble family, centered more on chivalry than religion before his serious injury at the Battle of Pamplona in 1520. While recovering, he experienced a conversion when he began reading the only books available to him, The Golden Legend *(about saints' lives) and the* Life of Christ. *After spending time at the monastery of Montserrat, where he devoted himself to prayer, fasting, and self-reflection, he began work on* The Spiritual Exercises, *a manual of discernment for the pilgrim journeying to God. After studying at the University of Paris, Ignatius, Francis Xavier (1506–1552), and other friends made vows of chastity and poverty, determining to travel to Jerusalem. When this became impossible, they went to Italy. The Society of Jesus (the Jesuits), founded by Ignatius and his early companions, was officially recognized by Pope Paul III in 1540 as a new order directly under the papacy. Its spirituality would be expressed most prominently in teaching and missionary work. The following letters of Ignatius reveal a new form of Catholic spiritual expression that was active and apostolic in its orientation. It was less a "response" to Protestantism than a model for Catholic life and work. Along with the works of other early Jesuits, it embodied a new spirit that so many had sought but not found in the late medieval church.*

From Joseph A. Munitiz and Philip Endean, eds. and trans., *Saint Ignatius of Loyola, Personal Writings: Reminiscences, Spiritual Diary, Select Letters, Including the Text of* The Spiritual Exercises (New York: Penguin Books, 1996), 165, 166, 230, 233–34, 257, 259, 262–63.

CONDUCT AT TRENT: ON HELPING OTHERS, 1546

Our main aim [to God's greater glory] during this undertaking at Trent is to put into practice (as a group that lives together in one appropriate place) preaching, confessions and readings, teaching children, giving good example, visiting the poor in the hospitals, exhorting those around us, each of us according to the different talents he may happen to have, urging on as many as possible to greater piety and prayer....

In their preaching they should not refer to points of conflict between Protestants and Catholics, but simply exhort all to upright conduct and to ecclesiastical practice, urging everyone to full self-knowledge and to greater knowledge and love of their Creator and Lord, with frequent allusions to the Council. At the end of each session, they should (as has been mentioned) lead prayers for the Council.

They should do the same with readings as with sermons, trying their best to influence people with greater love of their Creator and Lord as they explain the meaning of what is read; similarly, they should lead their hearers to pray for the Council....

They should spend some time, as convenient, in the elementary teaching of youngsters, depending on the means and disposition of all involved, and with more or less explanation according to the capacity of the pupils.... Let them visit the almshouses once or twice a day, at times that are convenient for the patients' health, hearing confessions and consoling the poor, if possible taking them something, and urging them to the sort of prayers mentioned above for confession. If there are three of ours in Trent, each should visit the poor at least once every four days.

When they are urging people in their dealings with them to go to confession and communion, to say mass frequently, to undertake the Spiritual Exercises and other good works, they should also be urging them to pray for the Council.

It was said that there are advantages in being slow to speak and measured in one's statements when doctrinal definitions are involved. The opposite is true when one is urging people to look to their spiritual progress. Then one should be eloquent and ready to talk, full of sympathy and affection.

SPREADING GOD'S WORD IN A GERMAN UNIVERSITY, 1549

The aim that they should have above all before their eyes is that intended by the Supreme Pontiff who has sent them: to help the University of Ingolstadt, and as far as is possible the whole of Germany, in all that concerns purity of faith, obedience to the Church, and firmness and soundness of doctrine and upright living....

They must be very competent in them, and teach solid doctrine without many technical terms (which are unpopular), especially if these are hard to understand. The lectures should be learned yet clear, sustained in argument yet not long-winded, and delivered with attention to style.... Besides these academic lectures, it seems opportune on feast days to hold sermons on Bible readings, more calculated to move hearts and form consciences than to produce learned minds.... They should make efforts to attract their students into a friendship of spiritual quality, and if possible towards confession and making the Spiritual Exercises, even in the full form, if they seem suitable to join the Society. . . .

On occasion they should give time to works of mercy of a more visible character, such as in hospitals and prisons and helping other kinds of poor; such works arouse a "sweet fragrance" in the Lord. Opportunity may also arise to act as peacemakers in quarrels and to teach basic Christian doctrine to the uneducated. Taking account of local conditions and the persons concerned, prudence will dictate whether they should act themselves or through others.

They should make efforts to make friends with the leaders of their opponents, as also with those who are most influential among the heretics or those who are suspected of it yet seem not absolutely immovable. They must try to bring them back from their error by sensitive skill and signs of love. . . . All must try to have at their finger-tips the main points concerning dogmas of faith that are subjects of controversy with heretics, especially at the time and place when they are present, and with those persons with whom they are dealing. Thus they will be able, whenever opportunity arises, to put forward and defend the Catholic truth, to refute errors and to strengthen the doubtful and wavering, whether by lectures and sermons or in the confessional and in conversations. . . .

It will be helpful to lead people, as far as possible, to open themselves to God's grace, exhorting them to a desire for salvation, to prayer, to alms, and to everything that conduces to receiving grace or increasing it. . . .

Let [the duke] understand also what glory it will mean for him if he is the first to introduce into Germany seminaries in the form of such colleges, to foster sound doctrine and religion.

THE FINAL WORD ON OBEDIENCE, 1553,
TO THE BROTHERS IN PORTUGAL

To form an idea of the exceptional intrinsic value of this obedience in the eyes of God Our Lord, one should weigh both the worth of the noble sacrifice offered, involving the highest human power, and the completeness of the self-offering undertaken, as one strips oneself of self, becoming a "living victim" pleasing to the Divine Majesty. Another indication is the intensity of the difficulty experienced as one conquers self for love of God, opposing the natural human inclination felt by us all to follow our own opinions. . . .

Let us be unpretentious and let us be gentle! God Our Lord will grant the grace to enable you, gently and lovingly, to maintain constantly the offering you have made to Him. . . .

All that has been said does not exclude your bringing before your superiors a contrary opinion that may have occurred to you, once you have prayed about the matter and you feel that it would be proper and in accord with your respect for God to do so. . . . Such is the model on which divine Providence "gently disposes all things," so that the lower via the middle, and the middle via the higher, are led to their final ends. . . . The same can be seen upon the earth with respect to all secular constitutions that are duly established, and with respect to the ecclesiastical hierarchy, which is subordinated to you in virtue of holy obedience to select among the many routes open to you that which will bring you back to Portugal as soon and as safely as possible. So I order you in the name of Christ Our Lord to do this, even if it will be so as to return soon to India. . . . Firstly, you are well aware how important for the upkeep and advancement of Christianity in those lands, as also in Guinea and Brazil, is the good order that the King of Portugal can grant from his kingdom. When a prince of such Christian desires and holy intentions as is the King of Portugal receives information from someone of your experience about the state of affairs in those parts, you can imagine what influence this will have on him to do much more in the service of God Our Lord and for the good of those countries that you will describe to him. . . .

You are also aware how important it is for the good of the Indies that the persons sent there should be suitable for the aim that one is pursuing in those and in other lands. . . . Quite apart from all these reasons, which apply to furthering the good of India, it seems to me that you would fire the King's enthusiasm for the Ethiopian project, which has been planned for so many years without anything effective having been seen. Similarly, with regard to the Congo and Brazil, you could give no small help from Portugal, which you cannot do from India as there are not the same commercial relations. If people in India consider that your presence is important given your post, you can continue to act as superior no less from Portugal than from Japan or China, and probably much better. Just as you have gone away on other occasions for longer periods, do the same now.

■ Discussion Questions

1. What does the Catholic life mean to Ignatius?
2. What advice does Ignatius offer about dealing with the problem of heresy?
3. What role will Jesuits play throughout Europe and the rest of the world according to Ignatius's instructions?
4. How does Ignatius think political leaders can be enlisted to support the aims of the reform movement?

3.
Hans Jacob Christoffel von Grimmelshausen
The Adventures of a Simpleton
1668–1669

Lutheranism was not the only challenge posed to the Catholic Church. A second wave of reform gained momentum under the influence of Frenchman John Calvin (1509–1564). Calvin had embraced the reform movement while studying in Paris in

From Hans Jacob Christoffel von Grimmelshausen, *The Adventures of Simplicius Simplicissimus*, trans. George Schulz-Behrend (Columbia: Camden House, 1993), 6–7.

1533–1534. Fleeing a government crackdown on Protestantism, Calvin eventually settled in Geneva, where he worked to build a godly city, making it a haven for reformers and a training ground for preachers. From here, Calvin's own brand of evangelical doctrine spread across Europe. The addition of Calvinism into the already heady mix of religious conflict fueled the last and most destructive war of religion, the Thirty Years War (1618–1648), which began in the Holy Roman Empire but eventually involved most European states. Hans Jacob Christoffel von Grimmelshausen (c. 1621–1676) experienced the war firsthand and then wrote about it in his novel, The Adventures of a Simpleton *(published in six books in 1668–1669). He had been a Lutheran schoolboy when Swedish troops pillaged his town, described in this excerpt. Later he served as a musketeer in the Catholic imperial armies and converted to Catholicism. In the novel, he writes from the point of view of a "simpleton," a naïve peasant who does not understand what is happening around him when in fact he had a keen eye for describing the horrors of war.*

Though I hadn't intended to take the peace-loving reader into my father's home and farm along with these merry cavalrymen, the orderly progress of my tale requires me to make known to posterity the sort of abysmal and unheard-of cruelties occasionally perpetrated in our German war, and to testify by my own example that all these evils were necessarily required for our own good by the kindness of our Lord. For, my dear reader, who would have told me that there is a God in heaven if the warriors hadn't destroyed my knan's house, if they hadn't forced me to be among the people who taught me well enough? Shortly before this event I could neither know nor imagine but that my knan, mother and Ursula, myself and the hired hands were the only humans on earth, for no people or dwellings were known to me except my knan's house, where I went in and out daily. But I soon discovered where people come from, and that they have no permanent abode, but often have to move on again before they can look around. I had been human in shape alone, and a Christian in name only; in reality I was an animal! But the Almighty looked upon my ignorance with forgiving eyes, and wanted me to come to the recognition of both Him and myself. And though he had a thousand different ways for this purpose, undoubtedly he wanted to use as an example to others the manner in which my knan and mother were punished for my negligent upbringing.

   The first thing these horsemen did in the nice black rooms of the house was to put in their horses. Then everyone took up a special job, a job having to do with death and destruction. Although some began butchering, heating water, and rendering lard, as if to prepare for a banquet, others raced through the house, ransacking upstairs and down; not even the privy chamber was safe, as if the golden fleece of Colchis might be hidden there. Still others bundled up big bags of cloth, household goods, and clothes, as if they wanted to hold a rummage sale somewhere. What they did not intend to take along they broke and spoiled. Some ran their swords into the hay and straw, as if there hadn't been hogs enough to stick. Some shook the feathers out of beds and put bacon slabs, hams, and other stuff in the ticking, as if they might sleep better on these. Others knocked down the hearth and broke the windows, as if announcing an everlasting summer. They flattened out copper and pewter dishes and baled the ruined goods. They burned up bedsteads, tables, chairs, and benches, though there were yards and yards of dry firewood outside the kitchen. Jars and crocks, pots and casseroles all were broken, either because they preferred their meat broiled or because they thought they'd eat only one meal with us. In the barn, the hired girl was handled so roughly that she was unable to walk away, I am ashamed to report. They stretched the hired man out flat on the ground, stuck a wooden wedge in his mouth to keep it open, and emptied a milk bucket full of stinking manure drippings down his throat; they called it a Swedish cocktail. He didn't relish it and made a very wry face. By this means they forced him to take a raiding party to some other place where they carried off men and cattle and brought them to our farm. Among these were my knan, mother, and Ursula.

Then they used thumbscrews, which they cleverly made out of their pistols, to torture the peasants, as if they wanted to burn witches. Though he had confessed to nothing as yet, they put one of the captured hayseeds in the bake-oven and lighted a fire in it. They put a rope around someone else's head and tightened it like a tourniquet until blood came out of his mouth, nose, and ears. In short, every soldier had his favorite method of making life miserable for peasants, and every peasant had his own misery. My knan was, as I thought, particularly lucky because he confessed with a laugh what others were forced to say in pain and martyrdom. No doubt because he was the head of the household, he was shown special consideration; they put him close to a fire, tied him by his hands and feet, and rubbed damp salt on the bottom of his soles. Our old nanny goat had to lick it off and this so tickled my knan that he could have burst laughing. This seemed so clever and entertaining to me—I had never seen or heard my knan laugh so long—that I joined him in laughter, to keep him company or perhaps to cover up my ignorance. In the midst of such glee he told them the whereabouts of hidden treasure much richer in gold, pearls, and jewelry than might have been expected on a farm.

I can't say much about the captured wives, hired girls, and daughters because the soldiers didn't let me watch their doings. But I do remember hearing pitiful screams from various dark corners and I guess that my mother and our Ursula had it no better than the rest. Amid all this horror I was busy turning a roasting spit and didn't worry about anything, for I didn't know the meaning of it. In the afternoon I helped water the horses and that way got to see our hired girl in the barn. She looked wondrously messed up and at first I didn't recognize her. In a sickly voice she said, "Boy, get out of this place, or the soldiers will take you with them. Try to get away; you can see they are up to no good!" That is all she could say.

■ Discussion Questions

1. Grimmelshausen's novel was very popular, appearing in six editions during his lifetime. Based on this passage, why do you think contemporary audiences found the book so appealing?

2. In what ways did Grimmelshausen's religious beliefs shape his account? What does this suggest about his understanding of the novel's broader function?

3. What does his account reveal about the methods of war at the time, and their impact on everyday life?

4.
Henry IV
Edict of Nantes
1598

The promulgation of the Edict of Nantes in 1598 by King Henry IV (r. 1589–1610) marked the end of the French Wars of Religion by recognizing French Protestants as a legally protected religious minority. Drawing largely on earlier edicts of pacification, the Edict of Nantes comprised ninety-two general articles, fifty-six secret articles, and two royal warrants. The two series of articles represented the edict proper and were registered by the highest courts of law in the realm (parlements). The following excerpts from the general articles reveal the triumph of political concerns over religious conformity on the one hand, and the limitations of religious tolerance in early modern France on the other.

Henry, By the Grace of God, King of *France,* and *Navarre,* To all Present, and to Come, greeteth. Among the infinite Mercies that God hath pleased to bestow upon us, that most Signal and Remarkable is, his having given us Power and Strength not to yield to the dreadful Troubles, Confusions, and Disorders, which were found at our coming to this Kingdom, divided into so many Parties and Factions, that the most Legitimate was almost the least, enabling us with Constancy in such manner to oppose the Storm, as in the end to surmount it, reducing this Estate to Peace and Rest. . . . For the general difference among our good Subjects, and the particular evils of the soundest parts of the State, we judged might be easily cured, after the Principal cause (the continuation of the Civil Wars) was taken away, in which we have, by the blessing of God, well and happily succeeded, all Hostility and Wars through the Kingdom being now ceased, and we hope he will also prosper us in our other affairs, which remain to be composed, and that by this means we shall arrive at the establishment of a good Peace, with tranquility and rest. . . . Amongst our said affairs . . . one of the principal hath been, the many complaints we received from divers of our Provinces and Catholick Cities, for that the exercise of the Catholick Religion was not universally re-established, as is provided by Edicts or Statutes heretofore made for the Pacification of the Troubles

From Henry IV, "Edict of Nantes" in Edmund Everard, *The Great Pressures and Grievances of the Protestants in France* (London: 1681); reprinted in *The Assassination of Henry IV,* trans. Joan Spencer (New York: Scribner, 1973), 316–25, 333, 343, 347.

arising from Religion; as also the Supplications and Remonstrances which have been made to us by our Subjects of the reformed Religion, as well upon the execution of what hath been granted by the said former Laws, as that they desire to have some addition for the exercise of their Religion, the liberty of their Consciences and the security of their Persons and Fortunes; presuming to have just reasons for desiring some inlargement of Articles, as not being without great apprehensions, because their Ruine hath been the principal pretext and original foundation of the late Wars, Troubles, and Commotions. Now not to burden us with too much business at once, as also that the fury of War was not compatible with the establishment of Laws, how good soever they might be, we have hitherto deferred from time to time giving remedy herein. But now that it hath pleased God to give us a beginning of enjoying some Rest, we think we cannot imploy our self better, than to apply to that which may tend to the glory and service of his holy name, and to provide that he may be adored and prayed unto by all our Subjects: and if it hath not yet pleased him to permit it to be in one and the same form of Religion, that it may at the least be with one and the same intention, and with such rules that may prevent amongst them all troubles and tumults. . . . For this cause . . . we have upon the whole judged it necessary to give to all our said Subjects one general Law, Clear, Pure, and Absolute, by which they shall be regulated in all differences which have heretofore risen among them, or may hereafter rise, wherewith the one and other may be contented, being framed according as the time requires: and having had no other regard in this deliberation than solely the Zeal we have to the service of God, praying that he would henceforward render to all our subjects a durable and Established peace. . . . We have by this Edict or Statute perpetual and irrevocable said, declared, and ordained, saying, declaring, and ordaining;

That the memory of all things passed on the one part and the other, since the beginning of the month of *March,* 1585. Until our coming to the Crown, and also during the other precedent troubles, and the occasion of the same, shall remain extinguished and suppressed, as things that had never been. . . .

We prohibit to all our Subjects of what State and Condition soever they be, to renew the memory thereof, to attaque, resent, injure, or provoke one the other by reproaches for what is past, under any pretext or cause whatsoever, by disputing, contesting, quarrelling, reviling, or offending by factious words; but to contain themselves, and live peaceably together as Brethren, Friends, and fellow-Citizens, upon penalty for acting to the contrary, to be punished for breakers of Peace, and disturbers of the public quiet.

We ordain, that the Catholick Religion shall be restored and re-established in all places, and quarters of this Kingdom and Countrey under our obedience, and where the exercise of the same hath been intermitted, to be there again, peaceably and freely exercised without any trouble or impediment. . . .

And not to leave any occasion of trouble and difference among our Subjects, we have permitted and do permit to those of the Reformed Religion, to live and dwell in all the Cities and places of this our Kingdom and Countreys under our obedience, without being inquired after, vexed, molested, or compelled to do any thing in Religion, contrary to their Conscience. . . .

We permit also to those of the said Religion to hold, and continue the Exercise of the same in all the Cities and Places under our obedience, where it hath by them been Established and made public by many and divers times, in the Year 1586, and in 1597, until the end of the Month of *August*. . . .

In like manner the said Exercise may be Established, and re-established in all the Cities and Places where it hath been established, or ought to be by the Statute of Pacification, made in the Year 1577. . . .

As also not to exercise the said Religion in our Court, nor in our Territories and Countries beyond the Mountains, nor in our City of *Paris,* nor within five Leagues of the said City. . . .

We prohibit all Preachers, Readers, and others who speak in public, to use any words, discourse, or propositions tending to excite the People to Sedition; and we enjoin them to contain and comport themselves modestly, and to say nothing which shall not be for the instruction and edification of the Auditors, and maintaining the peace and tranquillity established by us in our said Kingdom. . . .

They [French Protestants] shall also be obliged to keep and observe the Festivals of the Catholick Church, and shall not on the same dayes work, sell, or keep open shop, nor likewise the Artisans shall not work out of their shops, in their chambers or houses privately on the said Festivals, and other dayes forbidden, of any trade, the noise whereof may be heard without by those that pass by, or by the Neighbors. . . .

We ordain, that there shall not be made any difference or distinction upon the account of the said Religion, in receiving Scholars to be instructed in the Universities, Colledges, or Schools, nor of the sick or poor into Hospitals, sick houses or public Almshouses. . . .

We Will and Ordain, that all those of the Reformed Religion, and others who have followed their party, of what State, Quality or Condition soever they be, shall be obliged and constrained by all due and reasonable wayes, and under the penalties contained in the said Edict or Statute relating thereunto, to pay tythes to the Curates, and other Ecclesiasticks, and to all others to whom they shall appertain. . . .

To the end to re-unite so much the better the minds and good will of our Subjects, as is our intention, and to take away all complaints for the future; We declare all those who make or shall make profession of the said Reformed Religion, to be capable of holding and exercising all Estates, Dignities, Offices, and public charges whatsoever. . . .

We declare all Sentences, Judgments, Procedures, Seisures, Sales, and Decrees made and given against those of the Reformed Religion, as well living as dead, from the death of the deceased King *Henry* the Second our most honored Lord and Father in Law, upon the occasion of the said Religion, Tumults and Troubles since happening, as also the execution of the same Judgments and Decrees, from henceforward cancelled, revoked, and annulled. . . .

Those also of the said Religion shall depart and desist henceforward from all Practices, Negotiations, and Intelligences, as well within as without our Kingdom; and the said Assemblies and Councels established within the Provinces, shall readily separate, and also all the Leagues and Associations made or to be made under what pretext soever, to the prejudice of our present Edict, shall be cancelled and annulled, . . . prohibiting most expresly to all our Subjects to make henceforwards any Assesments or Leavy's of Money, Fortifications, Enrolments of men, Congregations and Assemblies of other than such as are permitted by our present Edict, and without Arms. . . .

We give in command to the People of our said Courts of Parliaments, Chambers of our Courts, and Courts of our Aids, Bayliffs, Chief-Justices, Provosts and other our Justices and Officers to whom it appertains, and to their Leivetenants, that they cause to be read, published, and Registred this present Edict and Ordinance in their Courts and Jurisdictions, and the same keep punctually, and the contents of the same to cause to be injoyned and used fully and peaceably to all those to whom it shall belong, ceasing and making to cease all troubles and obstructions to the contrary, for such is our pleasure: and in witness hereof we have signed these presents with our own hand; and to the end to make it a thing firm and stable for ever, we have caused to put and indorse our Seal to the same. Given at *Nantes* in the Month of *April* in the year of Grace 1598. and of our Reign the ninth

Signed

HENRY

■ Discussion Questions

1. What are the edict's principal objectives?
2. In what ways does the edict balance the demands of both French Catholics and Protestants?
3. What limits does the edict place on Protestants' religious rights?
4. Did Henry IV regard this edict as a permanent solution to the religious divisions in the realm? Why or why not?

5.
Galileo
Letter to the Grand Duchess Christina
1615

Italian-born and educated, Galileo Galilei (1564–1642) was among the most illustrious proponents of the new science in the seventeenth century. Early in his studies, he embraced the theory held by Nicolaus Copernicus (1473–1543) that the sun, not the earth, was at the center of the universe. Having improved on the newly invented telescope in 1609, Galileo was able to substantiate the heliocentric view through his observations of

From *Discoveries and Opinions of Galileo*, trans. Stillman Drake (New York: Doubleday, 1957), 175–86.

the moon and planets. Because Galileo's work challenged both traditional religious and scientific views, it sparked considerable controversy. In the letter excerpted here, written in 1615 to the Grand Duchess Christina of Tuscany, an important Catholic patron of learning, Galileo defends the validity of his findings while striving to separate scriptural authority from the study of natural phenomena.

GALILEO GALILEI TO THE MOST SERENE GRAND DUCHESS MOTHER:

Some years ago, as Your Serene Highness well knows, I discovered in the heavens many things that had not been seen before our own age. The novelty of these things, as well as some consequences which followed from them in contradiction to the physical notions commonly held among academic philosophers, stirred up against me no small number of professors—as if I had placed these things in the sky with my own hands in order to upset nature and overturn the sciences. . . .

Well, the passage of time has revealed to everyone the truths that I previously set forth. . . . But some, besides allegiance to their original error, possess I know not what fanciful interest in remaining hostile not so much toward the things in question as toward their discoverer. No longer being able to deny them, these men now take refuge in obstinate silence, but being more than ever exasperated by that which has pacified and quieted other men, they divert their thoughts to other fancies and seek new ways to damage me. . . .

Persisting in their original resolve to destroy me and everything mine by any means they can think of, these men are aware of my views in astronomy and philosophy. They know that as to the arrangement of the parts of the universe, I hold the sun to be situated motionless in the center of the revolution of the celestial orbs while the earth rotates on its axis and revolves about the sun. . . .

Now as to the false aspersions which they so unjustly seek to cast upon me, I have thought it necessary to justify myself in the eyes of all men, whose judgment in matters of religion and of reputation I must hold in great esteem. I shall therefore discourse of the particulars which these men produce to make this opinion detested and to have it condemned not merely as false but as heretical. To this end they make a shield of their hypocritical zeal for religion. They go about invoking the Bible, which they would have minister to their deceitful purposes. Contrary to the sense of the Bible and the intention of the holy Fathers, if I am not mistaken, they would extend such authorities until even in purely physical matters—where faith is not involved—they would have us altogether abandon reason and the evidence of our senses in favor of some biblical passage, though under the surface meaning of its words this passage may contain a different sense. . . .

The reason produced for condemning the opinion that the earth moves and the sun stands still is that in many places in the Bible one may read that the sun moves and the earth stands still. Since the Bible cannot err, it follows as a necessary consequence that anyone takes an erroneous and heretical position who maintains that the sun is inherently motionless and the earth movable.

With regard to this argument, I think in the first place that it is very pious to say and prudent to affirm that the holy Bible can never speak untruth—whenever its true meaning is understood. But I believe nobody will deny that it is often very abstruse, and may say things which are quite different from what its bare words signify. Hence in expounding the Bible if one were always to confine oneself to the unadorned grammatical meaning, one might fall into error. Not only contradictions and propositions far from true might thus be made to appear in the Bible, but even grave heresies and follies. Thus it would be necessary to assign to God feet, hands, and eyes, as well as corporeal and human affections, such as anger, repentance, hatred, and sometimes even the forgetting of things past and ignorance of those to come. These propositions uttered by the Holy Ghost were set down in that manner by the sacred scribes in order to accommodate them to the capacities of the common people, who are rude and unlearned. For the sake of those who deserve to be separated from the herd, it is necessary that wise expositors should produce the true senses of such passages, together with the special reasons for which they were set down in these words. This doctrine is so widespread and so definite with all theologians that it would be superfluous to adduce evidence for it.

Hence I think that I may reasonably conclude that whenever the Bible has occasion to speak of any physical conclusion (especially those which are very abstruse and hard to understand), the rule has been observed of avoiding confusion in the minds of the common people which would render them contumacious toward the higher mysteries. Now the Bible, merely to condescend to popular capacity, has not hesitated to obscure some very important pronouncements, attributing to God himself some qualities extremely remote from (and even contrary to) His essence. Who, then, would positively declare that this principle has been set aside, and the Bible has confined itself rigorously to the bare and restricted sense of its words, when speaking but casually of the earth, of water, of the sun, or of any other created thing? Especially in view of the fact that these things in no way concern the primary purpose of the sacred writings, which is the service of God and the salvation of souls—matters infinitely beyond the comprehension of the common people.

This being granted, I think that in discussions of physical problems we ought to begin not from the authority of scriptural passages, but from sense-experiences and necessary demonstrations; for the holy Bible and the phenomena of nature proceed alike from the divine Word, the former as the dictate of the Holy Ghost and the latter as the observant executrix of God's commands. It is necessary for the Bible, in order to be accommodated to the understanding of every man, to speak many things which appear to differ from the absolute truth so far as the bare meaning of the words is concerned. But Nature, on the other hand, is inexorable and immutable; she never transgresses the laws imposed upon her, or cares a whit whether her abstruse reasons and methods of operations are understandable to men. For that reason it appears that nothing physical which sense-experience sets before our eyes, or which necessary demonstrations prove to us, ought to be called in question (much less condemned) upon the testimony of biblical passages which may have some different meaning beneath their words. For the Bible is not chained in every expression to conditions as strict as those which govern all physical effects; nor is God any less excellently revealed in Nature's actions than in the sacred statements of the Bible. . . .

From this I do not mean to infer that we need not have an extraordinary esteem for the passages of holy Scripture. On the contrary, having arrived at any certainties in physics, we ought to utilize these as the most appropriate aids in the true exposition of the Bible and in the investigation of those meanings which are necessarily contained therein, for these must be concordant with demonstrated truths. I should judge that the authority of the Bible was designed to persuade men of those articles and propositions which, surpassing all human reasoning, could not be made credible by science, or by any other means than through the very mouth of the Holy Spirit.

Yet even in those propositions which are not matters of faith, this authority ought to be preferred over that of all human writings which are supported only by bare assertions or probable arguments, and not set forth in a demonstrative way. This I hold to be necessary and proper to the same extent that divine wisdom surpasses all human judgment and conjecture.

But I do not feel obliged to believe that that same God who has endowed us with senses, reason, and intellect has intended to forgo their use and by some other means to give us knowledge which we can attain by them. He would not require us to deny sense and reason in physical matters which are set before our eyes and minds by direct experience or necessary demonstrations. This must be especially true in those sciences of which but the faintest trace (and that consisting of conclusions) is to be found in the Bible. Of astronomy, for instance, so little is found that none of the planets except Venus are so much as mentioned, and this only once or twice under the name of "Lucifer." If the sacred scribes had had any intention of teaching people certain arrangements and motions of the heavenly bodies, or had they wished us to derive such knowledge from the Bible, then in my opinion they would not have spoken of these matters so sparingly in comparison with the infinite number of admirable conclusions which are demonstrated in that science. . . .

From these things it follows as a necessary consequence that, since the Holy Ghost did not intend to teach us whether heaven moves or stands still, whether its shape is spherical or like a discus or extended in a plane, nor whether the earth is located at its center or off to one side, then so much the less was it intended to settle for us any other conclusion of the same kind. And the motion or rest of the earth and the sun is so closely linked with the things just named, that without a determination of the one, neither side can be taken in the other matters. Now if the Holy Spirit has purposely neglected to teach us propositions of this sort as irrelevant to the highest goal (that is, to our salvation), how can anyone affirm that it is obligatory to take sides on them, and that one belief is required by faith, while the other side is erroneous? Can an opinion be heretical and yet have no concern with the salvation of souls? Can the Holy Ghost be asserted not to have intended teaching us something that does concern our salvation? I would say here something that was heard from an ecclesiastic of the most eminent degree: "That the intention of the Holy Ghost is to teach us how one goes to heaven, not how heaven goes."...

From this it is seen that the interpretation which we impose upon passages of Scripture would be false whenever it disagreed with demonstrated truths. And therefore we should seek the incontrovertible sense of the Bible with the assistance of demonstrated truth, and not in any way try to force the hand of Nature or deny experiences and rigorous proofs in accordance with the mere sound of words that may appeal to our frailty....

To that end they would forbid him the use of reason, divine gift of Providence, and would abuse the just authority of holy Scripture—which, in the general opinion of theologians, can never oppose manifest experiences and necessary demonstrations when rightly understood and applied. If I am correct, it will stand them in no stead to go running to the Bible to cover up their inability to understand (let alone resolve) their opponents' arguments.

■ Discussion Questions

1. What do you think Galileo's goal in writing this letter to the Grand Duchess was?

2. What is the basis of the attacks by Galileo's critics?

3. According to Galileo, what role should the Bible play in scientific inquiry?

4. How does this document lend support to historians who have credited Galileo for helping to popularize the principles and methods of the new science?

6.
The Trial of Suzanne Gaudry
1652

Even as the new science gained support, most Europeans continued to believe in demonic "black magic," especially at this time of religious wars, economic decline, and social strife. This belief found violent expression in a wave of witchcraft persecutions across Europe between 1560 and 1640. The following selections from the trial records of Suzanne Gaudry attest to the predominant notion that witches were agents of the devil. Although conducted at a time when the number of witch hunts and persecutions were in decline, her trial attests to the persistence of a deeply felt fear among many people regarding the presence of diabolical forces in everyday life.

From Alan C. Kors and Edward Peters, eds., *Witchcraft in Europe, 1100–1700: A Documentary History* (Philadelphia: University of Pennsylvania Press, 1972), 266–75.

At Ronchain, May 28, 1652. . . . Interrogation of Suzanne Gaudry, prisoner at the court of Rieux. Questioned about her age, her place of origin, her mother and father.

—Said that she is named Suzanne Gaudry, daughter of Jean Gaudry and Marguerite Gerné, both natives of Rieux, but that she is from Esgavans, near Odenarde, where her family had taken refuge because of the wars, that she was born the day that they made bonfires for the Peace between France and Spain, without being able otherwise to say her age.

Asked why she has been taken here.

—Answers that it is for the salvation of her soul.

—Says that she was frightened of being taken prisoner for the crime of witchcraft.

Asked for how long she has been in the service of the devil.

—Says that about twenty-five or twenty-six years ago she was his lover, that he called himself Petit-Grignon, that he would wear black breeches, that he gave her the name Magin, that she gave him a pin with which he gave her his mark on the left shoulder, that he had a little flat hat; said also that he had his way with her two or three times only.

Asked how many times she has been at the nocturnal dance.

—Answers that she has been there about a dozen times, having first of all renounced God, Lent and baptism; that the site of the dance was at the little marsh of Rieux, understanding that there were diverse dances. The first time, she did not recognize anyone there, because she was half blind. The other times, she saw and recognized there Noelle and Pasquette Gerné, Noelle the wife of Nochin Quinchou and the other of Paul Doris, the widow Marie Nourette, not having recognized others because the young people went with the young people and the old people with the old. [. . .]

Interrogated on how and in what way they danced.

—Says that they dance in an ordinary way, that there was a guitarist and some whistlers who appeared to be men she did not know; which lasted about an hour, and then everyone collapsed from exhaustion.

Inquired what happened after the dance.

—Says that they formed a circle, that there was a king with a long black beard dressed in black, with a red hat, who made everyone do his bidding, and that after the dance he made a . . . [the word is missing in the text], and then everyone disappeared. . . .

Questioned if she has abused the Holy Communion.

—Says no, never, and that she has always swallowed it. Then says that her lover asked her for it several times, but that she did not want to give it to him.

After several admonitions were sent to her, she has signed this

Mark

X

Suzanne Gaudry

SECOND INTERROGATION, MAY 29, 1652,
IN THE PRESENCE OF THE AFORE-MENTIONED

This prisoner, being brought back into the chamber, was informed about the facts and the charges and asked if what she declared and confessed yesterday is true.

—Answers that if it is in order to put her in prison it is not true; then after having remained silent said that it is true.

Asked what is her lover's name and what name has he given himself.

—Said that his name is Grinniou and that he calls himself Magnin.

Asked where he found her the first time and what he did to her.

—Answers that it was in her lodgings, that he had a hide, little black breeches, and a little flat hat; that he asked her for a pin, which she gave to him, with which he made his mark on her left shoulder. Said also that at the time she took him oil in a bottle and that she had thoughts of love.

Asked how long she has been in subjugation to the devil.

—Says that it has been about twenty-five or twenty-six years, that her lover also then made her renounce God, Lent, and baptism, that he has known her carnally three or four times, and that he has given her satisfaction. And on the subject of his having asked her if she wasn't afraid of having a baby, says that she did not have that thought.

Asked how many times she found herself at the nocturnal dance and carol and who she recognized there.

—Answers that she was there eleven or twelve times, that she went there on foot with her lover, where the third time she saw and recognized Pasquette and Noelle Gerné, and Marie Homitte, to whom she never spoke, for the reason that they did not speak to each other. And that the sabbat took place at the little meadow. . . .

Asked what occurred at the dance and afterwards.

—Says that right after the dance they put themselves in order and approached the chief figure, who had a long black beard, dressed also in black, with a red hat, at which point they were given some powder, to do with it what they wanted; but that she did not want to take any.

Charged with having taken some and with having used it evilly.

—Says, after having insisted that she did not want to take any, that she took some, and that her lover advised her to do evil with it; but that she did not want to do it.

Asked if, not obeying his orders, she was beaten or threatened by him, and what did she do with this powder.

—Answers that never was she beaten; she invoked the name of the Virgin [and answered] that she threw away the powder that she had, not having wanted to do any evil with it.

Pressed to say what she did with this powder. Did she not fear her lover too much to have thrown it away?

—Says, after having been pressed on this question, that she made the herbs in her garden die at the end of the summer, five to six years ago, by means of the powder, which she threw there because she did not know what to do with it. [. . .]

Charged once more with having performed some malefice with this powder, pressed to tell the truth.

—Answers that she never made any person or beast die; then later said that she made Philippe Cornié's red horse die, about two or three years ago, by means of the powder, which she placed where he had to pass, in the street close to her home. Asked why she did that and if she had had any difficulty with him.

—Says that she had had some difficulty with his wife, because her cow had eaten the leeks.[...]

After having been admonished to think of her conscience, was returned to prison after having signed this

Mark

X

Suzanne Gaudry

DELIBERATION OF THE COURT OF MONS — JUNE 3, 1652

The under-signed advocates of the Court of Mons have seen these interrogations and answers. They say that the aforementioned Suzanne Gaudry confesses that she is a witch, that she has given herself to the devil, that she has renounced God, Lent, and baptism, that she has been marked on the shoulder, that she has cohabited with him and that she has been to the dances, confessing only to have cast a spell upon and caused to die a beast of Philippe Cornié; but there is no evidence for this, excepting a prior statement. For this reason, before going further, it will be necessary to become acquainted with, to examine and to probe the mark, and to hear Philippe Cornié on the death of the horse and on when and in what way he died....

DELIBERATION OF THE COURT OF MONS — JUNE 13, 1652

[The Court] has reviewed the current criminal trial of Suzanne Gaudry, and with it the trial of Antoinette Lescouffre, also a prisoner of the same office.

It appeared [to the Court] that the office should have the places probed where the prisoners say that they have received the mark of the devil, and after that, they must be interrogated and examined seriously on their confessions and denials, this having to be done, in order to regulate all this definitively....

DELIBERATION OF THE COURT OF MONS — JUNE 22, 1652

The trials of Antoinette Lescouffre and Suzanne Gaudry having been described to the undersigned, advocates of the Court of Mons, and [the Court] having been told orally that the peasants taking them to prison had persuaded them to confess in order to avoid imprisonment, and that they would be let go, by virtue of which it could appear that the confessions were not so spontaneous:

They are of the opinion that the office, in its duty, would do well, following the two preceding resolutions, to have the places of the marks that they have taught us about probed, and if it is found that these are ordinary marks of the devil, one can proceed to their examination; then next to the first confessions, and if they deny [these], one can proceed to the torture, given that they issue from bewitched relatives, that at all times they have been suspect, that they fled to avoid the crime [that is to say, prosecution for the crime of witchcraft], and that by their confessions they have confirmed [their guilt], notwithstanding that they have wanted to revoke [their confessions] and vacillate. . . .

THIRD INTERROGATION, JUNE 27, ## IN THE PRESENCE OF THE AFORE-MENTIONED

This prisoner being led into the chamber, she was examined to know if things were not as she had said and confessed at the beginning of her imprisonment.
—Answers no, and that what she has said was done so by force.
Asked if she did not say to Jean Gradé that she would tell his uncle, the mayor, that he had better be careful . . . and that he was a Frank.
—Said that that is not true.
Pressed to say the truth, that otherwise she would be subjected to torture, having pointed out to her that her aunt was burned for this same subject.
—Answers that she is not a witch.
Interrogated as to how long she has been in subjection to the devil, and pressed that she was to renounce the devil and the one who misled her.
—Says that she is not a witch, that she has nothing to do with the devil thus that she did not want to renounce the devil, saying that he has not misled her, and upon inquisition of having confessed to being present at the carol, she insisted that although she had said that, it is not true, and that she is not a witch.
Charged with having confessed to having made a horse die by means of a powder that the devil had given her.
—Answers that she said it, but because she found herself during the inquisition pressed to say that she must have done some evil deed; and after several admonitions to tell the truth:
She was placed in the hands of the officer of the *haultes oeuvres* [the officer in charge of torture], throwing herself on her knees, struggling to cry, uttering several exclamations, without being able, nevertheless, to shed a tear. Saying at every moment that she is not a witch.

THE TORTURE

On this same day, being at the place of torture.
This prisoner, before being strapped down, was admonished to maintain herself in her first confessions and to renounce her lover.
—Said that she denies everything she has said, and that she has no lover. Feeling herself being strapped down, says that she is not a witch, while struggling to cry.
Asked why she fled outside the village of Rieux.

—Says that she cannot say it, that God and the Virgin Mary forbid her to; that she is not a witch. And upon being asked why she confessed to being one, said that she was forced to say it.

Told that she was not forced, that on the contrary she declared herself to be a witch without any threat.

—Says that she confessed it and that she is not a witch, and being a little stretched [on the rack] screams ceaselessly that she is not a witch, invoking the name of Jesus and of Our Lady of Grace, not wanting to say any other thing.

Asked if she did not confess that she had been a witch for twenty-six years.

—Says that she said it, that she retracts it, crying Jésus-Maria, that she is not a witch.

Asked if she did not make Philippe Cornié's horse die, as she confessed.

—Answers no, crying Jésus-Maria, that she is not a witch.

The mark having been probed by the officer, in the presence of Doctor Bouchain, it was adjudged by the aforesaid doctor and officer truly to be the mark of the devil.

Being more tightly stretched upon the torture-rack, urged to maintain her confessions.

—Said that it was true that she is a witch and that she would maintain what she had said.

Asked how long she has been in subjugation to the devil.

—Answers that it was twenty years ago that the devil appeared to her, being in her lodgings in the form of a man dressed in a little cow-hide and black breeches.

Interrogated as to what her lover was called.

—Says that she said Petit-Grignon, then, being taken down [from the rack] says upon interrogation that she is not a witch and that she can say nothing.

Asked if her lover has had carnal copulation with her, and how many times.

—To that she did not answer anything; then, making believe that she was ill, not another word could be drawn from her.

As soon as she began to confess, she asked who was alongside of her, touching her, yet none of those present could see anyone there. And it was noticed that as soon as that was said, she no longer wanted to confess anything.

Which is why she was returned to prison.

VERDICT

July 9, 1652

In the light of the interrogations, answers and investigations made into the charge against Suzanne Gaudry, coupled with her confessions, from which it would appear that she has always been ill-reputed for being stained with the crime of witchcraft, and seeing that she took flight and sought refuge in this city of Valenciennes, out of fear of being apprehended by the law for this matter; seeing how her close family were also stained with the same crime, and the perpetrators executed; seeing by her own confessions that she is said to have made a pact with the devil, received the mark from him, which in the report of *sieur* Michel de Roux was judged by the medical doctor of Ronchain and the officer of *haultes oeuvres* of Cambrai, after having proved it, to be not a natural mark but a mark of the devil, to which they have sworn with an oath; and that following this, she had renounced God, Lent, and baptism and had let herself be known carnally by him, in which she received satisfaction. Also, seeing that she is said to have been a part of nocturnal carols and dances. Which are crimes of divine lèse-majesty:

For expiation of which the advice of the under-signed is that the office of Rieux can legitimately condemn the aforesaid Suzanne Gaudry to death, tying her to a gallows, and strangling her to death, then burning her body and burying it there in the environs of the woods.

At Valenciennes, the 9th of July, 1652. To each [member of the Court] 4 *livres*, 16 *sous*. . . . And for the trip of the aforementioned Roux, including an escort of one soldier, 30 *livres*.

■ Discussion Questions

1. According to the trial record, why was Suzanne Gaudry targeted for persecution? What does this reveal about contemporary beliefs in witches and their powers?

2. How would you characterize the legal procedures used in this trial? How might the procedures help to explain the widespread consistency in the content of confessions throughout the period of witchcraft persecutions?

3. What does this document suggest about the religious anxieties of the times?

■ Comparative Questions

1. What similarities and/or differences do you see between Luther and Ignatius's models of Christian life?

2. What do *The Adventures of a Simpleton* and the witchcraft trial suggest about the role of violence in seventeenth-century European society and culture?

3. How do the Edict of Nantes and Galileo's letter support scholars who argue that amid the conflicts of this period, many European leaders and thinkers increasingly gave precedence to secular concerns over religious ones?

4. Despite a gradual trend toward secularization in seventeenth-century Europe, what do *The Adventures of a Simpleton,* the Edict of Nantes, Galileo's letter, and Suzanne Gaudry's trial records reveal about the continued importance of religion in shaping Europeans' understanding of the everyday world?

5. In what ways is Galileo's emphasis on the value of observation and personal experience reflected in the procedures of the Gaudry trial? What does this suggest about the impact of the new science on traditional beliefs?

13

State Building and the Search for Order, 1648–1690

T HE WARS OVER RELIGION not only had left bitter memories in late seventeenth-century Europe but also had ruined economies and weakened governments. In response, many people sought to impose order on the turbulent world in a variety of ways. As the first four documents reveal, politically, the quest for stability fueled the development of two rival systems of state building—absolutism and constitutionalism—with France and England, respectively, taking the lead. Despite their differences, rulers within both systems centralized power and expanded bureaucracies, casting an increasingly wide net over their subjects' lives. Although not everyone submitted willingly to the expansion of state power, such resistance was typically fruitless. Even so, as the final document suggests, the emergence of a new literary genre—the novel—during this period points to other, less overt forces countering the search for order.

1.
Louis de Rouvroy, Duke of Saint-Simon
Memoirs
1694–1723

A nobleman and godson of King Louis XIV (r. 1643–1715), Louis de Rouvroy (1675–1755), the Duke of Saint-Simon, was raised at the royal palace of Versailles. He recorded his life and impressions of the court for almost three decades, beginning at the age of nineteen. The result was his multivolume Memoirs, *which painted an intimate portrait of Louis XIV and the workings of the absolutist state. Louis de Rouvroy was not an entirely objective observer, however. Having never achieved great success within the court, he often viewed it through the lens of his own resentment. The ex-*

From *The Memoirs of the Duke of Saint Simon*, vol. II, trans. Bayle St. John (Philadelphia: Gebbie and Co., 1890), 363–69.

cerpt here provides insight into both the reasons behind Louis XIV's move to Versailles and his method of rule there.

Let me touch now upon some other incidents in his career, and upon some points in his character.

He early showed a disinclination for Paris. The troubles that had taken place there during the minority made him regard the place as dangerous; he wished, too, to render himself venerable by hiding himself from the eyes of the multitude; all these considerations fixed him at St. Germains soon after the death of the Queen, his mother. It was to that place he began to attract the world by fêtes and gallantries, and by making it felt that he wished to be often seen.

His love for Madame de la Vallière, which was at first kept secret, occasioned frequent excursions to Versailles, then a little card castle, which had been built by Louis XIII. — annoyed, and his suite still more so, at being frequently obliged to sleep in a wretched inn there, after he had been out hunting in the forest of Saint Leger. That monarch rarely slept at Versailles more than one night, and then from necessity; the King, his son, slept there, so that he might be more in private with his mistress; pleasures unknown to the hero and just man, worthy son of Saint Louis, who built the little château.

These excursions of Louis XIV. by degrees gave birth to those immense buildings he erected at Versailles; and their convenience for a numerous court, so different from the apartments at St. Germains, led him to take up his abode there entirely shortly after the death of the Queen. He built an infinite number of apartments, which were asked for by those who wished to pay their court to him; whereas at St. Germains nearly everybody was obliged to lodge in the town, and the few who found accommodation at the château were strangely inconvenienced.

The frequent fêtes, the private promenades at Versailles, the journeys, were means on which the King seized in order to distinguish or mortify the courtiers, and thus render them more assiduous in pleasing him. He felt that of real favors he had not enough to bestow; in order to keep up the spirit of devotion, he therefore unceasingly invented all sorts of ideal ones, little preferences and petty distinctions, which answered his purpose as well.

He was exceedingly jealous of the attention paid him. Not only did he notice the presence of the most distinguished courtiers, but those of inferior degree also. He looked to the right and to the left, not only upon rising but upon going to bed, at his meals, in passing through his apartments, or his gardens of Versailles, where alone the courtiers were allowed to follow him; he saw and noticed everybody; not one escaped him, not even those who hoped to remain unnoticed. He marked well all absentees from the court, found out the reason of their absence, and never lost an opportunity of acting towards them as the occasion might seem to justify. With some of the courtiers (the most distinguished), it was a demerit not to make the court their ordinary abode; with others 'twas a fault to come but rarely; for those who never or scarcely ever came it was certain disgrace. When their names were in any way mentioned, "I do not know them," the King would reply haughtily. Those who presented themselves but seldom were thus characterized: "They are people I never see"; these decrees were irrevocable. He could not bear people who liked Paris.

Louis XIV took great pains to be well informed of all that passed everywhere; in the public places, in the private houses, in society and familiar intercourse. His spies and tell-tales were infinite. He had them of all species; many who were ignorant that their information reached him; others who knew it; others who wrote to him direct, sending their letters through channels he indicated; and all these letters were seen by him alone, and always before everything else; others who sometimes spoke to him secretly in his cabinet, entering by the back stairs. These unknown means ruined an infinite number of people of all classes who never could discover the cause; often ruined them very unjustly; for the King, once prejudiced, never altered his opinion, or so rarely, that nothing was more rare. He had, too, another fault, very dangerous for others and often for himself, since it deprived him of good subjects. He had an excellent memory; in this way, that if he saw a man who, twenty years before, perhaps, had in some manner offended him, he did not forget the man, though he might forget the offense. This was enough, however, to exclude the person from all favor. The representations of a minister, of a general, of his confessor even, could not move the King. He would not yield.

The most cruel means by which the King was informed of what was passing—for many years before anybody knew it—was that of opening letters. The promptitude and dexterity with which they were opened passes understanding. He saw extracts from all the letters in which there were passages that the chiefs of the post-office, and then the minister who governed it, thought ought to go before him; entire letters, too, were sent to him, when their contents seemed to justify the sending. Thus the chiefs of the post, nay, the principal clerks were in a position to suppose what they pleased and against whom they pleased. A word of contempt against the King or the government, a joke, a detached phrase, was enough. It is incredible how many people, justly or unjustly, were more or less ruined, always without resource, without trial, and without knowing why. The secret was impenetrable; for nothing ever cost the King less than profound silence and dissimulation. . . .

He liked splendor, magnificence, and profusion in everything: you pleased him if you shone through the brilliancy of your houses, your clothes, your table, your equipages. Thus a taste for extravagance and luxury was disseminated through all classes of society; causing infinite harm, and leading to general confusion of rank and to ruin.

■ Discussion Questions

1. How did Louis XIV use court etiquette as a form of power?

2. Why might nobles have resided at Versailles? What benefits did they gain?

3. What is Saint-Simon's attitude toward Louis XIV's style of governing?

4. In what ways did court life embody the principles of absolutism?

2.
British Parliament
The English Bill of Rights
1689

King Louis XIV (r. 1643–1715) had many admirers in Europe, including King James II (r. 1685–1688) of England. Unlike Louis, however, James faced a major challenge to his power: Parliament. James and Parliament had been at odds for decades concerning the nature of royal authority, and James's absolutist policies proved too much for Parliament to bear. As a result, in 1688 they ousted the king and offered the throne to Prince William of Orange (1650–1702) and his wife, Mary (1662–1694), the eldest of James's adult daughters. In exchange, William and Mary agreed to accept the Bill of Rights, which legally defined the role of Parliament as the monarchy's partner in government. The bill not only marked the victory of constitutionalism over absolutism in England but also formed the cornerstone of the idea that government should ensure certain rights by law to protect its citizens from the dangers of arbitrary power.

Whereas the said late King James II having abdicated the government, and the throne being thereby vacant, his Highness the prince of Orange (whom it hath pleased Almighty God to make the glorious instrument of delivering this kingdom from popery and arbitrary power) did (by the advice of the lords spiritual and temporal, and diverse principal persons of the Commons) cause letters to be written to the lords spiritual and temporal, being Protestants, and other letters to the several counties, cities, universities, boroughs, and Cinque Ports, for the choosing of such persons to represent them, as were of right to be sent to parliament, to meet and sit at Westminster upon the two and twentieth day of January, in this year 1689, in order to such an establishment as that their religion, laws, and liberties might not again be in danger of being subverted; upon which letters elections have been accordingly made.

And thereupon the said lords spiritual and temporal and Commons, pursuant to their respective letters and elections, being now assembled in a full and free representation of this nation, taking into their most serious consideration the best means for attaining the ends aforesaid, do in the first place (as their ancestors in like case have usually done), for the vindication and assertion of their ancient rights and liberties, declare:

1. That the pretended power of suspending laws, or the execution of laws, by regal authority, without consent of parliament is illegal.

2. That the pretended power of dispensing with the laws, or the execution of law by regal authority, as it hath been assumed and exercised of late, is illegal.

From Great Britain, *The Statutes*, vol. II, rev. ed. (London: Eyre and Spottiswoode, 1871), 10–12.

3. That the commission for erecting the late court of commissioners for ecclesiastical causes, and all other commissions and courts of like nature, are illegal and pernicious.

4. That levying money for or to the use of the crown by pretense of prerogative, without grant of parliament, for longer time or in other manner than the same is or shall be granted, is illegal.

5. That it is the right of the subjects to petition the king, and all commitments and prosecutions for such petitioning are illegal.

6. That the raising or keeping a standing army within the kingdom in time of peace, unless it be with consent of parliament, is against law.

7. That the subjects which are Protestants may have arms for their defense suitable to their conditions, and as allowed by law.

8. That election of members of parliament ought to be free.

9. That the freedom of speech, and debates or proceedings in parliament, ought not to be impeached or questioned in any court or place out of parliament.

10. That excessive bail ought not to be required, nor excessive fines imposed, nor cruel and unusual punishments inflicted.

11. That jurors ought to be duly impaneled and returned, and jurors which pass upon men in trials for high treason ought to be freeholders.

12. That all grants and promises of fines and forfeitures of particular persons before conviction are illegal and void.

13. And that for redress of all grievances, and for the amending, strengthening, and preserving of the laws, parliament ought to be held frequently.

And they do claim, demand, and insist upon all and singular the premises, as their undoubted rights and liberties: and that no declarations, judgments, doings, or proceedings, to the prejudice of the people in any of the said premises, ought in any wise to be drawn hereafter into consequence or example.

To which demand of their rights they are particularly encouraged by the declaration of his Highness the prince of Orange, as being the only means for obtaining a full redress and remedy therein.

Having therefore an entire confidence that his said Highness the prince of Orange will perfect the deliverance so far advanced by him, and will still preserve them from the violation of their rights, which they have here asserted, and from all other attempt upon their religion, rights, and liberties:

The said lords spiritual and temporal, and commons, assembled at Westminster, do resolve that William and Mary, prince and princess of Orange, be, and be declared, king and queen of England, France, and Ireland, the dominions thereunto belonging, to hold the crown and royal dignity of the said kingdoms and dominions to them the said prince and princess during their lives. . . .

Upon which their said Majesties did accept the crown and royal dignity of the kingdoms of England, France, and Ireland, and the dominions thereunto belonging, according to the resolution and desire of the said lords and commons contained in the said declaration.

■ Discussion Questions

1. In what ways does the Bill of Rights limit the powers of the crown?

2. What role does the bill grant Parliament in government?

3. How does the bill give weight to the attitude of some members of Parliament at the time that they had "made" the new king and queen?

3.
Ludwig Fabritius
The Revolt of Stenka Razin
1670

Despite its geographical and cultural isolation from the rest of Europe, Russia followed France's lead down the path of absolutism. In the process, Tsar Alexei (r. 1645–1676) legally combined millions of slaves and free peasants into a single serf class bound to the land and their aristocratic masters. Not everyone passively accepted this fate, however. In 1667, a Cossack named Stenka Razin (c. 1630–1671) led a revolt against serfdom that gained considerable support among people whose social and economic status was threatened by the tsar's policies, including soldiers from peasant stock. Razin's ultimate defeat at the hands of the tsar explains the close ties between the Russian government's enhanced power and the enforcement of serfdom. A Dutch soldier, Ludwig Fabritius (1648–1729), who lived in Russia from 1660 to 1677 while employed as a military expert in the Russian army, wrote the following account of one stage of the revolt.

Then Stenka with his company started off upstream, rowing as far as Tsaritsyn, whence it took him only one day's journey to Panshin, a small town situated on the Don. Here he began straightaway quietly gathering the common people around him, giving them money, and promises of great riches if they would be loyal to him and help to exterminate the treacherous boyars.[1]

This lasted the whole winter, until by about spring he had assembled 4,000 to 5,000 men. With these he came to Tsaritsyn and demanded the immediate surrender of the fortress; the rabble soon achieved their purpose, and although the governor tried to take refuge in a tower, he soon had to give himself up as he was deserted by one and all. Stenka immediately had the wretched governor hanged; and all the goods they found belonging to the Tsar and his officers as well as to the merchants were confiscated and distributed among the rabble.

From Anthony Glenn Cross, ed., *Russia under Western Eyes, 1517–1825* (London: Elek Books, 1971), 120–23.
[1]This term refers to a class of noblemen.

Stenka now began once more to make preparations. Since the plains are not cultivated, the people have to bring their corn from Nizhniy-Novgorod and Kazan down the Volga in big boats known as *nasady*, and everything destined for Astrakhan has first to pass Tsaritsyn. Stenka Razin duly noted this, and occupied the whole of the Volga, so that nothing could get through to Astrakhan. Here he captured a few hundred merchants with their valuable goods, taking possession of all kinds of fine linen, silks, striped silk material, sables, soft leather, ducats, talers, and many thousands of rubles in Russian money and merchandise of every description. . . .

In the meantime four regiments of *streltsy* [sharpshooters] were dispatched from Moscow to subdue these brigands. They arrived with their big boats and as they were not used to the water, were easily beaten. Here Stenka Razin gained possession of a large amount of ammunition and artillery-pieces and everything else he required. While the above-mentioned [sharpshooters] were sent from Moscow, about 5,000 men were ordered up from Astrakhan by water and by land to capture Stenka Razin. As soon as he had finished with the former, he took up a good position, and, being in possession of reliable information regarding our forces, he left Tsaritsyn and came to meet us half way at Chernyy Yar, confronting us before we had suspected his presence or received any information about him. We stopped at Chernyy Yar for a few days and sent out scouts by water and by land, but were unable to obtain any definite information. On 10 July [*sic:* June] a council of war was held at which it was decided to advance and seek out Stenka. The next morning, at 8 o'clock, our look-outs on the water came hurriedly and raised the alarm as the Cossacks were following at their heels. We got out of our boats and took up battle positions. General Knyaz Semen Ivanovich Lvov went through the ranks and reminded all the men to do their duty and to remember the oath they had taken to His Majesty the Tsar, to fight like honest soldiers against these irresponsible rebels, whereupon they all unanimously shouted: "Yes, we will give our lives for His Majesty the Tsar, and will fight to the last drop of our blood."

In the meantime Stenka prepared for battle and deployed on a wide front; to all those who had no rifle he gave a long pole, burnt a little at one end, and with a rag or small hook attached. They presented a strange sight on the plain from afar, and the common soldiers imagined that, since there were so many flags and standards, there must be a host of people. They [the common soldiers] held a consultation and at once decided that this was the chance for which they had been waiting so long, and with all their flags and drums they ran over to the enemy. They began kissing and embracing one another and swore with life and limb to stand together and to exterminate the treacherous boyars, to throw off the yoke of slavery, and to become free men.

The general looked at the officers and the officers at the general, and no one knew what to do; one said this, and another that, until finally it was decided that they and the general should get into the boats and withdraw to Astrakhan. But the rascally [sharpshooters] of Chernyy Yar stood on the walls and towers, turning their weapons on us and opened fire; some of them ran out of the fortress and cut us off from the boats, so that we had no means of escape. In the meantime those curs of ours who had gone over to the Cossacks came up from behind. We numbered about eighty men, officers, noblemen, and clerks. Murder at once began. Then, however, Stenka Razin ordered that no more officers were to be killed, saying that there must be a few good men among them who should be pardoned, whilst those others who had not lived in amity with their men should be condemned to well-deserved punishment by the Ataman and his *Krug*. A *Krug* is a meeting convened by the order of the Ataman, at which the Cossacks stand in a circle with the standard in the center; the Ataman then takes his place beside his best officers, to whom he divulges his wishes, ordering them to make these known to the common brothers and to hear their opinion on the matter. . . .

A *Krug* was accordingly called and Stenka asked through his chiefs how the general and his officers had treated the soldiers under their command. Thereupon the unscrupulous curs [sharpshooters], as well as soldiers, unanimously called out that there was not one of them who deserved to remain alive, and they all asked that their father Stepan Timofeyevich Razin should order them to be cut down. This was granted with the exception of General Knyaz Semen Ivanovich Lvov, whose life was specially spared by Stenka himself. The officers were now brought in order of rank out of the tower, into which they had been thrown bound hand and foot the previous day, their ropes were cut and they were led outside the gate. When all the bloodthirsty curs had lined up, each was eager to deal his former superior the first blow, one with the sword, another with the lance, another with the scimitar, and others again with martels, so that as soon as an officer was pushed into the ring, the curs immediately killed him with their many wounds; indeed, some were cut to pieces and straightaway thrown into the Volga. My stepfather, Paul Rudolf Beem, and Lt. Col. Wundrum and many other officers, senior and junior, were cut down before my eyes.

My own time had not yet come: this I could tell by the wonderful way in which God rescued me, for as I—half-dead—now awaited the final blow, my [former] orderly, a young soldier, came and took me by my bound arms and tried to take me down the hill. As I was already half-dead, I did not move and did not know what to do, but he came back and took me by the arms and led me, bound as I was, through the throng of curs, down the hill into the boat and immediately cut my arms free, saying that I should rest in peace here and that he would be responsible for me and do his best to save my life. . . . Then my guardian angel told me not to leave the boat, and left me. He returned in the evening and brought me a piece of bread which I enjoyed since I had had nothing to eat for two days.

The following day all our possessions were looted and gathered together under the main flag, so that both our bloodthirsty curs and the Cossacks got their share.

■ Discussion Questions

1. What do you think motivated Razin and his followers to take action?

2. Why were Razin and his forces able to defeat the tsar's soldiers?

3. With whom do you think Fabritius's sympathies lay, and why?

4.
A True and Exact Relation of the Raising
of the Siege of Vienna
1683

As the decision by Tsar Alexei (r. 1645–1676) to enserf millions of Russian peasants suggests, rulers in central and eastern Europe developed their own form of absolutism, which reflected the conditions and challenges specific to their regions. The following anonymous eyewitness account of the raising of the siege of the Austrian capital, Vienna, in 1683 provides an example of just how formidable the conditions and challenges could be. Although the Holy Roman Emperor Leopold I (r. 1658–1705) had expanded his authority over the patchwork of ethnic groups under his rule, he still faced the growing presence of the Ottoman Turks to the east. As they pushed into the heart of Austrian Habsburg territory and surrounded Vienna in 1683, the Turks seemed poised for victory. All appeared lost for the Austrian troops until a Polish detachment under the leadership of King Jan Sobieski (r. 1674–1696) arrived. Together they took the Turkish army by surprise and saved the beleaguered city. For the eyewitness, the impact of this "signal victory" extended far beyond the walls of Vienna, opening the door for Austrian dominance of eastern Europe. His optimism was not unfounded, for by 1699, the Turkish sultan had relinquished almost all of Hungary to the Austrians.

SEPTEMBER 12TH

After a Siege of Sixty days, accompanied with a Thousand Difficulties, Sicknesses, Want of Provisions, and great Effusion of Blood, after a Million of Cannon and Musquet Shot, Bombs, Granadoes, and all sorts of Fire Works, which has changed the Face of the fairest and most flourishing City in the World, disfigured and ruined most part of the best Palaces of the same, and chiefly those of the Emperor; and damaged in many places the Beautiful Tower and Church of St. *Stephen,* with many Sumptuous Buildings. After a Resistance so vigorous, and the Loss of so many brave Officers and Soldiers, whose Valor and Bravery deserve Immortal Glory. After so many Toils endured, so many Watchings and so many Orders so prudently distributed by Count *Staremburgh,* and so punctually executed by the other Officers.

After so many new Retrenchments, Pallizadoes, Parapets, new Ditches in the Ravelins, Bastions, Courtins, and principal Streets and Houses in the Town: Finally, after a Vigorous Defense and a Resistance without parallel, Heaven favorably heard the Prayers and Tears of a Cast-down and Mournful People, and retorted

From "A True and Exact Relation of the Raising of the Siege of Vienna and the Victory Obtained Over the Ottoman Army" (London: 1683), 59–62, 65–66.

the Terror on a powerful Enemy, and drove him from the Walls of *Vienna,* who since the Fifteenth of *July* last early in the Morning, to the Twelfth of *September,* had so Vigorously attacked it with Two hundred thousand Men; and by endless Workings, Trenchings, and Minings, reduced it almost to its last gasp.

Count *Staremburgh,* who sustained this great Burden, assisted by so many Gallant Officers, having given Notice to the Christian Army, by Discharge of Musquets from the Tower of St. *Stephen,* of the Extremity whereto the City was reduced, they discovered on the Twelfth of this Month, early in the Morning, the Christian Troops marching down the Neighboring Mountains of *Kalemberg,* and heard continually the Discharges of their Artillery against the *Turks,* who being advanced thither, were fortified with Parapets of Earth and great Stones, to hinder the Descent of the Christian Army from the Mountains, who notwithstanding did advance. The Vanguard of the Horse and Foot, seconded by the Polish Horse, had a long Skirmish with the *Turks,* disputing every Foot of Ground; but seeing themselves totally vanquished by the Christian Forces, who had surmounted all the Difficulties of the Mountains, and drawn down their Cannon in spight of them, they retired Fighting, leaving to the Christians all their Camps full of Pavillions, Tents, Barracks, and Eight Pieces of Cannon (with which they had raised a Battery on that side Four days before) and retreated towards their Principal Camp, between the Villages of *Hernalls, Haderkling* and *Jezing;* but as they passed by the Bastion of *Melck* they fired their Cannon furiously on them: The Christians being ravish'd with the Victory, pursued them with so much heat, that they were not only forced to leave their great Camps, but likewise all their others; flying towards *Hungary:* And it is certain, had not the Night come on, they had totally defeated and routed the *Ottoman Army.* [. . .]

In the Night the Christians made themselves Masters of all the *Turks* Camp. Afterwards Four Companies of our Foot entered into the Enemies Approaches with Torches and lighted Straw, but found nothing but Dead Bodies; they took possession of the Enemies Artillery, some whereof were brought into the City. All the night long we saw Fires at a distance, the *Turk* having fired as many of their Camps as so sudden a flight would give them leave, and retreated from the *Island* by favor of a Bridge which they had made below the River, upon one of the Arms of the *Danube,* the Christians having seized the Bridge above, on the same River.

On Monday Morning we saw all the Camps and Fields covered with Soldiers as well *Poles* as *Germans.* The *City* was relieved on *Sunday* about Five of the Clock in the Afternoon, and every bodies' curiosity carried them to see the Camp, after they had been shut up above two Months.

The King of *Poland* having in the mean time with the greatest Vigor repulsed the Enemy on his side and put them to flight, leaving the Plunder of their Camp behind them, which consisted of a very Rich Tent of the Grand Visier, his Colors, Two Poles with the Horse Tails, their usual Signal of War, and his Guidon or Standard, set with Diamonds, his Treasure designed for the Payment of the Army, and in short, all his Equipage was possess'd by the *Polanders.* As for the rest of the Tents, Baggage, Artillery, Ammunition, and Provisions enough to load Eight thousand Waggons, was divided among our Army.

Night coming on, we could no longer pursue, having followed the Enemy about a Mile from their Camp, and our Army having been all that time without Eating and Drinking, we were forced to found a Retreat to refresh them. We had all that Night to rest in, and the Enemy to save themselves. The next day being the Thirteenth we continued not the pursuit for the same reason, which without doubt we might have done with great advantage, since they fled in much disorder toward St. *Godart* to get over the River *Raab.* We are building a Bridge at *Alltemburgh* in *Hungary,* and our Armies will march very suddenly. On Sunday Night, after the Battle, his Imperial Majesty came to *Cloister Nuburgh,* Four hours from *Vienna,* from whence he sent the next day to compliment the King of *Poland* and the Electors upon their good success the day before.

On the Fourteenth, Count *Staremburgh* came to his Imperial Majesty (who received him with all manner of demonstrations of Affection and Esteem) and gave him a Relation of several considerable passages during the Siege: A short time after the Emperor embarked on the *Danube,* and landed above the Bridge before the Town, and entered the City at the *Stuben Gate,* at Landing he was received by the Electors of *Bavaria* and *Saxony,* who were attended by their Guards and a great many Noble Men. It being impossible to remove in so short a time such a number of Dead Bodies, both *Turks, Christians,* and *Horses,* whereof the stench was so great on the Road, that it was enough to have caused an Infection. [...]

September 19th

The Emperor is gone this day to Lintz: We are now beginning to cleanse the City of its Rubbish, and carry off the Dead Carcasses of Man and Beast. The *Turks* had a *French Engineer* in their Camp, who hath done very much hurt to this City, and ruin'd us 50 Pieces of Cannon: There was also a great many *French* among the *Janizaries,* and many were found among the Dead with *French* Silver and Gold in their Pockets. There are daily brought in a great number of *Turks* Prisoners since the flight of the Grand Visier. It is intended to set the *Turks* that are already, and shall be hereafter taken, at Work on the reparation of our *Bastions* and *Courtins.* The Sieur *Kaunitz,* the Emperors Resident at the Port, who was found in the *Grand Visier* Tent, is now in this City.

This moment comes the News that *Friday* last the *17th,* a part of the *Turks* Army fled away in such haste, within sight of *Raab,* as if ours were at their backs; the Officer who brought it, added that on his way from *Raab* he met with but two *Turks,* whom he brought Prisoners to *Bruckham* of *Ceytha,* where he sold them for four Pecks of Oats. All the Enemies or Rebels who had got into the Isle of *Schut,* are retired thence. There are gone down from hence some Boats full of Infantry towards *Hungary.* We are in hopes to hear shortly of some great Enterprize on the *Turks.* Here are daily brought in abundance of young Children whom the *Turks* had taken Captive; they ravish'd the young Maids and Women, and cut off the Heads of the old Men and Women.

Here is News from *Gratz,* That Count *Budiani* (who hath desired Count *Strasoldo* to intercede for him to the Emperor) had commanded 8000 *Hussars* of his Troops, under the Command of his Son and the Count *Nadasti,* to fall on 2000 *Turks* encamped near *Canisa,* and that they have put them all to the Sword. *Baron Buroni* is dead, and his Son revolted from the Rebels, and begs the Emperor's Pardon. The *Turks* who are Prisoners, unanimously affirm, That the Grand Visier hath caused *Ibrahim Bassa* Visier of *Buda* to be strangled for first giving Ground at the Battle before *Vienna.* Part of the *Ottoman Army* is arrived near *Greekish Weissenberg.*

Since this Signal Victory obtained by the Christian Army (who some days had refreshed themselves) we are certainly informed they passed *Presbourgh* the 23rd of *September,* in pursuit of the scattered Forces of the Ottoman Army, who fled to *Stollweissembourgh;* so that a few days will bring us an Accompt of what has passed between them. This Victory hath already given this advantage to our Affairs, that the Count of *Trausmondorse* [Trautmannsdorf] had taken and confiscated the Castles and Revenues of those who had done Homage to the *Turk;* and it was resolved to do the like in *Hungary.*

■ Discussion Questions

1. What does this account reveal about military technology and tactics at the time?
2. How does the eyewitness portray Leopold I? What does this portrayal suggest about his method of rule?
3. How do the religious differences between the two camps shape the content and tone of this account of the raising of the siege?

5.
Madame de Lafayette
The Princess of Clèves
1678

Like the Duke of Saint-Simon, French author Marie-Madeline de La Vergne (b. 1634), Countess of Lafayette, was well acquainted with the court of Louis XIV (r. 1643–1715). She also had close ties to intellectual circles in Paris, where she cultivated her formidable writing talents. In 1678, she published anonymously The Princess of Clèves, *which was an overnight literary sensation. The following letters help explain why. Set during the reign of King Henry II (r. 1547–1559), the book centers on the character of Mademoiselle de Chartres, who, upon captivating the court with her wit and beauty, weds the Prince of Clèves. Their union proves an unhappy one, and the princess falls in love with another man, Nemours. She never succumbs to her desire, however, even after her husband's death. The book's portrayal of her emotional struggle scandalized many readers by challenging conventional notions of marriage and proper aristocratic behavior. At*

From Marie-Madeleine de Lafayette, *The Princess of Clèves,* trans. and ed. John D. Lyons (New York: Norton, 1994), 121–22.

the same time, the book abandoned the idealized and lengthy style of the romantic genre, giving birth to a new literary form, the novel.

MADAME DE LAFAYETTE TO JOSEPH MARIE DE LESCHERAINE

13 April 1678

A little book which appeared fifteen years ago and that people attributed to me makes them want to credit me with *The Princess of Clèves*. But I assure you that I had nothing to do with it and that M. de La Rochefoucauld, to whom the book has also been attributed, had as little to do with it as I did. He declared this under oath so many times that he cannot be doubted, especially about something that could be admitted without shame. As for me, I am flattered that people suspect me of being the author, and I believe that I would acknowledge the book as mine if I could be sure that the author would never show up and ask for it back. I find it a very pleasant work, well written without being perfectly polished, so full of admirably subtle details that it has to be read more than once. And most of all, I find in it a perfect representation of the world of the court and of the way one lives there. The book does not seem like a romance, and there is nothing overdone in it. Assuredly it is not a romance but rather a book of memoirs, and I have been told that such was its title, but they changed it.

So there, Monsieur, is my opinion of *Madame de Clèves*. I would ask yours as well. People are so divided over this book that they could come to blows. Some condemn what others admire in it. So, no matter what you say, don't be afraid of being the only one to say it.

ROGER DE BUSSY-RABUTIN TO MARIE DE SÉVIGNÉ

26 June 1678

But I forgot to tell you that I have finally given *The Princess of Clèves* an impartial reading, not at all prejudiced by the good and bad things people have written. I found the first part admirable; the second didn't seem as good. In the first volume, except a few words that are repeated too often — just a small number — everything is pleasing, everything is natural, nothing is stilted. In the second part, Madame de Clèves's confession is preposterous, and could only be told in a true history; but when one is making a story up it is absurd to depict the heroine as having a sentiment that is so out of the ordinary. The author, by doing so, was thinking of ways to be different from the old romances and was not paying attention to common sense. A wife rarely tells her husband that a man is in love with her and *never* tells her husband that she is in love with another man, and especially not by throwing herself at his feet, a gesture that can make him think she has committed the ultimate offense. Besides, it is implausible that passionate love and virtue should remain for a long time equal in strength. In court society if a woman hasn't completely rejected a suitor in two or three weeks, or at most a month, she is only trying to make herself appear more desirable. And if, against all the odds and in spite of custom, the conflict between love and virtue should last until her husband's death, she would be delighted to harmonize virtue and love by marrying a man of his [Nemours's] quality, the handsomest gallant of his day. The first incident in the gardens at Coulommiers is not plausible and smacks of romance. It is very a calculated arrangement that when the Princess confesses to her husband that she loves another man, M. de Nemours, at just the right moment, is behind the fence listening to them; I don't even see why he had to know her confession, and in any event it should have been arranged so that he learned about [it] in some other way. It's like a romance, as well, when people talk to themselves. Besides the fact that it is not customary for people to talk to themselves, it isn't possible to know what someone says to herself unless she writes her own story: and even then she would say only what she thought. The letter to the Vidame is also like the letters in a romance, obscure, too long, and not at all natural. Just the same, in this second volume everything is just as well narrated, and the turns of phrase are just as beautiful as in the first volume.

Roger de Rabutin, comte de Bussy

■ Discussion Questions

1. In the first letter, how does Madame de Lafayette confront the prejudice that it was improper in seventeenth-century France for noblewomen to publish their writings and use it to her advantage?

2. Why is Roger de Bussy-Rabutin critical of *The Princess of Clèves* in the second letter?

3. What do Roger de Bussy-Rabutin's criticisms suggest about the development of the novel as a new type of literature?

■ Comparative Questions

1. What do both Saint-Simon and Roger de Bussy-Rabutin reveal about court culture during the reign of Louis XIV?

2. Based on the first three documents, what comparisons could be drawn about the relationship between the individual and the state in England, France, and Russia? What do these comparisons suggest about the basis of authority in constitutional and absolutist governments?

3. What do the accounts of Stenka Razin's revolt and the raising of the siege of Vienna suggest about the role of the military in the growth of absolutism in central and eastern Europe?

14

The Atlantic System and Its Consequences, 1690–1740

T HE GROWTH OF EUROPEAN domestic economies and overseas colonization during the eighteenth century infused Europe with money, new products, and a
new sense of optimism about the future. Yet, as the first document here illustrates,
the good times came at a horrible price for the millions of African slaves who
formed the economic backbone of the colonial system. Changes were also under-
way on the political front, with the stabilization of the European state system.
Consequently, states such as Russia shone more brightly over the political landscape while others lost their luster. The second document brings Russia's new
prominence to life in its leader's own words. The third and fourth documents that
follow reveal that intellectual circles were also ablaze with change as scholars and
writers cast political, social, and religious issues in a new critical and secular light.
Yet at the same time, the final document attests that religion continued to assert a
powerful hold on Europeans, many of whom yearned for a renewal of Christian
beliefs and practices.

1.
Olaudah Equiano
The Interesting Narrative of the Life of Olaudah Equiano
Written by Himself
1789

*The autobiography of Olaudah Equiano (c. 1745–1797) puts a human face on the
eighteenth-century Atlantic slave trade and its human consequences. As he describes,
he was born in what is now Nigeria and was captured by local raiders and sold into
slavery in his early teens. He gained his freedom in 1766 and soon thereafter became
a vocal supporter of the English abolitionist movement. He published his autobiography in 1789, a best seller in its day, with numerous editions published in Britain and*

From Paul Edwards, ed., *Equiano's Travels: His Autobiography*, abridged (London: Heinemann,
1967), 25–32.

America. In the following excerpt, Equiano recounts his journey on the slave ship that took him away from his homeland, his freedom, and his very identity. Millions of others shared this same fate. Scholars have recently challenged this account, pointing to new evidence that suggests Equiano was born a slave in South Carolina, so probably early parts of his autobiography drew on the oral history of other slaves rather than on Equiano's personal experience. Regardless of where the truth lies, his book is invaluable as one of the very few texts written in English during the eighteenth century by a person of African descent.

The first object which saluted my eyes when I arrived on the coast was the sea, and a slave ship which was then riding at anchor and waiting for its cargo. These filled me with astonishment, which was soon converted into terror when I was carried on board. I was immediately handled and tossed up to see if I were sound by some of the crew, and I was now persuaded that I had gotten into a world of bad spirits and that they were going to kill me. Their complexions too differing so much from ours, their long hair and the language they spoke (which was very different from any I had ever heard) united to confirm me in this belief. Indeed such were the horrors of my views and fears at the moment that, if ten thousand worlds had been my own, I would have freely parted with them all to have exchanged my condition with that of the meanest slave in my own country. When I looked round the ship too and saw a large furnace or copper boiling and a multitude of black people of every description chained together, every one of their countenances expressing dejection and sorrow, I no longer doubted of my fate; and quite overpowered with horror and anguish, I fell motionless on the deck and fainted. When I recovered a little I found some black people about me, who I believed were some of those who had brought me on board and had been receiving their pay; they talked to me in order to cheer me, but all in vain. I asked them if we were not to be eaten by those white men with horrible looks, red faces, and loose hair. They told me I was not, and one of the crew brought me a small portion of spirituous liquor in a wine glass, but being afraid of him I would not take it out of his hand. One of the blacks therefore took it from him and gave it to me, and I took a little down my palate, which instead of reviving me, as they thought it would, threw me into the greatest consternation at the strange feeling it produced, having never tasted such any liquor before. Soon after this the blacks who brought me on board went off, and left me abandoned to despair.

I now saw myself deprived of all chance of returning to my native country or even the least glimpse of hope of gaining the shore, which I now considered as friendly; and I even wished for my former slavery in preference to my present situation, which was filled with horrors of every kind, still heightened by my ignorance of what I was to undergo. I was not long suffered to indulge my grief; I was soon put down under the decks, and there I received such a salutation in my nostrils as I had never experienced in my life: so that with the loathsomeness of the stench and crying together, I became so sick and low that I was not able to eat, nor had I the least desire to taste anything. I now wished for the last friend, death, to relieve me; but soon, to my grief, two of the white men offered me eatables, and on my refusing to eat, one of them held me fast by the hands and laid me across I think the windlass, and tied my feet while the other flogged me severely. I had never experienced anything of this kind before, and although, not being used to the water, I naturally feared that element the first time I saw it, yet nevertheless could I have got over the nettings I would have jumped over the side, but I could not; and besides, the crew used to watch us very closely who were not chained down to the decks, lest we should leap into the water: and I have seen some of these poor African prisoners most severely cut for attempting to do so, and hourly whipped for not eating. This indeed was often the case with myself. In a little time after, amongst the poor chained men I found some of my own nation, which in a small degree gave ease to my mind. I inquired of these what was to be done with us; they gave me to understand we were to be carried to these white people's country to work for them. I then was a little revived, and thought if it were no worse than working, my situation was not so desperate: but still I feared I should be put to death, the white people looked and acted, as I thought, in so savage a manner; for I had never seen among my people such instances of brutal cruelty, and this not only shewn towards us blacks but also to some of the whites themselves. One white man in particular I saw, when we were permitted to be on deck, flogged so unmercifully with a large rope near the foremast that he died in consequence of it; and they tossed him over the side as they would have done a brute. This made me fear these people the more, and I expected nothing less than to be treated in the same manner. . . . At last, when the ship we were in had got in all her cargo, they made ready with many fearful noises, and we were all put under deck so that we could not see how they managed the vessel. But this disappointment was the last of my sorrow. The stench of the hold while we were on the coast was so intolerably loathsome that it was dangerous to remain there for any time, and some of us had been permitted to stay on the deck for the fresh air; but now that the whole ship's cargo were confined together it became absolutely pestilential. The closeness of the place and the heat of the climate, added to the number in the ship, which was so crowded that each had scarcely room to turn himself, almost suffocated us. This produced copious perspirations, so that the air soon became unfit for respiration from a variety of loathsome smells, and brought on a sickness among the slaves, of which many died, thus falling victims to the improvident avarice, as I may call it, of their purchasers. This wretched situation was again aggravated by the galling of the chains, now become insupportable, and the filth of the necessary tubs, into which the children often fell and were almost suffocated. The shrieks of the women and the groans of the dying rendered the whole a scene of horror almost inconceivable. Happily perhaps for myself I was soon reduced so low here that it was thought necessary to keep me almost always on deck, and from my extreme youth I was not put in fetters. In this situation I expected every hour to share the fate of my companions, some of whom were almost daily brought upon deck at the point of death, which I began to hope would soon put an end to my miseries. . . . At last we came in sight of the island of Barbados, at which the whites on board gave a great shout and made many signs of joy to us.

We did not know what to think of this, but as the vessel drew nearer we plainly saw the harbour and other ships of different kinds and sizes, and we soon anchored amongst them off Bridgetown. Many merchants and planters now came on board, though it was in the evening. They put us in separate parcels and examined us attentively. They also made us jump, and pointed to the land, signifying we were to go there.... We were not many days in the merchant's custody before we were sold after their usual manner, which is this: On a signal given, (as the beat of a drum) the buyers rush at once into the yard where the slaves are confined, and make choice of that parcel they like best. The noise and clamor with which this is attended and the eagerness visible in the countenances of the buyers serve not a little to increase the apprehensions of the terrified Africans, who may well be supposed to consider them as the ministers of that destruction to which they think themselves devoted. In this manner, without scruple, are relations and friends separated, most of them never to see each other again. I remember in the vessel in which I was brought over, in the men's apartment there were several brothers who, in the sale, were sold in different lots; and it was very moving on this occasion to see and hear their cries at parting. O, ye nominal Christians! might not an African ask you, Learned you this from your God who says unto you, Do unto all men as you would men should do unto you?

■ Discussion Questions

1. What are Equiano's impressions of the white men on the ship and their treatment of the slaves? How does this treatment reflect the slave traders' primary concerns?

2. What message do you think Equiano sought to convey to his readers? Based on this message, to whom do you think his book especially appealed?

2.

Tsar Peter I
Letter to His Son, Alexei
October 11, 1715
and
Alexei's Response
October 31, 1715

During the eighteenth century, European states turned much of their attention to the political and military scene burgeoning within Europe, vying to keep one step ahead

From *A Source Book for Russian History from Early Times to 1917*, vol. II (New Haven and London: Yale University Press, 1972), 338–39.

of their rivals. Russian Tsar Peter I (r. 1689–1725) was especially successful at this game, transforming Russia into a great European power with all the trappings of a Western absolutist state, including a strong army and centralized bureaucracy, during his reign. Peter wrote the following letter to Alexei, who was then his only son and heir, during the Great Northern War against Sweden, which Peter ultimately won to Russia's great advantage. The letter explains the tsar's relentless drive toward greatness on the European stage. Alexei's response reveals not only the striking differences in personality between the two men but also the tension that marked their tumultuous relationship.

[Peter to Alexei, October 11, 1715:]

Declaration to my son:

Everyone knows how, before the beginning of this war, our people were hemmed in by the Swedes, who not only stole the essential ports of our fatherland . . . but cut us off from communication with the whole world. And also later, in the beginning of this war (which enterprise was and is directed by God alone), oh, what great persecution we had to endure from those eternal enemies of ours because of our incompetence in the art of war, and with what sorrow and endurance we went to this school and, with the help of the above-mentioned guide, achieved a creditable degree [of effectiveness]. We were thus found worthy of looking on this enemy now trembling before us, trembling, perhaps, even more than we did before him. All this has been accomplished with the help of God through my modest labors and through those of other equally zealous and faithful sons of Russia.

However, when, considering this great blessing given by God to our fatherland, I think of my successor, a grief perhaps as strong as my joy gnaws me, when I see you, my heir, unfit for the management of state affairs (for it is not the fault of God, who has not deprived you of mind or health; for although not of a very strong constitution, you are not very weak either). But above all, you have no wish to hear anything about military affairs, which opened to us the way from darkness to light, so that we who were unknown before are now honored. I do not teach you to be inclined to wage war without a just cause, but to love this art and to endow and learn it by all means, for it is one of the two activities necessary for government: order and defense.

I have no wish to give you many examples, but I will mention only the Greeks, who are of the same religion as we. Did they not perish because they laid their arms aside, and were they not vanquished because of their peaceableness? Desirous of tranquil living, they always gave way to their enemy, who changed their tranquillity into endless servitude to tyrants. Perhaps you think that it can all be left to the generals; but this is really not so, for everyone looks up to his chief, to comply with his desires, which is an obvious fact. Thus, in the days of my brother's reign [Theodore, 1676–82], everyone liked clothes and horses above all things, and now they like arms. They may not be really interested in one or the other; but in what the chief is interested all take an interest, and to what he is indifferent, all are indifferent. And if they turn away so lightly from the frivolous pastimes, which are only a pleasure to man, how much more easily will they abandon so burdensome a game as war!

Furthermore, you do not learn anything because you have no desire to learn it, and you have no knowledge of military affairs. Lacking all knowledge, how can you direct these affairs? How can you reward the diligent and punish the negligent when you yourself do not understand their work? You will be forced to look into people's mouths like a young bird. Do you pretend to be unfit for military work because of weak health? But that is no reason. I ask of you not work, but good will, which no malady can destroy. Ask anyone who remembers my brother whom I spoke of but now, who was, beyond comparison, sicklier than you and could not ride spirited horses, but he had a great liking for them and was always looking at them and kept them before his eyes. . . . So you see, not everything is done by great labor, but also by a strong desire. You say to yourself, perhaps, that many rulers do not themselves go to war, and yet campaigns are still carried on. This is true when, although not going themselves, they have a desire for it, as had the late French king [Louis XIV], who went to war himself but little, and who yet had a great taste for it and showed such magnificent deeds in war that his wars were called the theater and school for the whole world. But he had a taste not only for war, but also for other affairs and for manufactures, through all of which he procured glory for his state more than anybody else.

Now that I have gone into all this, I return again to my original point, thinking of you. I am a man, and subject to death. To whom shall I leave all this sowing, done with God's help, and that harvest which has already grown? To one who, like the idle slave in the Gospel, buried his talent in the ground (which means that he threw away everything that God had given him)? I also keep thinking of your wicked and stubborn disposition; for how many times I used to scold you for that, and not only scold but beat you, and also how many years I have now gone without speaking to you, and all without success! . . .

I have pondered this with much grief, and, seeing that I can in no wise dispose you toward good, I have deemed it appropriate to write to you this last admonition, and to wait a short time for you to mend your ways, and that *not hypocritically* [Peter's emphasis]. If you do not, know that I shall totally disinherit you like a gangrenous member; and do not imagine that, because you are my only son, I write this only to frighten you; I will do it indeed (with God's consent), because I have never spared my own life for my fatherland and people, nor do I now; therefore how can I spare you, unworthy one? Better a good stranger than an unworthy kinsman.

Peter
October 11, 1715
Saint Petersburg

[Alexei to Peter, October 31, 1715:]

Most gracious sovereign and father:

I have read [the letter] that was given me on your behalf on October 27, 1715, after the funeral of my wife. I have nothing to say about it, except that if you wish to disinherit me of the Russian crown because of my worthlessness, let it be as you will. Most humbly I ask you for this very thing, Sire, for I consider myself unqualified and unfit for this task, being most deficient in memory (without which it is impossible to accomplish anything). All my mental and physical capacities are weakened by various illnesses, and I have become unfit to rule such a people, which task requires a man less rotten than I. Therefore, I do not make a claim, nor will I make claim in the future, to the inheritance of the Russian throne after you — God give you health for many years — even if I did not have a brother (but now, thank God, I have one [note: Prince Peter, born to Peter and Catherine on October 29, 1715], God give him health); let God be my witness [in this matter], and to show that I testify truthfully I write this with my own hand.

I entrust my children to your will and ask only for maintenance for myself to the end of my life. This is submitted to your decision and merciful will.

Your most humble slave and son Alexei
Saint Petersburg
October 31, 1715

■ Discussion Questions

1. Why do you think Peter regarded the "art of war" as so important to government, and what did he gain by practicing it?

2. In what ways was Peter critical of his son, and why?

3. Whom does Peter single out as a political role model, and why is this significant?

4. What do these letters reveal about the tsar's personality?

3.

Montesquieu
Persian Letters: Letter 37
1721

As Europe's economy expanded, so did its intellectual horizons with the birth of the Enlightenment in the 1690s. Charles-Louis de Secondat, Baron of Montesquieu (1689–1755), was an especially important literary figure on this front. In 1721 he published Persian Letters, *in which he uses fictional characters to explore an array of*

From Montesquieu, *Persian Letters*, vol. I, trans. John Davidson (London: Privately printed, 1892), 85–86.

topics with the critical, reasoning spirit characteristic of the period. Letter 37 points to one of his and other Enlightenment authors' main targets: the French king Louis XIV (r. 1643–1715) and his absolutist state. Written by one of the book's two main characters, a Persian traveler in France named Usbek, to a friend back home, the letter explicitly criticizes the king's vanity, ostentation, and life at court. The letter implicitly passes even more serious judgment on the aging ruler in noting his esteem for "oriental policies." Montesquieu condemns these same policies elsewhere in his letters as inhumane and unjust.

USBEK TO IBBEN, AT SMYRNA

The King of France is old. We have no examples in our histories of such a long reign as his. It is said that he possesses in a very high degree the faculty of making himself obeyed: he governs with equal ability his family, his court, and his kingdom: he has often been heard to say, that, of all existing governments, that of the Turks, or that of our august Sultan, pleased him best: such is his high opinion of Oriental statecraft.[1]

I have studied his character, and I have found certain contradictions which I cannot reconcile. For example, he has a minister who is only eighteen years old,[2] and a mistress [Madame de Maintenon] who is fourscore; he loves his religion, and yet he cannot abide those [the Jansenists] who assert that it ought to be strictly observed; although he flies from the noise of cities, and is inclined to be reticent, from morning till night he is engaged in getting himself talked about; he is fond of trophies and victories, but he has as great a dread of seeing a good general at the head of his own troops, as at the head of an army of his enemies. It has never I believe happened to anyone but himself, to be burdened with more wealth than even a prince could hope for, and yet at the same time steeped in such poverty as a private person could ill brook.

He delights to reward those who serve him; but he pays as liberally the assiduous indolence of his courtiers, as the labors in the field of his captains; often the man who undresses him, or who hands him his serviette at table, is preferred before him who has taken cities and gained battles; he does not believe that the greatness of a monarch is compatible with restriction in the distribution of favors; and, without examining into the merit of a man, he will heap benefits upon him, believing that his selection makes the recipient worthy; accordingly, he has been

---

[1]When Louis XIV was in his sixteenth year, some courtiers discussed in his presence the absolute power of the Sultans, who dispose as they like of the goods and the lives of their subjects. "That is something like being a king," said the young monarch. Marshal d'Estrées, alarmed at the tendency revealed in that remark, rejoined, "But, sire, several of these emperors have been strangled even in my time." [Ed.]

[2]Barbezieux, son of Louvois, Louis's youngest minister, held office at twenty-three, not eighteen; and he was dead in 1713. [Ed.]

known to bestow a small pension upon a man who had run off two leagues from the enemy, and a good government on another who had gone four.

Above all, he is magnificent in his buildings; there are more statues in his palace gardens [at Versailles] than there are citizens in a large town. His body-guard is as strong as that of the prince before whom all the thrones of the earth tremble;[3] his armies are as numerous, his resources as great, and his finances as inexhaustible.

Paris, the 7th of the moon of Maharram, 1713.

■ Discussion Questions

1. What contradictions does Usbek see in Louis's character, and what do they reveal about his method of rule?

2. In what ways does this letter reflect Montesquieu's general interest in the foundation of good government?

3. Based on this letter, why do you think that scholars regard Montesquieu as a herald of the Enlightenment?

[3]The Shah of Persia. [Ed.]

4.

Mary Astell
Reflections upon Marriage
1706

Like Montesquieu, English author Mary Astell (1666–1731) helped to usher in the Enlightenment by surveying society with a critical eye. First published anonymously in 1700, Reflections upon Marriage, *one of her best-known books, highlights Astell's keen interest in the institution of marriage, education, and relations between the sexes. Only the third edition (published in 1706) divulged her gender, but still not her name. As the following excerpt reveals, Astell held a dim view of women's inequality in general and of their submissive role in marriage in particular. She argues that one should abhor the use of arbitrary power within the state, and so, too, within the family. Among the book's principal goals was to present spinsterhood as a viable alternative to marriage. Perhaps not surprisingly, Astell herself never married.*

These Reflections being made in the Country, where the Book that occasion'd them came but late to Hand, the *Reader* is desir'd to excuse their Unseasonableness as well as other Faults; and to believe that they have no other Design than to Correct some Abuses, which are not the less because Power and Prescription seem

From Bridget Hill, ed., *The First English Feminist: Reflections upon Marriage and Other Writings by Mary Astell* (New York: St. Martin's Press, 1986), 69–76.

to Authorize them. If any are so needlessly curious as to inquire from what Hand they come, they may please to know, that it is not good Manners to ask, since the Title-Page does not tell them: We are all of us sufficiently Vain, and without doubt the Celebrated Name of *Author*, which most are so fond of, had not been avoided but for very good Reasons: To name but one; *Who will care to pull upon themselves an Hornet's nest?* 'Tis a very great Fault to regard rather who it is that Speaks, than what is Spoken; and either to submit to Authority, when we should only yield to Reason; or if Reason press too hard, to think to ward it off by Personal Objections and Reflections. Bold Truths may pass while the Speaker is Incognito, but are not endur'd when he is known; few Minds being strong enough to bear what Contradicts their Principles and Practices without Recriminating when they can. And tho' to tell the Truth be the most Friendly Office, yet whosoever is so hardy as to venture at it, shall be counted an Enemy for so doing.

Thus far the old Advertisement, when the Reflections first appear'd, A.D.1700.

But the *Reflector,* who hopes *Reflector* is not bad English, now Governor is happily of the feminine Gender, had as good or better have said nothing; For People by being forbid, are only excited to a more curious Inquiry. A certain Ingenuous Gentleman (as she is inform'd) had the Good-Nature to own these Reflections, so far as to affirm that he had the Original M.S. in his Closet, a Proof she is not able to produce, and so to make himself responsible for all their Faults, for which she returns him all due Acknowledgment. However, the Generality being of Opinion, that a Man would have had more Prudence and Manners than to have Publish'd such unseasonable Truths, or to have betray'd the *Arcana Imperii* of his Sex, she humbly confesses, that the Contrivance and Execution of this Design, which is unfortunately accus'd of being so destructive to the government, of the Men I mean, is entirely her own. She neither advis'd with Friends, nor turn'd over Antient or Modern Authors, nor prudently submitted to the Correction of such as are, or such as *think* they are good Judges, but with an *English* Spirit and Genius, set out upon the Forlorn Hope, meaning no hurt to any body, nor designing any thing but the Public Good, and to retrieve, if possible, the Native Liberty, the Rights and Privileges of the Subject.

Far be it from her to stir up Sedition of any sort, none can abhor it more; and she heartily wishes that our Masters wou'd pay their Civil and Ecclesiastical Governors the same Submission, which they themselves extract from their Domestic Subjects. Nor can she imagine how she any way undermines the Masculine Empire, or blows the Trumpet of Rebellion to the Moiety of Mankind. Is it by exhorting Women, not to expect to have their own Will in any thing, but to be entirely Submissive, when once they have made choice of a Lord and Master, tho' he happen not to be so Wise, so Kind, or even so Just a Governor as was expected? She did not indeed advise them to think his Folly Wisdom, nor his Brutality that Love and Worship he promised in his Matrimonial Oath, for this required a Flight of Wit and Sense much above her poor Ability, and proper only to Masculine Understandings. However she did not in any manner prompt them to Resist, or to Abdicate the Perjur'd Spouse, tho' the Laws of GOD and the Land make special Provision for it, in a case wherein, as is to be fear'd, few Men can truly plead Not Guilty.

Tis true, thro' Want of Learning, and of that Superior Genius which Men as Men lay claim to, she was ignorant of the *Natural Inferiority* of our Sex, which our Masters lay down as a Self-Evident and Fundamental Truth.[1] She saw nothing in the Reason of Things, to make this either a Principle or a Conclusion, but much to the contrary; it being Sedition at least, if not Treason to assert it in this Reign. For if by the Natural Superiority of their Sex, they mean that every Man is by Nature superior to every Woman, which is the obvious meaning, and that which must be stuck to if they would speak Sense, it wou'd be a Sin in *any* Woman to have Dominion over *any* Man, and the greatest Queen ought not to command but to obey her Footman, because no Municipal Laws can supersede or change the Law of Nature; so that if the dominion of the Men be such, the *Salique Law,*[2] as unjust as *English Men* have ever thought it, ought to take place over all the Earth, and the most glorious Reigns in the *English, Danish, Castilian,* and other Annals, were wicked Violations of the Law of Nature!

If they mean that *some* Men are superior to *some* Women, this is no great Discovery; had they turn'd the Tables they might have seen that *some* Women are Superior to *some* Men. Or had they been pleased to remember their Oaths of Allegiance and Supremacy, they might have known that *One* Woman is superior to *All* the Men in these Nations, or else they have sworn to very little purpose. And it must not be suppos'd, that their Reason and Religion wou'd suffer them to take Oaths, contrary to the Law of Nature and Reason of things.

By all which it appears, that our Reflector's Ignorance is very pitiable, it may be her Misfortune but not her Crime, especially since she is willing to be better inform'd, and hopes she shall never be so obstinate as to shut her Eyes against the Light of Truth, which is not to be charg'd with Novelty, how late soever we may be bless'd with the Discovery. Nor can Error, be it as Antient as it may, ever plead Prescription against Truth. And since the only way to remove all Doubts, to answer all Objections, and to give the Mind entire Satisfaction, is not by *Affirming,* but by *Proving,* so that every one may see with their *own* Eyes, and Judge according to the best of their *own* Understandings, She hopes it is no Presumption to insist on this Natural Right of Judging for her self, and the rather, because by quitting it, we give up all the Means of Rational Conviction. Allow us then as many Glasses as you please to help our Sight, and as many good Arguments as you can afford to Convince our Understandings: But don't exact of us we beseech you, to affirm that we see such things as are only the Discovery of Men who have quicker Senses; or that we understand and Know what we have by Hearsay only, for to be so excessively Complaisant, is neither to see nor to understand.

---

[1] Possibly a reference to William Nichols, D.D., *The Duty of Inferiours Towards Their Superiours in Five Practical Discourses* (1701), in which he argued that man possesses "a higher state of natural perfection and dignity, and thereupon puts in a just claim of superiority, which everything which is of more worth has a right to, over that which has less" (pp. 87–88). [Ed.]

[2] *Salique Law:* A law excluding women from the throne of France. [Ed.]

That the Custom of the World has put Women, generally speaking, into a State of Subjection, is not deny'd; but the Right can no more be prov'd from the Fact, than the Predominancy of Vice can justifie it. A certain great Man has endeavour'd to prove by Reasons not contemptible, that in the Original State of things the Woman was the Superior, and that her Subjection to the Man is an Effect of the Fall, and the Punishment of her Sin. And that Ingenious Theorist Mr. *Whiston*[3] asserts, That before the Fall there was a greater equality between the two Sexes. However this be 'tis certainly no Arrogance in a Woman to conclude, that she was made for the Service of GOD, and that this is her End. Because GOD made all Things for Himself, and a Rational Mind is too noble a Being to be Made for the Sake and Service of any Creature. The Service she at any time becomes oblig'd to pay to a Man, is only a Business by the Bye. Just as it may be any Man's Business and Duty to keep Hogs; he was not Made for this, but if he hires himself out to such an Employment, he ought conscientiously to perform it. Nor can anything be concluded to the contrary from St. *Paul's* Argument, *I Cor. II.* For he argues only for Decency and Order, according to the present Custom and State of things. Taking his Words strictly and literally, they prove too much, in that *Praying and Prophecying in the Church* are allow'd the Women, provided they do it with their Head Cover'd, as well as the Men; and no inequality can be inferr'd from hence, their Reverence to the Sacred Oracles who engage them in such Disputes. And therefore the blame be theirs, who have unnecessarily introduc'd them in the present Subject, and who by saying that the *Reflections* were not agreeable to Scripture, oblige the Reflector to shew that those who affirm it must either mistake her Meaning, or the Sense of Holy Scripture, or both, if they think what they say, and do not find fault merely because they resolve to do so. For had she ever writ any thing contrary to those sacred Truths, she wou'd be the first in pronouncing its Condemnation.

But what says the Holy Scripture? It speaks of Women as in a State of Subjection, and so it does of the *Jews* and *Christians* when under the Dominion of the *Chaldeans* and *Romans,* requiring of the one as well as of the other a quiet submission to them under whose Power they liv'd. But will any one say that these had a *Natural Superiority* and Right to Dominion? that they had a superior Understanding, or any Pre-eminence, except what their greater Strength acquir'd? Or that the other were subjected to their Adversaries for any other Reason but the Punishment of their sins, and in order to their Reformation? Or for the Exercise of their Vertue, and because the Order of the World and the Good of Society requir'd it?

If Mankind had never sinn'd, Reason wou'd always have been obey'd, there wou'd have been no struggle for Dominion, and Brutal Power wou'd not have pre-

---

[3]William Whiston (1667–1752), divine, mathematician and Newtonian. Author of many works including *A New Theory of the Earth* (1696). He succeeded Newton as the Lucasian Professor and did much to popularize Newton's ideas. In 1710 he was deprived of his chair for casting doubt on the doctrine of the Trinity. [Ed.]

vail'd. But in the laps'd State of Mankind, and now that Men will not be guided by their Reason but by their Appetites, and do not what they *ought* but what they *can*, the Reason, or that which stands for it, the Will and Pleasure of the Governor is to be the Reason of those who will not be guided by their own, and must take place for Order's sake, altho' it shou'd not be conformable to right Reason. Nor can there be any Society great or little, from Empires down to private Families, with a last Resort, to determine the Affairs of that Society by an irresistible Sentence. Now unless this Supremacy be fix'd somewhere, there will be a perpetual Contention about it, such is the love of Dominion, and let the Reason of things be what it may, those who have least Force, or Cunning to supply it, will have the Disadvantage. So that since Women are acknowledg'd to have least Bodily strength, their being commanded to obey is in pure kindness to them and for their Quiet and Security, as well as for the Exercise of their Vertue. But does it follow that Domestic Governors have more Sense than their Subjects, any more than that other Governors have? We do not find that any Man thinks the worse of his own Understanding because another has superior Power; or concludes himself less capable of a Post of Honor and Authority, because he is not Prefer'd to it. How much time wou'd lie on Men's hands, how empty wou'd the Places of Concourse be, and how silent most Companies, did Men forbear to Censure their Governors, that is in effect to think themselves Wiser. Indeed Government wou'd be much more desirable than it is, did it invest the Possessor with a superior Understanding as well as Power. And if mere Power gives a Right to Rule, there can be no such thing as Usurpation; but a Highway-Man so long as he has strength to force, has also a Right to require our Obedience.

Again, if Absolute Sovereignty be not necessary in a State, how comes it to be so in a family? or if in a Family why not in a State; since no Reason can be alledg'd for the one that will not hold more strongly for the other? If the Authority of the Husband so far as it extends, is sacred and inalienable, why not of the Prince? The Domestic Sovereign is without Dispute Elected, and the Stipulations and Contract are mutual, is it not then partial in Men to the last degree, to contend for, and practice that Arbitrary Dominion in their Families, which they abhor and exclaim against in the State? For if Arbitrary Power is evil in itself, and an improper Method of Governing Rational and Free Agents, it ought not to be Practis'd any where; Nor is it less, but rather more mischievous in Families than in Kingdoms, by how much 100,000 Tyrants are worse than one. What tho' a Husband can't deprive a Wife of Life without being responsible to the Law, he may however do what is much more grievous to a generous Mind, render Life miserable, for which she has no Redress, scarce Pity which is afforded to every other Complainant. It being thought a Wife's Duty to suffer everything without Complaint. *If all Men are born free*, how is it that all Women are born slaves? as they must be if the being subjected to the *inconstant, uncertain, unknown, arbitrary Will* of Men, be the *perfect Condition of Slavery?* and if the Essence of Freedom consists, as our Masters say it does, in having a *standing Rule to live by?* And why is Slavery so much condemn'd and strove against in one Case, and so highly applauded, and held so necessary and so sacred in another?

■ **Discussion Questions**

1. According to Mary Astell, what is women's customary status in society, and why? What evidence does Astell present to challenge this status?

2. What does the language Astell uses reveal about her style of thinking and basic intellectual beliefs?

3. Why do you think scholars characterize *Reflections upon Marriage* as a "feminist" work?

5.
Pietist Spiritual Songbook
1705

Even as the new secular spirit of the Enlightenment began to emerge in the 1690s, most Europeans remained sincere Christians. Some people sought to deepen their faith further still during this period, giving rise to various religious revivals, including the Protestant movement known as Pietism. *Although Pietism first appeared in Lutheran Germany in the late seventeenth century, its concerns spread rapidly to Protestant denominations in Holland, Switzerland, and Scandinavia. In its most basic form, Pietism opposed the rigidity of academic theology in favor of practical and experiential piety. Its success was fueled in part by the popularity of a printing program in the Prussian town of Halle, which was also an important center of pietist study. By making inexpensive and readable editions of books available to the public, the Halle program offered the laity hands-on spiritual and moral guidance imbued with pietist ideals. The songbook excerpted here was published in Halle in 1705, with a preface by Johann Anastasius Freylinghausen (1670–1739).*

PREFACE

Dear Reader:

The Old and the New Testaments, all of church history, and experience itself testifies that it is always a mark of special grace by which God visits his people or promises to visit them in the future, when and wherever spiritual loving hymns flow out from the mouths of spiritual children in songs of praise. . . .

[This can be seen in the songs sung by the children of Israel, by David and Solomon, by the prophets, by the Magnificat of Mary, and the Benedictus of Zacharias, by the songs indicated in the New Testament as sung by the apostolic communities, and by the songs sung thereafter, in particular by the hymns gathered by the Bohemian brethren.]

From Peter C. Erb, ed., *Pietists: Selected Writings* (New York: Paulist Press, 1983), 167–68, 172–75.

All the examples given to this point demonstrate the truth of the proposition that God visits his people in song; this can be demonstrated even more strongly by the experience of our own times in which the good hand of God has led us. In the last few years he has allowed the preaching of repentance and of the gospel, in particular in Germany, to ring forth with new strength, and he has sealed this not insignificant fruit. Not to acknowledge this or not to wish to acknowledge this is an indication of the most dangerous blindness. Likewise God has placed a new song in the hearts and mouths of many of his children and servants so that they might praise him with this song and by it elevate both present and coming grace. [The results of these new songs can be seen in the many songbooks of our day.]

Just as one does with all other good things, so also in the appropriation and use of this gift one is not to remain hanging to the wretched and petty instruments of this world, but is to look up to God the Father of light from whom all good and all perfect gifts come from above and who grants through the one spirit the many gifts for the improvement and building up of the body of Jesus Christ. One is to acknowledge and praise this same wisdom and faithful concern which God demonstrates toward his congregation and to use it for teaching and instruction, particularly for daily encouragement and a walking in faith, love, and hope, as well as for consolation and all struggle and suffering in this short pilgrim journey. One is to do this in humility and out of a simple heart.

For this end the present new songbook of the saints, elect and beloved of God, has been published in the good hope that through the grace of the Lord this end will be reached. . . .

HYMN

Praise God! one step toward eternity
Is once again completed.
In the movement of this time
My heart ardently turns to you
O source, out of which my heart flows
And all grace flows
Into my soul as life.

I count the hours, days, and years,
And time seems never-ending
Until I completely
Embrace you, O life.
Then what is mortal in me
Will be completely swallowed up in you
And I will be immortal.

With the fire of love
My heart glows so that it ignites
What is in me, and my mind

Binds itself so to you
That you in me and I in you
And I yet always more
Will press nearer into you.

Oh, that you would come quickly;
I count the moments.
Ah, come, before my heart grows cold
And turns to death.
Come, in your glory.
Behold, your bride has prepared herself;
The loins are girded.

And since the oil of the Spirit
Is poured out upon me,
You are closer to me in my interior,
And I have flowed into you.
Thus, the light of life enlightens me,
And my lamp is prepared
To receive you joyously.

"Come" is the voice of your bride.
"Come" calls your pious beloved.
She calls and shouts loudly.
Come quickly, Jesus, come.
So come then, my bridegroom;
You know me, O lamb of God,
That I am betrothed to you.

But the proper time and hour
Are totally left to you.
I know that it is pleasing to you
That I with heart and tongue
Promise to come to you, and, therefore,
From now on direct my way
Toward you.

I am satisfied that nothing
Can separate me from your love
And that free before every man
I dare call you the bridegroom,
And you, O true prince of life,
will be wedded to me there
And give me your inheritance.
Therefore, I praise you with thanks

That the day (night, hour, year) is ended
And that from this time
one more step is completed.
I step forth again speedily
Until I come to the gate
Of Jerusalem above.
When hands are careless
And knees shake,

Offer me your hands quickly
In the chest of my faith
So that through your strength, my heart
Might be strengthened, and heavenwards
I might rise up without intermission.

Go, soul, fresh in faith
And be not now afraid.
Do not be enticed from the true path
by the desires of the world.
If you think you are too slow,
Hasten, as the eagle flys
with wings of sweet love.

O Jesus, my soul
Has already flown up to you.
You have, because you are totally love,
Completely exhausted me.
Leave off, what are times and hours,
I am already in eternity
Because I live in Jesus.

■ Discussion Questions

1. According to the preface, why is singing important to Christians in general and Pietists in particular?

2. In what ways does the hymn reflect this importance? What message does it convey?

3. What kind of emotional effect do you think the hymn may have had on a congregation, and why?

■ Comparative Questions

1. Both Louis XIV and Peter I cast themselves as absolute rulers. Do the documents support this claim? If so, how?

2. In what ways does Astell's discussion of the evils of arbitrary power foreshadow Montesquieu's concerns?

3. Although *Persian Letters* and Equiano's narrative belong to different literary genres, how do they adopt similar methods to describe eighteenth-century Europeans and their customs?

4. In what ways do Equiano, Astell, and Freylinghausen challenge conventional Christian authority and beliefs? What does this suggest about the place of Christianity in European society and culture at the time?

15

The Promise of Enlightenment, 1740–1789

THE FOLLOWING DOCUMENTS represent some of the many voices of the Enlightenment, an intellectual and cultural movement during the eighteenth century that captured the minds of middle- and upper-class people across Europe and in British North America. Enlightenment writers were united by their belief that reason was the key to humanity's advancement as the basis of truth, liberty, and justice. They cultivated and disseminated their ideals through letters, published works, and personal exchanges, particularly at gatherings known as *salons*, which were organized by upper-class women. By midcentury, people as diverse as the king of Prussia and a French artisan began to echo the Enlightenment principle that progress depended on destroying all barriers to reason, including religious intolerance. As the fifth document reveals, the Enlightenment's message spread further still into the North American colonies, where it had revolutionary consequences.

1.
Marie-Thérèse Geoffrin and M. d'Alembert
The Salon of Madame Geoffrin
1765

From its beginnings as an intellectual movement against absolutism, the Enlightenment became a formidable force of change by the mid-eighteenth century. The role of salons was crucial in this regard, providing an arena for the discussion and dissemination of Enlightenment ideas by bringing innovative intellectuals, writers, and artists together in private homes on a regular basis. Madame Marie-Thérèse Geoffrin (1699–1777) presided over the most influential salon in Paris at the time, as de-

From *Historical and Literary Memoirs and Anecdotes,* trans. Robert Bland and Anne Plumptre, 2nd ed. vol. 3, (London: H. Colburn, 1815), 400–05. Reprinted in Brian Tierney and Joan Scott, *Western Societies: A Documentary History,* vol. 2, (New York: McGraw Hill, 1984), 186–87.

scribed in the memoirs of a beneficiary of her patronage, M. d'Alembert. In addition to nurturing the intellectual scene in Paris, Geoffrin also cultivated it abroad by corresponding with important European leaders, including Polish King Stanislaw, to whom she wrote the letter that follows in 1765. Together, these two documents elucidate the life of a woman who was actively engaged in Enlightenment thinking.

MEMOIR D'ALEMBERT

Much has been said respecting Madame Geoffrin's goodness, to what a point it was active, restless, obstinate. But it has not been added, and which reflects the greatest honor upon her, that, as she advanced in years, this habit constantly increased. For the misfortune of society, it too often happens that age and experience produce a directly contrary effect, even in very virtuous characters, if virtue be not in them a powerful sentiment indeed, and of no common stamp. The more disposed they have been at first to feel kindness towards their fellow creatures, the more, finding daily their ingratitude, do they repent of having served them, and even consider it almost as a reproach to themselves to have loved them. Madame Geoffrin had learnt, from a more reflected study of mankind, from taking a view of them more *enlightened* by reason and justice, that they are more weak and vain than wicked; that we ought to compassionate their weakness, and bear with their vanity, that they may bear with ours. . . .

The passion of *giving,* which was an absolute necessity to her, seemed born with her, and tormented her, if I may say so, even from her earliest years. While yet a child, if she saw from the window any poor creature asking alms, she would throw whatever she could lay her hands upon to them; her bread, her linen, and even her clothes. She was often scolded for this *intemperance* of charity, sometimes even punished, but nothing could alter the disposition, she would do the same the very next day. . . .

Always occupied with those whom she loved, always anxious about them, she even anticipated every thing which might interrupt their happiness. A young man,[1] for whom she interested herself very much, who had till that moment been wholly absorbed in his studies, was suddenly seized with an unfortunate passion, which rendered study, and even life itself insupportable to him. She succeeded in curing him. Some time after she observed that the same young man mentioned to her, with great interest, an amiable woman with whom he had recently become acquainted. Madame Geoffrin, who knew the lady, went to her. "I am come," she said, "to intreat a favor of you. Do not evince too much friendship for **** or too

---

[1] This young man was M. d'Alembert himself.
From Charles de Moüy, ed., *Correspondance inédite du roi Stanislaw-Auguste Poniatowski et de Madame Geoffrin* (Geneva: Slatkine, 1970; reprint of 1875 edition). Trans. Lynn Hunt as published in *Connecting with the Past,* 164–68.

much desire to see him, he will be soon in love with you, he will be unhappy, and I shall be no less so to see him suffer; nay, you yourself will be a sufferer, from consciousness of the sufferings you occasion him." This woman, who was truly amiable, promised what Madame Geoffrin desired, and kept her word.

As she had always among the circle of her society persons of the highest rank and birth, as she appeared even to seek an acquaintance with them, it was supposed that this flattered her vanity. But here a very erroneous opinion was formed of her; she was in no respect the dupe of such prejudices, but she thought that by managing the humors of these people, she could render them useful to her friends. "You think," said she, to one of the latter, for whom she had a particular regard, "that it is for my own sake I frequent ministers and great people. Undeceive yourself, — it is for the sake of you, and those like you who may have occasion for them. . . ."

MME. GEOFFRIN WRITES TO THE KING OF POLAND

I am sending to you a banker named Claudel who is returning to Warsaw. He will have with him a printed memoir on a new kind of mill. The more I have learned about it, the more I see that this machine is very well-known. Your Majesty is best advised to invite a miller to come from France; he will know how to set it up and show how to use it, and use of it can spread from there.

Prince Sulkowski [a Polish nobleman] met Mr. Hennin at my salon. Mr. Hennin had been for a long time in Warsaw, and they talked together about Poland. I see with pain that it has a very bad government [Stanislaw was elected king only in 1764]; it seems almost impossible to make it better. . . .

I sent you the catalogue of the diamonds of Madame de Pompadour [King Louis XV's mistress had died recently and her diamonds were auctioned off]. . . .

Do not forget, my dear son, to send the memoir on commerce to Mr. Riancourt when he returns. . . .

I cannot report any news yet on your project for paintings; I am very sad about the death of poor Carle Vanloo [a leading French painter who died in July 1765]. It was a horrible loss for the arts.

■ Discussion Questions

1. Based on these documents, how would you characterize Geoffrin's personality? In what ways was she "enlightened"?

2. What impressions do the documents offer of her salon and how it functioned?

3. What does Geoffrin's letter to Stanislaw suggest about the range of her interests? How was this typical of Enlightenment thinkers?

2.
Jacques-Louis Ménétra
Journal of My Life
1764–1802

Although the philosophes—the writers of the Enlightenment—directed their message to the educated elite, Journal of My Life *by Jacques-Louis Ménétra (b. 1738) suggests that at least some people from the lower classes heard it too. Born in Paris, Ménétra learned to read and write in local parish schools. Following his father's example, he became a master glazier. He began his journal in 1764 and organized it principally around his recollections of his journey-man's "tour de France" from 1757 to 1764. The document here reveals not only his quick wit and sense of adventure but also his affinity for the intellectual spirit of criticism that characterized the Enlightenment. As the excerpt demonstrates, alongside the tales of his amusements, Ménétra commented on many of the fundamental issues of the day, including the question of religious tolerance. It is printed as originally written, without punctuation.*

I went to Paris to see Denongrais   Madame la Police had been interfering with business   she made up her mind to sell her property and to retire with her cuckold of a husband to her native village for she'd put by quite a bit in the course of her work   I was all for it   She said to me   I see clearly from what you've just said that you never loved me   She was right for never had a woman touched my heart except for sensual pleasure and nothing else   I promised her to come say my farewells and they've yet to be said

Since it was the good season we went to Champigny and went with some friends of mine to what are called *guinguettes* [open-air cafés with music and dancing—Trans.] Sundays and holidays we went to dance in front of the castle and other days usually with the people from the *guinguette* we played tennis or went visiting the local festivals   One holiday in a village one league from Montigny people were playing tennis on the square when Du Tillet showed up accompanied by the lord the magistrate or sheriff and the priest   I heard somebody say That's the Parisian over there I wondered what this was all about   It's because they know you're good at tennis said my friend   they're going to propose a match In fact six young men came and politely gave each of us a racket   My friend said no since he didn't know how to play but he said   But as for my friend he'll give you a good show   I declined   They insisted   the lord the sheriff and the priest joined in   I played   applause   hands were heard to clap   They took us to the castle (and) gave us refreshment

I was greatly applauded   I promised again that the fellows from Montigny and I would be waiting for them next Sunday   People came from all around I was

From Jacques-Louis Ménétra, *Journal of My Life,* intro. Daniel Roche, trans. Arthur Goldhammer (New York: Columbia University Press, 1986), 129–30.

all over the court and we had a good time   we won and whatever else they were well entertained   My friend went all out because M Trudaine had wanted to see me play and when I passed in front of him he and the people around him said to me Courage   So I answered that that was one thing I wasn't lacking

One day I followed the game warden   Since I had no rifle I let him run all over the fields and went to a village where I had seen the curate pay his respects to M Trudaine   who recognized me   and said I was pretty nimble at tennis and took me to his presbytery for a drink

After some idle talk we finally got onto the subject of religion   We talked about the mysteries of the sacraments . . . I spoke passionately about the sufferings that had been inflicted on men who worshiped the same God except for a few matters of opinion And (I said that) the Roman religion should be tolerant if it followed the maxims of its lawgiver   that because of its mysteries it was absurd and that all mysteries were in my opinion nothing but lies   And that so long as they sold indulgences and gave remission for sins in exchange for money   fear of hell which was like purgatory just an invention of the first impostors   that Jesus had never spoken of purgatory   And that all those sacraments were nothing but pure inventions to make money and impress the vulgar And that he himself who was a very intelligent man was not capable of making his God   chewing him and then swallowing him   That we mistreated those peoples who did not share our belief (and who) according to the Church should have been damned because all the priests went around saying   Outside the Church there is no salvation And that we accused those who worship idols of being idolators when we prostrate ourselves before statues   We even worship a piece of dough which we eat in the firm belief that it is God And those idolators only worship all those things to keep from being hurt by them and other things in the hope of getting some good out of them while we on the other hand we were real man-eaters   After praying to him and worshipping him in order to satisfy him we've got to eat him too

He answered me with objections as many others had answered me   His one and only response was to say to me   All these mysteries must be believed because the Church believes them   he said to me   My friend you are enlightened   It is necessary that for the sake of government nations live always in ignorance and credulity   I answered him So be it . . .

■ Discussion Questions

1. Why do you think Ménétra was so critical of the Catholic Church?

2. How do Ménétra's criticisms echo those of great Enlightenment thinkers?

3. What does the priest mean when he describes Ménétra as enlightened?

4. How would you characterize Ménétra's style of writing?

3.

Adam Smith
An Inquiry into the Nature and Causes of the Wealth of Nations
1776

*Intellectuals in Paris were not alone in their faith in the power of human reason to il-
luminate the meaning of the world around them. Like-minded thinkers across Europe
embraced the Enlightenment spirit in their own pursuit of knowledge. For Scottish
philosopher Adam Smith (1723–1790), this pursuit centered on explaining what he
described as "the progress of opulence" that was so visible in the economic boom of the
period. He set forth his explanation in masterful fashion in* An Inquiry into the Nature and Causes of the Wealth of Nations *published in 1776. The excerpt here reveals one of the pillars of Smith's argument, namely that economic markets should be
left to their own devices, free from the government regulations that prevailed in his
day. In this way, Smith declared, individual self-interest "led by an invisible hand" of
competition could come to the fore, which was naturally compatible with society's
general welfare.*

By restraining, either by high duties, or by absolute prohibitions, the importation
of such goods from foreign countries as can be produced at home, the monopoly
of the home market is more or less secured to the domestic industry employed in
producing them. Thus the prohibition of importing either live cattle or salt provisions from foreign countries secures to the graziers of Great Britain the monopoly
of the home market for butcher's-meat. The high duties upon the importation of
corn, which in times of moderate plenty amount to a prohibition, give a like advantage to the growers of that commodity. The prohibition of the importation of
foreign woollens is equally favorable to the woollen manufactures. The silk manufacture, though altogether employed upon foreign materials, has lately obtained
the same advantage. The linen manufacture has not yet obtained it, but is making
great strides towards it. Many other sorts of manufacturers have, in the same manner, obtained in Great Britain, either altogether, or very nearly a monopoly against
their countrymen. The variety of goods of which the importation into Great
Britain is prohibited, either absolutely, or under certain circumstances, greatly ex-
ceeds what can easily be suspected by those who are not well acquainted with the
laws of the customs.

That this monopoly of the home market frequently gives great encouragement to that particular species of industry which enjoys it, and frequently turns
towards that employment a greater share of both the labor and stock of the society than would otherwise have gone to it, cannot be doubted. But whether it tends

From Adam Smith, *An Inquiry into the Nature and Causes of the Wealth of Nations,* 2nd ed.,
vol. II (Oxford: Clarendon Press, 1880), 25–30.

either to increase the general industry of the society, or to give it the most advantageous direction, is not, perhaps, altogether so evident.

The general industry of the society never can exceed what the capital of the society can employ. As the number of workmen that can be kept in employment by any particular person must bear a certain proportion to his capital, so the number of those that can be continually employed by all the members of a great society, must bear a certain proportion to the whole capital of that society, and never can exceed that proportion. No regulation of commerce can increase the quantity of industry in any society beyond what its capital can maintain. It can only divert a part of it into a direction into which it might not otherwise have gone; and it is by no means certain that this artificial direction is likely to be more advantageous to the society than that into which it would have gone of its own accord.

Every individual is continually exerting himself to find out the most advantageous employment for whatever capital he can demand. It is his own advantage, indeed, and not that of the society, which he has in view. But the study of his own advantage naturally or rather necessarily, leads him to prefer that employment which is most advantageous to the society.

First, every individual endeavors to employ his capital as near home as he can, and consequently as much as he can in the support of domestic industry; provided always that he can thereby obtain the ordinary, or not a great deal less than the ordinary, profits of stock.

Thus, upon equal or nearly equal profits, every wholesale merchant naturally prefers the home trade to the foreign trade of consumption, and the foreign trade of consumption to the carrying trade. In the home trade his capital is never so long out of his sight as it frequently is in the foreign trade of consumption. He can know better the character and situation of the persons whom he trusts, and, if he should happen to be deceived, he knows better the laws of the country from which he must seek redress. In the carrying trade, the capital of the merchant is, as it were, divided between two foreign countries, and no part of it is ever necessarily brought home, or placed under his own immediate view and command. The capital which an Amsterdam merchant employs in carrying corn from Konigsberg to Lisbon, and fruit and wine from Lisbon to Konigsberg, must generally be the one half of it at Konigsberg and the other half at Lisbon. No part of it need ever come to Amsterdam. The natural residence of such a merchant should either be at Konigsberg or Lisbon, and it can only be some very particular circumstance which can make him prefer the residence of Amsterdam. The uneasiness, however, which he feels at being separated so far from his capital, generally determines him to bring part both of the Konigsberg goods which he destines for the market of Lisbon, and of the Lisbon goods which he destines for that of Konigsberg, to Amsterdam; and though this necessarily subjects him to a double charge of loading and unloading, as well as to the payment of some duties and customs, yet for the sake of having some part of his capital always under his own view and command, he willingly submits to this extraordinary charge; and it is in this manner that every country which has any considerable share of the carrying trade, becomes always the emporium, or general market, for the goods of all the different countries whose trade it carries on. The merchant, in order to save a second loading and unloading, endeavors always to sell in the home market as much of the goods of all those different countries as he can, and thus, so far as he can, to convert his carrying trade into a foreign trade of consumption. A merchant, in the same manner, who is engaged in the foreign trade of consumption, when he collects goods for foreign markets, will always be glad, upon equal or nearly equal profits, to sell as great a part of them at home as he can. He saves himself the risk and trouble of exportation, when, so far as he can, he thus converts his foreign trade of consumption into a home trade. Home is in this manner the center, if I may say so, round which the capitals of the inhabitants of every country are continually circulating, and towards which they are always tending, though by particular causes they may sometimes be driven off and repelled from it towards more distant employments. But a capital employed in the home trade, it has already been shown, necessarily puts into motion a greater quantity of domestic industry, and gives revenue and employment to a greater number of the inhabitants of the country, than an equal capital employed in the foreign trade of consumption; and one employed in the foreign trade of consumption has the same advantage over an equal capital employed in the carrying trade. Upon equal, or only nearly equal profits, therefore, every individual naturally inclines to employ his capital in the manner in which it is likely to afford the greatest support to domestic industry, and to give revenue and employment to the greatest number of people of his own country.

Secondly, every individual who employs his capital in the support of domestic industry, necessarily endeavors so to direct that industry, that its produce may be of the greatest possible value.

The produce of industry is what it adds to the subject or materials upon which it is employed. In proportion as the value of this produce is great or small, so will likewise be the profits of the employer. But it is only for the sake of profit that any man employs a capital in the support of industry; and he will always, therefore, endeavor to employ it in the support of that industry of which the produce is likely to be of the greatest value, or to exchange for the greatest quantity either of money or of other goods.

But the annual revenue of every society is always precisely equal to the exchangeable value of the whole annual produce of its industry, or rather is precisely the same thing with that exchangeable value. As every individual, therefore, endeavors as much as he can both to employ his capital in the support of domestic industry, and so to direct that industry that its produce may be of the greatest value, every individual necessarily labors to render the annual revenue of the society as great as he can. He generally, indeed, neither intends to promote the public interest, nor knows how much he is promoting it. By preferring the support of domestic to that of foreign industry, he intends only his own security; and by directing that industry in such a manner as its produce may be of the greatest value, he intends only his own gain, and he is in this, as in many other cases, led by an invisible hand to promote an end which was no part of his intention. Nor is it always the worse for the society that it was no part of it. By pursuing his own interest he frequently promotes that of the society more effectually than when he really intends to promote it. I have never known much good done by those who affected to trade for the public good. It is an affectation, indeed, not very common among merchants, and very few words need be employed in dissuading them from it.

What is the species of domestic industry which his capital can employ, and of which the produce is likely to be of the greatest value, every individual, it is evident, can, in his local situation, judge much better than any statesman or lawgiver can do for him. The statesman, who should attempt to direct private people in what manner they ought to employ their capitals, would not only load himself with a most unnecessary attention, but assume an authority which could safely be trusted, not only to no single person, but to no council or senate whatever, and which would nowhere be so dangerous as in the hands of a man who had folly and presumption enough to fancy himself fit to exercise it.

To give the monopoly of the home market to the produce of domestic industry, in any particular art or manufacture, is in some measure to direct private people in what manner they ought to employ their capitals, and must, in almost all cases, be either a useless or a hurtful regulation. If the produce of domestic can be brought there as cheap as that of foreign industry, the regulation is evidently useless. If it cannot, it must generally be hurtful. It is the maxim of every prudent master of a family, never to attempt to make at home what it will cost him more to make than to buy. The tailor does not attempt to make his own shoes, but buys them of the shoemaker. The shoemaker does not attempt to make his own clothes, but employs a tailor. The farmer attempts to make neither the one nor the other, but employs those different artificers. All of them find it for their interest to employ their whole industry in a way in which they have some advantage over their neighbors, and to purchase with a part of its produce, or, what is the same thing, with the price of a part of it, whatever else they have occasion for.

What is prudence in the conduct of every private family, can scarce be folly in that of a great kingdom. If a foreign country can supply us with a commodity cheaper than we ourselves can make it, better buy it of them with some part of the produce of our own industry, employed in a way in which we have some advantage. The general industry of the country, being always in proportion to the capital which employs it, will not thereby be diminished, no more than that of the above-mentioned artificers, but only left to find out the way in which it can be employed with the greatest advantage. It is certainly not employed to the greatest advantage, when it is thus directed towards an object which it can buy cheaper than it can make. The value of its annual produce is certainly more or less diminished, when it is thus turned away from producing commodities evidently of more value than the commodity which it is directed to produce. According to the supposition, that commodity could be purchased from foreign countries cheaper than it can be made at home. It could, therefore, have been purchased with a part only of the commodities, or, what is the same thing, with a part only of the price of the commodities, which the industry employed by an equal capital would have produced at home, had it been left to follow its natural course. The industry of the country, therefore, is thus turned away from a more to a less advantageous employment, and the exchangeable value of its annual produce, instead of being increased, according to the intention of the lawgiver, must necessarily be diminished by every such regulation.

■ Discussion Questions

1. Why does Smith argue against the regulation of commerce? What evidence does he cite to support his argument?

2. Why does Smith think that allowing individuals to pursue economic gain freely is advantageous to society as a whole?

3. How does this excerpt support the view held by scholars that Smith helped to lay the theoretical foundations of modern capitalist society?

4. How does Smith reflect broader Enlightenment ideas?

4.
Frederick II
Political Testament
1752

The Enlightenment's triumph is perhaps best reflected in the politics of the second half of the eighteenth century. Rather than working to suppress the philosophes' calls for change, rulers across continental Europe embraced them as a means of enhancing their power and prestige. They did so at their own discretion, however, and often with an iron hand, as the case of King Frederick II of Prussia (r. 1740–1786) vividly reveals. A devotee of the Enlightenment as well as an exemplary soldier and statesman, Frederick transformed Prussia into a leading European state during his reign. In his Political Testament *of 1752, he outlines his political philosophy, which blended Enlightenment ideals with an uncompromising view of his own power.*

One must attempt, above all, to know the special genius of the people which one wants to govern in order to know if one must treat them leniently or severely, if they are inclined to revolt . . . to intrigue. . . .

[The Prussian nobility] has sacrificed its life and goods for the service of the state, its loyalty and merit have earned it the protection of all its rulers, and it is one of the duties [of the ruler] to aid those [noble] families which have become impoverished in order to keep them in possession of their lands: for they are to be regarded as the pedestals and the pillars of the state. In such a state no factions or rebellions need be feared . . . it is one goal of the policy of this state to preserve the nobility.

From George L. Mosse, Rondo E. Cameron, Henry Bertram Hill, and Michael B. Petrovich, eds., *Europe in Review* (Chicago: Rand McNally and Company, 1957), 111–12.

A well conducted government must have an underlying concept so well integrated that it could be likened to a system of philosophy. All actions taken must be well reasoned, and all financial, political and military matters must flow towards one goal: which is the strengthening of the state and the furthering of its power. However, such a system can flow but from a single brain, and this must be that of the sovereign. Laziness, hedonism and imbecility, these are the causes which restrain princes in working at the noble task of bringing happiness to their subjects . . . a sovereign is not elevated to his high position, supreme power has not been confined to him in order that he may live in lazy luxury, enriching himself by the labor of the people, being happy while everyone else suffers. The sovereign is the first servant of the state. He is well paid in order that he may sustain the dignity of his office, but one demands that he work efficiently for the good of the state, and that he, at the very least, pay personal attention to the most important problems. . . .

You can see, without doubt, how important it is that the King of Prussia govern personally. Just as it would have been impossible for Newton to arrive at his system of attractions if he had worked in harness with Leibnitz and Descartes, so a system of politics cannot be arrived at and continued if it has not sprung from a single brain. . . . All parts of the government are inexorably linked with each other. Finance, politics and military affairs are inseparable; it does not suffice that one be well administered; they must all be . . . a Prince who governs personally, who has formed his [own] political system, will not be handicapped when occasions arise where he has to act swiftly: for he can guide all matters towards the end which he has set for himself. . . .

Catholics, Lutherans, Reformed, Jews and other Christian sects live in this state, and live together in peace: if the sovereign, actuated by a mistaken zeal, declares himself for one religion or another, parties will spring up, heated disputes ensue, little by little persecutions will commence and, in the end, the religion persecuted will leave the fatherland and millions of subjects will enrich our neighbors by their skill and industry.

It is of no concern in politics whether the ruler has a religion or whether he has none. All religions, if one examines them, are founded on superstitious systems, more or less absurd. It is impossible for a man of good sense, who dissects their contents, not to see their error; but these prejudices, these errors and mysteries were made for men, and one must know enough to respect the public and not to outrage its faith, whatever religion be involved.

■ Discussion Questions

1. Based on this excerpt, in what ways does the term *enlightened despot* apply to Frederick II? How is he enlightened? How is he despotic?

2. What reasons does Frederick advance in favor of religious tolerance?

3. According to Frederick, what should be the one goal of government?

5.
Thomas Jefferson
Declaration of Independence
July 4, 1776

Even while calling for change, the philosophes preferred to work within established institutions rather than abolish them altogether. Nonetheless, their ideals could have a revolutionary impact, as they did in Britain's North American colonies. Since the early 1760s, many colonists had increasingly come to resent British rule and turned to a variety of sources, including Enlightenment writings, to build a case for independence. Tensions came to a head in 1775, and war quickly ensued. Deeply imbued with Enlightenment thought, Thomas Jefferson (1743–1826) was an eloquent spokesman for the American cause as the Declaration of Independence *attests. Although others helped revise the document, Jefferson wrote the original draft himself. A Virginia planter and lawyer, Jefferson went on to become governor of Virginia, minister to France, secretary of state, vice president and president of the United States (1801–1809). The* Declaration *was at once a stirring expression of the belief in natural or human rights and a masterful work of political propaganda.*

The unanimous Declaration of the thirteen united States of America,

When in the Course of human events, it becomes necessary for one people to dissolve the political bands which have connected them with another, and to assume among the powers of the earth, the separate and equal station to which the Laws of Nature and of Nature's God entitle them, a decent respect to the opinions of mankind requires that they should declare the causes which impel them to the separation.

We hold these truths to be self-evident, that all men are created equal, that they are endowed by their Creator with certain unalienable Rights, that among these are Life, Liberty and the pursuit of Happiness. — That to secure these rights, Governments are instituted among Men, deriving their just powers from the consent of the governed, — That whenever any Form of Government becomes destructive of these ends, it is the Right of the People to alter or to abolish it, and to institute new Government, laying its foundation on such principles and organizing its powers in such form, as to them shall seem most likely to effect their Safety and Happiness. Prudence, indeed, will dictate that Governments long established should not be changed for light and transient causes; and accordingly all experience hath shewn, that mankind are more disposed to suffer, while evils are sufferable, than to right themselves by abolishing the forms to which they are accustomed. But when a long train of abuses and usurpations, pursuing invariably the same Object evinces a design to reduce them under absolute Despotism, it is their

From National Archives Web site, "The Declaration of Independence: A Transcription," www.archives.gov/national-archives-experience/charters/declaration_transcript.html.

right, it is their duty, to throw off such Government, and to provide new Guards for their future security. — Such has been the patient sufferance of these Colonies; and such is now the necessity which constrains them to alter their former Systems of Government. The history of the present King of Great Britain is a history of repeated injuries and usurpations, all having in direct object the establishment of an absolute Tyranny over these States. To prove this, let Facts be submitted to a candid world.

He has refused his Assent to Laws, the most wholesome and necessary for the public good.

He has forbidden his Governors to pass Laws of immediate and pressing importance, unless suspended in their operation till his Assent should be obtained; and when so suspended, he has utterly neglected to attend to them.

He has refused to pass other Laws for the accommodation of large districts of people, unless those people would relinquish the right of Representation in the Legislature, a right inestimable to them and formidable to tyrants only.

He has called together legislative bodies at places unusual, uncomfortable, and distant from the depository of their public Records, for the sole purpose of fatiguing them into compliance with his measures.

He has dissolved Representative Houses repeatedly, for opposing with manly firmness his invasions on the rights of the people.

He has refused for a long time, after such dissolutions, to cause others to be elected; whereby the Legislative powers, incapable of Annihilation, have returned to the People at large for their exercise; the State remaining in the mean time exposed to all the dangers of invasion from without, and convulsions within.

He has endeavored to prevent the population of these States; for that purpose obstructing the Laws for Naturalization of Foreigners; refusing to pass others to encourage their migrations hither, and raising the conditions of new Appropriations of Lands.

He has obstructed the Administration of Justice, by refusing his Assent to Laws for establishing Judiciary powers.

He has made Judges dependent on his Will alone, for the tenure of their offices, and the amount and payment of their salaries.

He has erected a multitude of New Offices, and sent hither swarms of Officers to harass our people, and eat out their substance.

He has kept among us, in times of peace, Standing Armies without the Consent of our legislatures.

He has affected to render the Military independent of and superior to the Civil power.

He has combined with others to subject us to a jurisdiction foreign to our constitution, and unacknowledged by our laws; giving his Assent to their Acts of pretended Legislation:

For Quartering large bodies of armed troops among us:

For protecting them, by a mock Trial, from punishment for any Murders which they should commit on the Inhabitants of these States:

For cutting off our Trade with all parts of the world:

For imposing Taxes on us without our Consent:

For depriving us in many cases, of the benefits of Trial by Jury:

For transporting us beyond Seas to be tried for pretended offenses

For abolishing the free System of English Laws in a neighboring Province, establishing therein an Arbitrary government, and enlarging its Boundaries so as to render it at once an example and fit instrument for introducing the same absolute rule into these Colonies:

For taking away our Charters, abolishing our most valuable Laws, and altering fundamentally the Forms of our Governments:

For suspending our own Legislatures, and declaring themselves invested with power to legislate for us in all cases whatsoever.

He has abdicated Government here, by declaring us out of his Protection and waging War against us.

He has plundered our seas, ravaged our Coasts, burnt our towns, and destroyed the lives of our people.

He is at this time transporting large Armies of foreign Mercenaries to compleat the works of death, desolation and tyranny, already begun with circumstances of Cruelty & perfidy scarcely paralleled in the most barbarous ages, and totally unworthy the Head of a civilized nation.

He has constrained our fellow Citizens taken Captive on the high Seas to bear Arms against their Country, to become the executioners of their friends and Brethren, or to fall themselves by their Hands.

He has excited domestic insurrections amongst us, and has endeavoured to bring on the inhabitants of our frontiers, the merciless Indian Savages, whose known rule of warfare, is an undistinguished destruction of all ages, sexes and conditions.

In every stage of these Oppressions We have Petitioned for Redress in the most humble terms: Our repeated Petitions have been answered only by repeated injury. A Prince whose character is thus marked by every act which may define a Tyrant, is unfit to be the ruler of a free people.

Nor have We been wanting in attentions to our Brittish brethren. We have warned them from time to time of attempts by their legislature to extend an unwarrantable jurisdiction over us. We have reminded them of the circumstances of our emigration and settlement here. We have appealed to their native justice and magnanimity, and we have conjured them by the ties of our common kindred to disavow these usurpations, which, would inevitably interrupt our connections and correspondence. They too have been deaf to the voice of justice and of consanguinity. We must, therefore, acquiesce in the necessity, which denounces our Separation, and hold them, as we hold the rest of mankind, Enemies in War, in Peace Friends.

We, therefore, the Representatives of the united States of America, in General Congress, Assembled, appealing to the Supreme Judge of the world for the rectitude of our intentions, do, in the Name, and by Authority of the good People of these Colonies, solemnly publish and declare, That these United Colonies are, and of Right ought to be Free and Independent States; that they are Absolved from all Allegiance to the British Crown, and that all political connection between them and the State of Great Britain, is and ought to be totally dissolved; and that as Free and Independent States, they have full Power to levy War, conclude Peace, contract Alliances, establish Commerce, and to do all other Acts and Things which Independent States may of right do. And for the support of this Declaration, with a firm reliance on the protection of divine Providence, we mutually pledge to each other our Lives, our Fortunes and our sacred Honor.

■ Discussion Questions

1. How would you describe Jefferson's political philosophy? What were its defining ideals?
2. What links do you see between these ideals and Enlightenment thought?
3. How does the Declaration reflect changing conceptions of the basis of good government and state power in the eighteenth century?
4. What segments of colonial society were excluded from Jefferson's vision of universal human rights? What does this suggest about the limitations of the Enlightenment?

■ Comparative Questions

1. How do Ménétra's and Frederick II's attitudes toward organized religion overlap?
2. What similarities and differences do you see between Frederick II's and Jefferson's views on the basis of good government?
3. What similarities and differences do you see in Madame Geoffrin's and Jefferson's expression of Enlightenment ideas with regard to both content and mode of transmission? Why is this significant to understanding the Enlightenment's development?
4. In what ways do the documents by Adam Smith, Frederick II, and Thomas Jefferson reflect Enlightenment thinkers' intense interest in the relationship between the individual and secular society?

16

The French Revolution and Napoleon, 1789–1815

W HEN THE ESTATES GENERAL convened at Versailles in May 1789, no one could have foreseen what lay ahead: ten years of upheaval that established the model of modern revolution and set the course of modern politics. The first three documents illuminate the French Revolution in the making, from the politically charged months preceding the convocation of the Estates General to the formation of a republic and a government of terror designed to destroy enemies of the Revolution. The end of the Reign of Terror in 1794 opened a new chapter in European history, one marked by the extraordinary rise of Napoleon Bonaparte (1769–1821). Between 1795 and 1804, Napoleon transformed himself from a humble artillery officer in the Revolutionary Army into first consul, and ultimately, emperor of France. The fourth document describes a key stage in this transformation, Napoleon's invasion of Egypt in 1798. Although the campaign ultimately failed, it foreshadowed Napoleon's subsequent attempts to colonize large parts of Europe along similar lines, as the fifth document reveals. Backed by the Grand Army, Napoleon's political strategy of mixing revolutionary values with authoritarian rule seemed unstoppable.

1.
Abbé Sieyès
What Is the Third Estate?
1789

Although in 1788 King Louis XVI (r. 1774–1792) agreed to call the Estates General, he left a thorny procedural question for the deputies to answer: Would the assembly vote by order or by head? The debate over this question galvanized the nation in the

From Lynn Hunt, ed. and trans., *The French Revolution and Human Rights: A Brief Documentary History* (Boston: Bedford/St. Martin's, 1996), 65–70.

months preceding the opening of the Estates General in May 1789, thanks in part to pamphlets like the one that follows. Written by a middle-class clergyman, Abbé Emmanuel-Joseph Sieyès (1748–1836), this pamphlet's message was clear: the privileged few should not determine the nation's future, as a traditional vote by order would ensure by allowing the clergy and nobility to join forces to block any decision contrary to their liking. Rather, government should rest in the hands of the people whose labor and skills sustain society, the Third Estate. In forging his argument, Sieyès forcefully condemned traditional political and social structures while granting the Third Estate a voice on the national stage.

The plan of this work is quite simple. We must ask ourselves three questions.

1. What is the Third Estate? Everything.
2. What has it been until now in the political order? Nothing.
3. What does it want? To become something. . . .

What does a Nation require to survive and prosper? *Private* employment and *public* offices.

Private employment includes four classes of work:

1. Since the land and water provide the raw material for the needs of mankind, the first class, in logical order, includes all those families attached to work in the countryside.

2. Between the initial sale of raw materials and their consumption or usage as finished goods, labor of various sorts adds more value to these goods. In this way human industry manages to improve on the blessings of Nature and to multiply the value of the raw materials two, ten, or a hundredfold. Such is the second class of work.

3. Between production and consumption, as also between the different stages of production, there are a host of intermediary agents, useful both to producers and consumers; these are the merchants and wholesale traders. Wholesale traders constantly weigh demand according to place and time and speculate on the profit that they can make on storage and transport; merchants actually sell the goods on the markets, whether wholesale or retail. This type of utility designates the third class of work.

4. Besides these three classes of hard-working and useful Citizens who occupy themselves with the *things* fit to be consumed or used, society also needs a multitude of private occupations and services *directly* useful or agreeable to the *person*. This fourth class embraces all those occupations from the most distinguished scientific and liberal professions down to the least esteemed domestic servants.

These are the kinds of work that sustain society. Who carries them out? The Third Estate.

In the present state of affairs public offices can also be ranked in four well-known categories: the Sword [the army], the Robe [the courts], the Church, and the Administration. Detailed analysis is not necessary to show that the Third Estate makes up everywhere $\frac{19}{20}$ths of their number, except that it is charged with all the really hard work, all the work that the privileged order refuses to perform. Only the lucrative and most honored places are taken by the members of the privileged order. Should we praise them for this? We could do so only if the Third [Estate] was unwilling or unable to fill these offices. We know the truth of the matter, but the Third Estate has nonetheless been excluded. They are told, "Whatever your services, whatever your talents, you will only go so far and no further. Honors are not for your sort." A few rare exceptions, noteworthy as they are bound to be, are only a mockery, and the language encouraged on these exceptional occasions is but an additional insult.

If this exclusion is a social crime committed against the Third Estate, can we say at least that it is useful to the public good? Ah! Are the effects of monopoly now known? If it discourages those whom it pushes aside, does it not also render those it favors less competent? Is it not obvious that every piece of work kept out of free competition will be made more expensively and less well?

When any office is deemed the prerogative of a separate order among the citizens, has no one noticed that a salary has to be paid not only to the man who does the work but also to all those of the same caste who do not and even to entire families of both those who work and those who do not? Has no one noticed that this state of affairs, so abjectly respected among us, nonetheless seems contemptible and shameful in the history of ancient Egypt and in the stories of voyages to the Indies? But let us leave aside those considerations which though broadening our purview and perhaps enlightening would only slow our pace. It suffices here to have made the point that the supposed usefulness of a privileged order to the public service is nothing but a mirage; that without that order, all that is most arduous in this service is performed by the Third Estate; that without the privileged the best places would be infinitely better filled; that such places should naturally be the prize and reward for recognized talents and services; and that if the privileged have succeeded in usurping all the lucrative and honored posts, this is at once an odious iniquity committed against the vast majority of the citizenry and an act of treason against the public good.

Who therefore dares to say that the Third Estate does not contain within itself all that is needed to form a complete Nation? The Third Estate is like a strong and robust man with one arm still in chains. If we remove the privileged order, the Nation will not be something less but something more. Thus, what is the Third Estate? All, but an all that is shackled and oppressed. What would it be without the privileged order? All, but an all that is free and flourishing. Nothing can be done without it [the Third Estate]; everything would be infinitely better without the other two orders.

It does not suffice to have demonstrated that the privileged, far from being useful to the Nation, can only weaken and harm it; it must be proved further that the noble order[1] is not even part of society itself: It may very well be a burden for the Nation but it cannot be a part of it.

First, it is not possible to assign a place to the caste of nobles among the many elements that make up a Nation. I know that there are too many individuals whose infirmities, incapacity, incurable laziness, or excessively bad morals make them essentially foreigners to the work of society. The exception and the abuse always accompany the rule, especially in a vast empire. But at least we can agree that the fewer the abuses, the better ordered the state. The worst-off state of all would be the one in which not only isolated individual cases but also an entire class of citizens would glory in inactivity amidst the general movement and would contrive to consume the best part of what is produced without having contributed anything to its making. Such a class is surely foreign to the Nation because of its *idleness.*

The noble order is no less foreign amongst us by reason of its *civil* and *public* prerogatives.

What is a Nation? A body of associates living under a *common* law and represented by the same *legislature.*

Is it not more than certain that the noble order has privileges, exemptions, and even rights that are distinct from the rights of the great body of citizens? Because of this, it does not belong to the common order, it is not covered by the law common to the rest. Thus its civil rights already make it a people apart inside the great Nation. It is truly *imperium in imperio* [a law unto itself].

As for its *political* rights, the nobility also exercises them separately. It has its own representatives who have no mandate from the people. Its deputies sit separately, and even when they assemble in the same room with the deputies of the ordinary citizens, the nobility's representation still remains essentially distinct and separate: it is foreign to the Nation by its very principle, for its mission does not emanate from the people, and by its purpose, since it consists in defending, not the general interest, but the private interests of the nobility.

---

[1][Sieyès's own note] I do not speak of the clergy here. In my way of thinking, the clergy is not an order but rather a profession charged with a public service. In the clergy, it is not the person who is privileged but the office, which is very different. . . . The word caste refers to a class of men who, without functions and without usefulness and by the sole fact that they exist, enjoy the privileges attached to their person. From this point of view, which is the true one in my opinion, there is only one order, that of the nobility. They are truly a people apart but a false people, which not being able to exist by itself by reason of its lack of useful organs, attaches itself to a real Nation like those plant growths which can only survive on the sap of the plants that they tire and suck dry. The Clergy, the Robe, the Sword, and the Administration are four classes of public trustees that are necessary everywhere. Why are they accused in France of *aristocraticism?* It is because the noble caste has usurped all the good positions; it has done so as if this was a patrimonial property exploited for its personal profit rather than in the spirit of social welfare.

The Third Estate therefore contains everything that pertains to the Nation and nobody outside of the Third Estate can claim to be part of the Nation. What is the Third Estate? EVERYTHING. . . .

By Third Estate is meant the collectivity of citizens who belong to the common order. Anybody who holds a legal privilege of any kind leaves that common order, stands as an exception to the common law, and in consequence does not belong to the Third Estate. . . . It is certain that the moment a citizen acquires privileges contrary to common law, he no longer belongs to the common order. His new interest is opposed to the general interest; he has no right to vote in the name of the people. . . .

What is the will of a Nation? It is the result of individual wills, just as the Nation is the aggregate of the individuals who compose it. It is impossible to conceive of a legitimate association that does not have for its goal the common security, the common liberty, in short, the public good. No doubt each individual also has his own personal aims. He says to himself, "protected by the common security, I will be able to peacefully pursue my own personal projects, I will seek my happiness where I will, assured of encountering only those legal obstacles that society will prescribe for the common interest, in which I have a part and with which my own personal interest is so usefully allied." . . .

Advantages which differentiate citizens from one another lie outside the purview of citizenship. Inequalities of wealth or ability are like the inequalities of age, sex, size, etc. In no way do they detract from the *equality* of citizenship. These individual advantages no doubt benefit from the protection of the law; but it is not the legislator's task to create them, to give privileges to some and refuse them to others. The law grants nothing; it protects what already exists until such time that what exists begins to harm the common interest. These are the only limits on individual freedom. I imagine the law as being at the center of a large globe; we the citizens, without exception, stand equidistant from it on the surface and occupy equal places; all are equally dependent on the law, all present it with their liberty and their property to be protected; and this is what I call the *common rights* of citizens, by which they are all alike. All these individuals communicate with each other, enter into contracts, negotiate, always under the common guarantee of the law. If in this general activity somebody wishes to get control over the person of his neighbor or usurp his property, the common law goes into action to repress this criminal attempt and puts everyone back in their place at the same distance from the law. . . .

It is impossible to say what place the two privileged orders ought to occupy in the social order: this is the equivalent of asking what place one wishes to assign to a malignant tumor that torments and undermines the strength of the body of a sick person. It must be *neutralized*. We must re-establish the health and working of all the organs so thoroughly that they are no longer susceptible to these fatal schemes that are capable of sapping the most essential principles of vitality.

■ Discussion Questions

1. What is the traditional status of the Third Estate? How does Sieyès want to change it, and why?

2. Why do you think Sieyès was so critical of nobility in particular? What do these criticisms reveal about his political principles?

3. How effective do you think this pamphlet is as a work of political propaganda, and why?

2.
National Assembly
The Declaration of the Rights of Man and of the Citizen
1789

Promulgated by the fledgling National Assembly in August 1789, The Declaration of the Rights of Man and of the Citizen *gave the Revolution a clear sense of purpose and direction after the dizzying series of events of that summer. In it, the delegates set forth the guiding principles of the new government, echoing many of the ideals of influential eighteenth-century thinkers. The document also marked the definitive end of the old regime by presenting the protection of individual rights, not royal prerogative, as the cornerstone of political authority. The deputies' work was not done, however, for they regarded the declaration as a preliminary step toward their primary goal: to write a constitution for the country that would transform it into an enlightened constitutional monarchy. This goal was met with the Constitution of 1791, to which the declaration was attached.*

The representatives of the French people, organized as a National Assembly, believing that the ignorance, neglect, or contempt of the rights of man are the sole cause of public calamities and of the corruption of governments, have determined to set forth in a solemn declaration the natural, inalienable, and sacred rights of man, in order that this declaration, being constantly before all the members of the social body, shall remind them continually of their rights and duties; in order that the acts of the legislative power, as well as those of the executive power, may be compared at any moment with the objects and purposes of all political institutions and may thus be more respected; and, lastly, in order that the grievances of the citizens, based hereafter upon simple and incontestable principles, shall tend to the maintenance of the constitution and redound to the happiness of all. Therefore the National Assembly recognizes and proclaims, in the presence and

From James Harvey Robinson, *Readings in European History,* vol. II (Boston: Ginn and Company, 1906), 409–11.

under the auspices of the Supreme Being, the following rights of man and of the citizen:

Article 1. Men are born and remain free and equal in rights. Social distinctions may be founded only upon the general good.

2. The aim of all political association is the preservation of the natural and imprescriptible rights of man. These rights are liberty, property, security, and resistance to oppression.

3. The principle of all sovereignty resides essentially in the nation. No body nor individual may exercise any authority which does not proceed directly from the nation.

4. Liberty consists in the freedom to do everything which injures no one else; hence the exercise of the natural rights of each man has no limits except those which assure to the other members of the society the enjoyment of the same rights. These limits can only be determined by law.

5. Law can only prohibit such actions as are hurtful to society. Nothing may be prevented which is not forbidden by law, and no one may be forced to do anything not provided for by law.

6. Law is the expression of the general will. Every citizen has a right to participate personally, or through his representative, in its formation. It must be the same for all, whether it protects or punishes. All citizens, being equal in the eyes of the law, are equally eligible to all dignities and to all public positions and occupations, according to their abilities, and without distinction except that of their virtues and talents.

7. No person shall be accused, arrested, or imprisoned except in the cases and according to the forms prescribed by law. Any one soliciting, transmitting, executing, or causing to be executed, any arbitrary order, shall be punished. But any citizen summoned or arrested in virtue of the law shall submit without delay, as resistance constitutes an offense.

8. The law shall provide for such punishments only as are strictly and obviously necessary, and no one shall suffer punishment except it be legally inflicted in virtue of a law passed and promulgated before the commission of the offense.

9. As all persons are held innocent until they shall have been declared guilty, if arrest shall be deemed indispensable, all harshness not essential to the securing of the prisoner's person shall be severely repressed by law.

10. No one shall be disquieted on account of his opinions, including his religious views, provided their manifestation does not disturb the public order established by law.

11. The free communication of ideas and opinions is one of the most precious of the rights of man. Every citizen may, accordingly, speak, write, and print with freedom, but shall be responsible for such abuses of this freedom as shall be defined by law.

12. The security of the rights of man and of the citizen requires public military forces. These forces are, therefore, established for the good of all and not for the personal advantage of those to whom they shall be intrusted.

13. A common contribution is essential for the maintenance of the public forces and for the cost of administration. This should be equitably distributed among all the citizens in proportion to their means.

14. All the citizens have a right to decide, either personally or by their representatives, as to the necessity of the public contribution; to grant this freely; to know to what uses it is put; and to fix the proportion, the mode of assessment and of collection and the duration of the taxes.

15. Society has the right to require of every public agent an account of his administration.

16. A society in which the observance of the law is not assured, nor the separation of powers defined, has no constitution at all.

17. Since property is an inviolable and sacred right, no one shall be deprived thereof except where public necessity, legally determined, shall clearly demand it, and then only on condition that the owner shall have been previously and equitably indemnified.

■ **Discussion Questions**

1. In delineating the rights of the individual, how did the National Assembly respond to Enlightenment writers' calls for reforms?

2. According to this document, what are the fundamental roles of government and the individual citizen?

3. How does the document define political sovereignty, and how is this definition related to the deputies' collective sense of identity and purpose?

3.
Olympe de Gouges
Letters on the Trial
1793

Despite the momentous events of the first two years of the Revolution, even more radical changes were yet to come. With pressures mounting at home and the threat of war looming abroad, in 1792 the National Convention abolished the monarchy and established the first French Republic. A year later the government instituted a set of policies known as the "Terror" to crush all its enemies. The following excerpts from the trial record of French author and activist Olympe de Gouges (1748–1793) illuminate the instruments and ideals of the Terror in action. De Gouges, the daughter of a butcher, had already gained fame by protesting women's exclusion from full political

From Darline Gay Levy, Harriet Branson Applewhite, and Mary Durham Johnson, eds. and trans., *Women in Revolutionary Paris, 1789–1795* (Urbana: University of Illinois Press, 1979), 255–59.

participation in the Revolution in her 1791 tract, Declaration of the Rights of Woman. *In 1793, she aimed the power of her pen at the Terror. Having caught the attention of the police, de Gouges was imprisoned, and upon her interrogation before the Revolutionary Tribunal in November, she met the same fate as thousands of others at the time: death by guillotine.*

Audience of ... 12 Brumaire, Year II of the Republic.
Case of Olympe de Gouges.

Questioned concerning her name, surname, age, occupation, place of birth, and residence. Replied that her name was Marie Olympe de Gouges, age thirty-eight, *femme de lettres,* a native of Montauban, living in Paris, rue du Harlay, Section Pont-Neuf.

The clerk read the act of accusation, the tenor of which follows.

Antoine-Quentin Fouquier-Tinville, public prosecutor before the Revolutionary Tribunal, etc.

States that, by an order of the administrators of police, dated last July 25, signed Louvet and Baudrais, it was ordered that Marie Olympe de Gouges, widow of Aubry, charged with having composed a work contrary to the expressed desire of the entire nation, and directed against whoever might propose a form of government other than that of a republic, one and indivisible, be brought to the prison called l'Abbaye, and that the documents be sent to the public prosecutor of the Revolutionary Tribunal. Consequently, the accused was brought to the designated prison and the documents delivered to the public prosecutor on July 26. The following August 6, one of the judges of the Revolutionary Tribunal proceeded with the interrogation of the above-mentioned de Gouges woman.

From the examination of the documents deposited, together with the interrogation of the accused, it follows that against the desire manifested by the majority of Frenchmen for republican government, and in contempt of laws directed against whoever might propose another form of government, Olympe de Gouges composed and had printed works which can only be considered as an attack on the sovereignty of the people because they tend to call into question that concerning which it [the people] formally expressed its desire; that in her writing, entitled *Les Trois urnes, ou le Salut de la patrie,* there can be found the project of the liberty-killing faction which wanted to place before the people the approbation of the judgment of the tyrant condemned by the people itself; that the author of this work openly provoked civil war and sought to arm citizens against one another by proposing the meeting of primary assemblies to deliberate and express their desire concerning either monarchical government, which the national sovereignty had abolished and proscribed; concerning the one and indivisible republican [form], which it had chosen and established by the organ of its representatives; or, finally, concerning the federative [form], which would be the source of incalculable evils and which would destroy liberty infallibly.

... The public prosecutor stated next that it is with the most violent indignation that one hears the de Gouges woman say to men who for the past four years have not stopped making the greatest sacrifices for liberty; who on August 10, 1792, overturned both the throne and the tyrant; who knew how to bravely face the arms and frustrate the plots of the despot, his slaves, and the traitors who had abused the public confidence — to men who have submitted tyranny to the avenging blade of the law — that Louis Capet [Louis XVI] still reigns among them.

There can be no mistaking the perfidious intentions of this criminal woman, and her hidden motives, when one observes her in all the works to which, at the very least, she lends her name, calumniating and spewing out bile in large doses against the warmest friends of the people, their most intrepid defender....

On the basis of the foregoing exposé the public prosecutor drew up this accusation against Marie Olympe de Gouges, widow Aubry, for having maliciously and purposefully composed writings attacking the sovereignty of the people (whose desire, when these were written, had been pronounced for republican government, one and indivisible) and tending towards the reestablishment of the monarchical government (which it [the people] had formally proscribed) as well as the federative [form] (against which it [the people] had forcefully protested); for having had printed up and distributed several copies of one of the cited works tending towards these ends, entitled, *Les Trois urnes, ou le Salut de la patrie;* for having been stopped in her distribution of a greater number of copies as well as in her posting of the cited work only by the refusal of the bill-poster and by her prompt arrest; for having sent this work to her son, employed in the army of the Vendée as *officier de l'état major;* for having, in other manuscripts and printed works — notably, in the manuscript entitled *La France sauvée, ou le Tyran détrôné* as well as in the poster entitled *Olympe de Gouges au Tribunal Révolutionnaire* — sought to degrade the constituted authorities, calumniate the friends and defenders of the people and of liberty, and spread defiance among the representatives and the represented, which is contrary to the laws....

Consequently, the public prosecutor asks that he be given official notice by the assembled Tribunal of this indictment, etc., etc.

In this case only three witnesses were heard, one of whom was the citizen bill-poster, who stated that, having been asked to post a certain number of copies of printed material with the title *Les Trois urnes,* he refused when he found out about the principles contained in this writing.

When the accused was questioned sharply about when she composed this writing, she replied that it was some time last May, adding that what motivated her was that seeing the storms arising in a large number of *départments* ... she had the idea of bringing all parties together by leaving them all free in the choice of the kind of government which would be most suitable for them; that furthermore, her intentions had proven that she had in view only the happiness of her country.

Questioned about how it was that she, the accused, who believed herself to be such a good patriot, had been able to develop, in the month of June, means which she called conciliatory concerning a fact which could not longer be in question because the people, at that period, had formally pronounced for republican government, one and indivisible, she replied that this was also the [form of government] she had voted for as the preferable one; that for a long while she had professed only republican sentiments. . . .

Asked to declare whether she acknowledged authorship of a manuscript work found among her papers entitled *La France sauvée ou le Tyran détrôné*, she replied yes.

Asked why she had placed injurious and perfidious declamations against the most ardent defenders of the rights of the people in the mouth of the person who in this work was supposed to represent the Capet woman [Marie-Antoinette], she replied that she had the Capet woman speaking the language appropriate for her; that besides, the handbill for which she was brought before the Tribunal had never been posted; that to avoid compromising herself she had decided to send twenty-four copies to the Committee of Public Safety, which, two days later, had her arrested.

The public prosecutor pointed out to the accused, concerning this matter, that if her placard entitled *Les Trois urnes* had not been made public, this was because the bill-poster had not been willing to take it upon himself. The accused was in agreement with this fact.

Questioned about whether, since her detention, she had not sent a copy to her son along with a letter, she said that the fact was exact and that her intention concerning this matter had been to apprise him of the cause of her arrest; that besides, she did not know whether her son had received it, not having heard from him in a long while and not knowing at all what could have become of him.

Asked to speak concerning various phrases in the placard entitled *Olympe de Gouges, défenseur de Louis Capet*, a work written by her at the time of the former's trial, and concerning the placard entitled *Olympe de Gouges au Tribunal Révolutionnaire* as well, she responded only with oratorical phrases and persisted in saying that she was and always had been a good *citoyenne*, that she had never intrigued.

Asked to express herself and to reply precisely concerning her sentiments with respect to the faithful representatives of the people whom she had insulted and calumniated in her writings, the accused replied that she had not changed, that she still held to her same opinion concerning them, and that she had looked upon them as ambitious persons.

In her defense the accused said that she had ruined herself in order to propagate the principles of the Revolution and that she was the founder of popular societies of her sex, etc.

During the résumé of the charge brought by the public prosecutor, the accused, with respect to the facts she was hearing articulated against her, never stopped her smirking. Sometimes she shrugged her shoulders; then she clasped her hands and raised her eyes towards the ceiling of the room; then, suddenly, she moved on to an expressive gesture, showing astonishment; then gazing next at the court, she smiled at the spectators, etc.

Here is the judgment rendered against her.

The Tribunal, based on the unanimous declaration of the jury, stating that (1) it is a fact that there exist in the case writings tending towards the reestablishment of a power attacking the sovereignty of the people [and] (2) that Marie Olympe de Gouges, calling herself widow Aubry, is proven guilty of being the author of these writings, and admitting the conclusions of the public prosecutor, condemns the aforementioned Marie Olympe de Gouges, widow Aubry, to the punishment of death in conformity with Article One of the law of last March 29, which was read, which is conceived as follows: "Whoever is convicted of having composed or printed works or writings which provoke the dissolution of the national representation, the reestablishment of royalty, or of any other power attacking the sovereignty of the people, will be brought before the Revolutionary Tribunal and punished by death," and declares the goods of the aforementioned Marie Olympe de Gouges acquired for the republic....

... The execution took place the same day [12 Brumaire] towards 4 P.M.; while mounting the scaffold, the condemned, looking at the people, cried out: "Children of the Fatherland, you will avenge my death." Universal cries of "Vive la République" were heard among the spectators waving hats in the air.

■ Discussion Questions

1. What was the basis of the charges against Gouges?

2. What do these charges and the ensuing judgment reveal about the political principles of the Terror?

3. How were these ideals at odds with those of Gouges?

4. Do you think that Gouges's gender influenced the tribunal's attitudes toward her? If so, why?

4.
Abd al-Rahman al-Jabartî
Napoleon in Egypt
1798

While the Directory government that came to power in 1795 worked to establish order in France, Napoleon (1769–1821) continued the Revolution's policy of conquest and annexation abroad, first in Italy (1796–1797) and then in Egypt (1798–1801). At the time, Egypt was France's most important trading partner outside of the Caribbean; it was also a key base for challenging British interests in Asia. Egyptian historian Abd al-Rahman al-Jabartî's (1753–c. 1826) account of the first six months of the French invasion offers a native's perspective of Napoleon. In the excerpt here, Jabartî views Napoleon's actions skeptically through the lens of his own culture. His skepticism proved well founded, for Napoleon failed to colonize Egypt. Even so, he retained his reputation as a great military leader, preparing the way for his mastery of

From *Napoleon in Egypt: Al-Jabartî's Chronicle of the French Occupation, 1798*, trans. Shmuel Moreh (Princeton: Markus Wiener, 1993), 24–33.

France and much of Europe through a blend of authoritarian policies and revolutionary principles similar to those used in Egypt.

On Monday news arrived that the French had reached Damanhûr and Rosetta, bringing about the flight of their inhabitants to Fuwwa and its surroundings. Contained in this news was mention of the French sending notices throughout the country demanding impost for the upkeep of the military. Furthermore they printed a large proclamation in Arabic, calling on the people to obey them and to raise their "Bandiera." In this proclamation were inducements, warnings, all manner of wiliness and stipulations. Some copies were sent from the provinces to Cairo and its text is:

In the name of God, the Merciful, the Compassionate. There is no god but God. He has no son, nor has He an associate in His Dominion.

On behalf of the French Republic which is based upon the foundation of liberty and equality, General Bonaparte, Commander-in-Chief of the French armies makes known to all the Egyptian people that for a long time the Sanjaqs[1] who lorded it over Egypt have treated the French community basely and contemptuously and have persecuted its merchants with all manner of extortion and violence. Therefore the hour of punishment has now come.

Unfortunately this group of Mamlûks,[2] imported from the mountains of Circassia and Georgia have acted corruptly for ages in the fairest land that is to be found upon the face of the globe. However, the Lord of the Universe, the Almighty, has decreed the end of their power.

O ye Egyptians, they may say to you that I have not made an expedition hither for any other object than that of abolishing your religion; but this is a pure falsehood and you must not give credit to it, but tell the slanderers that I have not come to you except for the purpose of restoring your rights from the hands of the oppressors and that I more than the Mamlûks, serve God. . . .

And tell them also that all people are equal in the eyes of God and the only circumstances which distinguish one from the other are reason, virtue, and knowledge. But amongst the Mamlûks, what is there of reason, virtue, and knowledge, which would distinguish them from others and qualify them alone to possess everything which sweetens life in this world? Wherever fertile land is found it is appropriated to the Mamlûks; and the handsomest female slaves, and the best horses, and the most desirable dwelling-places, all these belong to them exclusively. If the land of Egypt is a fief of the Mamlûks, let them then produce the title-deed, which God conferred upon them. But the Lord of the Universe is compassionate and equitable toward mankind, and with the help of the Exalted, from this day forward no Egyptian shall be excluded from admission to eminent positions nor from acquiring high ranks, therefore the intelligent and virtuous and learned

---

[1]**Sanjaqs:** Provincial governors in the Ottoman Empire. [Ed.]
[2]**Mamlûks:** Descendants of medieval slave-soldiers who enjoyed considerable political power until the French invasion. [Ed.]

("ulamā") amongst them, will regulate / their affairs, and thus the state of the whole population will be rightly adjusted. . . .

Blessing on blessing to the Egyptians who will act in concert with us, without any delay, for their condition shall be rightly adjusted, and their rank raised. Blessing also, upon those who will abide in their habitations, not siding with either of the two hostile parties, yet when they know us better, they will hasten to us with all their hearts. But woe upon woe to those who will unite with the Mamlūks and assist them in the war against us, for they will not find the way of escape, and no trace of them shall remain. . . .

Here is an explanation of the incoherent words and vulgar constructions which he put into this miserable letter.

His statement "In the name of God, the Merciful, the Compassionate. There is no god but God. He has no son, nor has He an associate in His Dominion." In mentioning these three sentences there is an indication that the French agree with the three religions, but at the same time they do not agree with them, not with any religion. They are consistent with the Muslims in stating the formula "In the name of God," in denying that He has a son or an associate. They disagree with the Muslims in not mentioning the two Articles of Faith, in rejecting the mission of Muhammad, and the legal words and deeds which are necessarily recognized by religion. They agree with the Christians in most of their words and deeds, but disagree with them by not mentioning the Trinity, and denying the mission and furthermore in rejecting their beliefs, killing the priests and destroying the churches. Then, their statement "On behalf of the French Republic, etc.," that is, this proclamation is sent from their Republic, that means their body politic, because they have no chief or sultan with whom they all agree, like others, whose function is to speak on their behalf. For when they rebelled against their sultan six years ago and killed him, the people agreed unanimously that there was not to be a single ruler but that their state, territories, laws, and administration of their affairs, should be in the hands of the intelligent and wise men among them. They appointed persons chosen by them and made them heads of the army, and below them generals and commanders of thousands, two hundreds, and tens, administrators and advisers, on condition that they were all to be equal and none superior to any other in view of the equality of creation and nature. They made this the foundation and basis of their system. This is the meaning of their statement "based upon the foundation of liberty and equality." . . . They follow this rule: great and small, high and low, male and female are all equal. Sometimes they break this rule according to their whims and inclinations or reasoning. Their women do not veil themselves and have no modesty; they do not care whether they uncover their private parts. Whenever a Frenchman has to perform an act of nature he does so wherever he happens to be, even in full view of people, and he goes away as he is, without washing his private parts after defecation. If he is a man of taste and refinement he wipes himself with whatever he finds, even with a paper with writing on it, otherwise he remains as he is. They have intercourse with any woman who pleases them and vice versa. Sometimes one of their women goes into a barber's shop, and invites him to shave her pubic hair. If he wishes he can take his fee in kind. It is their custom to shave both their moustaches and beard. Some of them leave the hair of their cheeks only. . . .

His saying *qad hattama* etc. (has decreed) shows that they are appointing themselves controllers of God's secrets, but there is no disgrace worse than disbelief. . . .

His statement *wa-qūlū li'l-muftariyīn* (but tell the slanderers) is the plural of *muftari* (slanderer) which means liar, and how worthy of this description they are. The proof of that is his saying "I have not come to you except for the purpose of restoring your rights from the hands of the oppressors," which is the first lie he uttered and a falsehood which he invented. Then he proceeds to something even worse than that, may God cast him into perdition, with his words: "I more than the Mamlūks serve God. . . ." There is no doubt that this is a derangement of his mind, and an excess of foolishness. . . .

His saying [all people] are equal in the eyes of God the Almighty, this is a lie and stupidity. How can this be when God has made some superior to others as is testified by the dwellers in the Heavens and on the Earth? . . .

May God hurry misfortune and punishment upon them, may He strike their tongues with dumbness, may He scatter their hosts, and disperse them, confound their intelligence, and cause their breath to cease. He has the power to do that, and it is up to Him to answer.

■ Discussion Questions

1. What strategy did Napoleon use in his proclamation to garner the support of the Egyptian people?

2. What does this strategy suggest about Napoleon's personal ambitions and method of rule?

3. Why is Jabartî critical of Napoleon's intentions as stated in his proclamation?

4. What do Jabartî's criticisms suggest about the differences between French and Egyptian culture?

5.
Napoleon Bonaparte
Instructions and Letters
1805–1809

Despite the failure of the Egyptian campaign, Napoleon Bonaparte retained the loyalty of his troops and admirers in France. Upon his return to Paris in October 1799, he drew upon the support of both groups to overturn the beleaguered French

From *The Mind of Napoleon: A Selection from His Written and Spoken Words*, ed. and trans. J. Christopher Herold (New York: Columbia University Press, 1955), 165–68.

government. The door was now open for Napoleon to pursue his vision of world empire, beginning with his centralization of state authority at home, followed by aggressive military campaigns abroad. He relied greatly on his own family to realize his vision, installing them in positions of power in the wake of French territorial conquests. As the documents below reveal, these appointees included his stepson, Eugène Beauharnais, in Italy, and his brothers Joseph in Spain and Jerome in Westphalia. His instructions and letters to them illuminate the political attitudes and tactics that helped propel him to such great heights of power. At the same time, however, they reveal his inability to appreciate the powerful tradition of independent states in Europe, which ultimately contributed to his defeat.

INSTRUCTIONS TO EUGÈNE BEAUHARNAIS, 1805, ON HIS NOMINATION AS VICEROY OF ITALY

Dissimulation is natural in a mature man; to you, it must be a matter of principle and self-control. When you have spoken your mind needlessly, admit to yourself that you have made a mistake, and you will not make it again. As for the nation you are about to govern, you must display a suitable esteem, the more so because you will discover reasons for liking it less. The time will come when you will realize that there is little difference between one nation and another. The purpose of your administration being the welfare of my Italian subjects, you must begin by sacrificing your prejudices against those customs of theirs which you resent so violently. In any post other than that of viceroy of Italy you must pride yourself on being a Frenchman; but here [in Italy] you must make them forget that you are French, and you cannot succeed in this unless you can convince the Italians that you like them. They know that there is no love without esteem. Cultivate their language and their society; give them special proofs of your esteem at your receptions; approve of what they approve and like what they like.

Speak as little as possible. Your knowledge is too limited and your education has been too neglected for you to engage freely in discussions. Be able to listen, and be assured that silence often produces the same effect as wisdom. Be not ashamed of asking questions. Although you are a viceroy, you are only twenty-three years old, and no matter what flatterers may tell you, everybody is secretly aware of what you know and accords you his esteem not so much for what he thinks you are as for what he hopes you will be.

LETTER TO EUGÈNE, 1805

Do not let the Italians forget that I am master to do as I like. This is necessary for all peoples, but especially for the Italians, who obey only a voice of command. They will esteem you only to the degree to which they fear you, and they will fear you only to the degree to which they are aware that their duplicity and treacherous character are known to you.

LETTER TO JOSEPH, THEN KING OF SPAIN, 1809

Five sixths of Madrid are good people. But honest people need encouragement, and this is possible only if the mob is kept in its place. Here [in Valladolid] they did the impossible to obtain a pardon for the ruffians who have been condemned. I refused to listen, I had them hanged, and I have realized since that at bottom those people [the intercessors] were very glad not to have been listened to. I believe it is necessary that, especially at the beginning, your government should show some vigor in dealing with the rabble. The rabble loves and esteems only those it fears, and only if you make yourself feared by the rabble can you make yourself loved and esteemed by the whole nation.

LETTER TO JÉRÔME, THEN KING OF WESTPHALIA, 1808

There are three things I commend to you. First, respect, gratitude, and loyalty to me and to the French people, to whom you owe everything. Second, strictest economy, so as not to bring out the contrast between the miserable conditions that are weighing down your subjects and unbridled luxury and waste. Economy is necessary at all times but especially at the beginning of a reign, when public opinion is being formed. Economy does not mean merely that you should have no debts but also that, of the six million francs on your civil list, you spend three million for your household, save a million and a half for unforeseen events—such as marriages, feasts, and building expenses—and save another million and a half to build up over the next ten years a reserve of fifteen million. . . . Finally, use your time to learn what you do not know—cavalry, infantry, and artillery tactics and the administration of justice and of finance. When you have fulfilled these conditions, you will deserve my esteem as well as that of France and of your subjects. To accomplish all this, there are a great many reflections you could make, a great many reforms you could put into practice, and much that you could change in your ways.

LETTER TO JÉRÔME, 1809

You are king and brother of the Emperor: these are ridiculous qualifications in war. You must be a soldier, and again a soldier, and nothing but a soldier. You must take no ministers with you, no diplomatic corps, no pomp. You must bivouac with your outposts, be on horseback night and day, go with the vanguard to get your intelligence at first hand—or else stay in your seraglio.

You are making war like a satrap. Is it me, good God! that you have learned this? . . .

■ Discussion Questions

1. Based on these instructions and letters, why do you think Napoleon's efforts to colonize Europe were so successful? Do you see any clue as to why in the end they ultimately failed?

2. Although Napoleon proclaimed he was master to do as he liked, how did he also recognize the importance of public opinion as a basis for state authority?

3. What does this recognition suggest about the ways in which he mixed authoritarian policies with revolutionary principles?

■ Comparative Questions

1. In his pamphlet, Sieyès openly rejected traditional political and social structures in favor of the Third Estate. How do the basic tenets of *The Declaration of the Rights of Man and of the Citizen* convey a similar message?

2. Based on the trial record of Olympe de Gouges, in what ways did the Terror undermine these tenets?

3. Taken collectively, how do the first three documents allow us to chart the course of the Revolution between 1789 and 1795?

4. How did Napoleon take advantage of this course of events, and use it to his advantage? What revolutionary ideals as expressed by Sieyès and *The Declaration of the Rights of Man and of the Citizen* did he embody in particular?

5. Al-Jabartî was highly critical of the French in Egypt because, from his perspective, they embraced ideals of equality and liberty yet often placed restrictions on their meanings in practice. Do you think a similar criticism could be applied to Napoleon's rule in Europe, and why? What does this suggest about the limitations of the Revolution's legacy?

17

Industrialization and Social Ferment, 1815–1850

W HEN NAPOLEON BONAPARTE met his match on the battlefield in 1813, the reestablishment of the conservative order now seemed within reach after more than two decades of near constant warfare. Yet voices of unrest continued to reverberate across Europe. Not only was the revolutionary legacy still powerful, as the first two documents suggest, but another force was also at work—industrialization. The third document exposes industrialization's effects on the everyday world as factories sprang up across much of Europe and railroads crisscrossed the landscape. The parallel impact of the French Revolution and the Industrial Revolution prompted people to search for new ways of understanding the changes unfolding around them. The fourth document illuminates one of the most significant ideological consequences of this search, the birth of communism. As the final document suggests, however, the immediate impact of communism was far less visible than the intensity of nationalist fervor unleashed by the revolutions of 1848.

1.
T. B. Macaulay
Speech on Parliamentary Reform
1831

Upon Napoleon's defeat in 1813, the allied powers worked to erase the imprint that the French Revolution and Napoleon's conquests had left on European society and politics. The allied powers faced many obstacles, however, including the new ideology of liberalism. Unlike their political rivals, liberals heralded individual rights and the need for broader political representation, two hallmarks of the French Revolution. Even so, they shared conservatives' fear of popular unrest. British politician Thomas B. Macaulay (1800–1859) sought to capitalize on this common ground in a speech he

From T. B. Macaulay, *Miscellanies,* vol. I (Boston: Houghton Mifflin, 1901), 1–19.

delivered to Parliament in support of a bill for electoral reform at the very moment when mass unrest gripped Europe. His words struck a chord, for the bill passed a year later, expanding the British electorate to more than 800,000. Although this represented a tiny fraction of the country's growing population, which reached more than twenty million by 1850, it marked a triumph over exclusive aristocratic politics and opened the door to yet more sweeping changes.

It is a circumstance, Sir, of happy augury for the motion before the House, that almost all those who have opposed it have declared themselves hostile on principle to parliamentary reform. . . . For what I feared was, not the opposition of those who are averse to all reform, but the disunion of reformers. I knew that, during three months, every reformer had been employed in conjecturing what the plan of the government would be. I knew that every reformer had imagined in his own mind a scheme. . . . I felt therefore great apprehension that one person would be dissatisfied with one part of the bill, that another person would be dissatisfied with another part, and that thus our whole strength would be wasted in internal dissensions. That apprehension is now at an end. I have seen with delight the perfect concord which prevails among all who deserve the name of reformers in this House. . . . I will not, Sir, at present express any opinion as to the details of the bill; but, having during the last twenty-four hours given the most diligent consideration to its general principles, I have no hesitation in pronouncing it a wise, noble, and comprehensive measure, skilfully framed for the healing of great distempers, for the securing at once of the public liberties and of the public repose, and for the reconciling and knitting together of all the orders of the state.

The honorable Baronet who has just sat down [Sir John Walsh] has told us, that the Ministers have attempted to unite two inconsistent principles in one abortive measure. Those were his very words. He thinks, if I understand him rightly, that we ought either to leave the representative system such as it is, or to make it perfectly symmetrical. I think, Sir, that the Ministers would have acted unwisely if they had taken either course. Their principle is plain, rational, and consistent. It is this, to admit the middle class to a large and direct share in the representation, without any violent shock to the institutions of our country. . . . The government has, in my opinion, done all that was necessary for the removal of a great practical evil, and no more than was necessary.

I consider this, Sir, as a practical question. I rest my opinion on no general theory of government. I distrust all general theories of government. I will not positively say, that there is any form of polity which may not, in some conceivable circumstances, be the best possible. I believe that there are societies in which every man may safely be admitted to vote. Gentlemen may cheer, but such is my opinion. I say, Sir, that there are countries in which the condition of the laboring classes is such that they may safely be entrusted with the right of electing Members of the Legislature. If the laborers of England were in that state in which I, from my soul, wish to see them, if employment were always plentiful, wages always high, food always cheap, if a large family were considered not as an encumbrance but as a blessing, the principal objection to Universal Suffrage would, I think, be removed. Universal Suffrage exists in the United States without producing any very frightful consequences; and I do not believe that the people of those States, or of any part of the world, are in any good quality naturally superior to our own countrymen. But, unhappily, the laboring classes in England, and in all old countries, are occasionally in a state of great distress. Some of the causes of this distress are, I fear, beyond the control of the government. We know what effect distress produces, even on people more intelligent than the great body of the laboring classes can possibly be. . . . It is therefore no reflection on the poorer class of Englishmen, who are not, and who cannot in the nature of things be, highly educated, to say that distress produces on them its natural effects, those effects which it would produce on the Americans, or on any other people, that it blinds their judgment, that it inflames their passions, that it makes them prone to believe those who flatter them, and to distrust those who would serve them. For the sake, therefore, of the whole society, for the sake of the laboring classes themselves, I hold it to be clearly expedient that, in a country like this one, the right of suffrage should depend on a pecuniary qualification.

But, Sir, every argument which would induce me to oppose Universal Suffrage induces me to support the plan which is now before us. I am opposed to Universal Suffrage, because I think that it would produce a destructive revolution. I support this plan, because I am sure that it is our best security against a revolution. . . . I do in my conscience believe that, unless the plan proposed, or some similar plan, be speedily adopted, great and terrible calamities will befall us. Entertaining this opinion, I think myself bound to state it, not as a threat, but as a reason. I support this bill because it will improve our institutions; but I support it also because it tends to preserve them. That we may exclude those whom it is necessary to exclude, we must admit those whom it may be safe to admit. At present we oppose the schemes of revolutionists with only one half, with only one quarter of our proper force. We say, and we say justly, that it is not by mere numbers, but by property and intelligence, that the nation ought to be governed. Yet, saying this, we exclude from all share in the government great masses of property and intelligence, great numbers of those who are most interested in preserving tranquillity, and who know best how to preserve it. We do more. We drive over to the side of revolution those whom we shut out from power. Is this a time when the cause of law and order can spare one of its natural allies? . . .

If it be said that there is an evil in change as change, I answer that there is also an evil in discontent as discontent. This, indeed, is the strongest part of our case. It is said that the system works well. I deny it. I deny that a system works well, which the people regard with aversion. We may say here, that it is a good system and a perfect system. But if any man were to say so to any six hundred and fifty-eight respectable farmers or shopkeepers, chosen by lot in any part of England, he would be hooted down, and laughed to scorn. Are these the feelings with which any part of the government ought to be regarded? Above all, are these the feelings with which the popular branch of the legislature ought to be regarded? It is almost as essential to the utility of a House of Commons, that it should possess the confidence of the people, as that it should deserve that confidence. Unfortunately, that which is in theory the popular part of our government is in practice the unpopular part. Who wishes to dethrone the King? Who wishes to turn the Lords out of their House? Here and there a crazy radical, whom the boys in the street point at as he walks along. Who wishes to alter the constitution of this House? The whole people. It is natural that it should be so. . . .

Now, . . . if I were convinced that the great body of the middle class in England look with aversion on monarchy and aristocracy, I should be forced, much against my will, to come to this conclusion, that monarchical and aristocratical institutions are unsuited to my country. Monarchy and aristocracy, valuable and useful as I think them, are still valuable and useful as means, and not as ends. The end of government is the happiness of the people: and I do not conceive that, in a country like this, the happiness of the people can be promoted by a form of government in which the middle classes place no confidence, and which exists only because the middle classes have no organ by which to make their sentiments known. But, Sir, I am fully convinced that the middle classes sincerely wish to uphold the Royal prerogatives and the constitutional rights of the Peers. . . .

Now therefore while everything at home and abroad forebodes ruin to those who persist in a hopeless struggle against the spirit of the age, now, while the crash of the proudest throne of the Continent is still resounding in our ears, now, while the roof of a British palace affords an ignominious shelter to the exiled heir of forty kings, now, while we see on every side ancient institutions subverted, and great societies dissolved, now, while the heart of England is still sound, now, while old feelings and old associations retain a power and a charm which may too soon pass away, now, in this your accepted time, now, in this your day of salvation, take counsel, not of prejudice, not of party spirit, not of the ignominious pride of a fatal consistency, but of history, of reason, of the ages which are past, of the signs of this most portentous time. Pronounce in a manner worthy of the expectation with which this great debate has been anticipated, and of the long remembrance which it will leave behind. Renew the youth of the state. Save property, divided against itself. Save the multitude, endangered by its own ungovernable passions. Save the aristocracy, endangered by its own unpopular power. Save the greatest, and fairest, and most highly civilized community that ever existed, from calamities which may in a few days sweep away all the rich heritage of so many ages of wisdom and glory. The danger is terrible. The time is short. If this bill should be rejected, I pray to God that none of those who concur in rejecting it may ever remember their votes with unavailing remorse, amidst the wreck of laws, the confusion of ranks, the spoliation of property, and the dissolution of social order.

■ Discussion Questions

1. According to Macaulay, what is the main goal of the reform bill?

2. Why do you think Macaulay is against universal manhood suffrage?

3. What strategy does Macaulay use to sway opponents of the bill to support it?

4. In what ways does Macaulay's speech reflect liberal principles?

2.
Joseph Mazzini
Life and Writings of Joseph Mazzini
1805–1872

The son of a Genoese doctor, Joseph Mazzini (1805–1872) embodied the growing force of nationalist sentiment in post-Napoleonic Europe. Politically fragmented, Italy had long been a battleground for European rulers, including Napoleon. Napoleon's annexation of Italian territories and establishment of satellite kingdoms sparked local resistance, sowing the seeds of the movement for Italian unification that emerged later in the century. Mazzini dedicated his life to nourishing these seeds; as he recounts in the following excerpt from his autobiography. The quest to free Italy from foreign rule and establish a republic consumed his very soul after the failed political revolts of 1820–1821. France was no longer the target, however; instead it was Austria, which had regained a political foothold in the region upon Napoleon's defeat.

One Sunday in April 1821, while I was yet a boy, I was walking in the Strada Nuova of Genoa with my mother, and an old friend of our family named Andrea Gambini. The Piedmontese insurrection had just been crushed; partly by Austria, partly through treachery, and partly through the weakness of its leaders.

The revolutionists, seeking safety by sea, had flocked to Genoa, and, finding themselves distressed for means, they went about seeking help to enable them to cross into Spain, where the revolution was yet triumphant. The greater number of them were crowded in S. Pier d'Arena, awaiting a chance to embark; but not a few had contrived to enter the city one by one, and I used to search them out from amongst our own people, detecting them either by their general appearance, by some peculiarity of dress, by their warlike air, or by the signs of a deep and silent sorrow on their faces.

The population were singularly moved. Some of the boldest had proposed to the leaders of the insurrection — Santarosa and Ansaldi, I think — to concentrate themselves in, and take possession of the city, and organize a new resistance; but Genoa was found to be deprived of all means of successful defense; the fortresses were without artillery, and the leaders had rejected the proposition, telling them *to preserve themselves for a better fate.*

Presently we were stopped and addressed by a tall black-bearded man, with a severe and energetic countenance, and a fiery glance that I have never since forgotten. He held out a white handkerchief towards us, merely saying, *For the refugees of Italy.* My mother and friend dropped some money into the handkerchief, and he turned from us to put the same request to others. I afterwards

From Joseph Mazzini, *Life and Writings of Joseph Mazzini: Autobiographical and Political,* vol. I (London: Smith, Elder, 1890), 1–4.

learned his name. He was one Rini, a captain in the National Guard, which had been instituted at the commencement of the movement. He accompanied those for whom he had thus constituted himself collector, and, I believe, died—as so many of ours have perished—for the cause of liberty in Spain.

That day was the first in which a confused idea presented itself to my mind—I will not say of country or of liberty—but an idea that we Italians *could* and therefore *ought* to struggle for the liberty of our country. I had already been unconsciously educated in the worship of equality by the democratic principles of my parents, whose bearing towards high or low was ever the same. Whatever the position of the individual, they simply regarded the *man*, and sought only the honest man. And my own natural aspirations towards liberty were fostered by constantly hearing my father and the friend already mentioned speak of the recent republican era in France; by the study of the works of Livy and Tacitus, which my Latin master had given me to translate; and by certain old French newspapers, which I discovered half-hidden behind my father's medical books. Amongst these last were some numbers of the *Chronique du Mois,* a Girondist publication belonging to the first period of the French Revolution.

But the idea of an existing wrong in my own country, against which it was a duty to struggle, and the thought that I too must bear my part in that struggle, flashed before my mind on that day for the first time, never again to leave me. The remembrance of those refugees, many of whom became my friends in after life, pursued me where-ever I went by day, and mingled with my dreams by night. I would have given I know not what to follow them. I began collecting names and facts, and studied, as best I might, the records of that heroic struggle, seeking to fathom the causes of its failure.

They had been betrayed and abandoned by those who had sworn to concentrate every effort in the movement; the new king [Carlo Felice] had invoked the aid of Austria; part of the Piedmontese troops had even preceded the Austrians at Novara; and the leaders had allowed themselves to be overwhelmed at the first encounter, without making an effort to resist. All the details I succeeded in collecting led me to think that they *might* have conquered, if all of them had done their duty;—then why not renew the attempt? . . .

■ **Discussion Questions**

1. According to Mazzini, why did the 1820–1821 revolts fail?

2. How did this failure shape the course of Mazzini's life?

3. What were some of the other influences at work?

3.
Factory Rules in Berlin
1844

Industrialization did not simply create new social classes, new jobs, and new problems; it also created new work habits regimented by the pace of machines and the time clock. It fell on factory owners and managers to instill these habits in their workforce to ensure efficient and consistent levels of production. This was no easy task, because most people, whether former peasants or skilled workers, were traditionally accustomed to controlling their own time. The list of rules distributed to the employees of the Foundry and Engineering Works of the Royal Overseas Trading Company in Berlin provides a telling example of one approach to this challenge. This document also illustrates the spread of industrialization eastward across continental Europe.

In every large works, and in the co-ordination of any large number of workmen, good order and harmony must be looked upon as the fundamentals of success, and therefore the following rules shall be strictly observed.

Every man employed in the concern named below shall receive a copy of these rules, so that no one can plead ignorance. Its acceptance shall be deemed to mean consent to submit to its regulations.

(1) The normal working day begins at all seasons at 6 a.m. precisely and ends, after the usual break of half an hour for breakfast, a hour for dinner and half an hour for tea, at 7 p.m., and it shall be strictly observed.

Five minutes before the beginning of the stated hours of work until their actual commencement, a bell shall ring and indicate that every worker employed in the concern has to proceed to his place of work, in order to start as soon as the bell stops.

The doorkeeper shall lock the door punctually at 6 a.m., 8:30 a.m., 1 p.m. and 4:30 p.m.

Workers arriving 2 minutes late shall lose half an hour's wages; whoever is more than 2 minutes late may not start work until after the next break, or at least shall lose his wages until then. Any disputes about the correct time shall be settled by the clock mounted above the gatekeeper's lodge.

These rules are valid both for time- and for piece-workers, and in cases of breaches of these rules, workmen shall be fined in proportion to their earnings. The deductions from the wage shall be entered in the wage-book of the gatekeeper whose duty they are; they shall be unconditionally accepted as it will not be possible to enter into any discussions about them.

(2) When the bell is rung to denote the end of the working day, every workman, both on piece- and on day-wage, shall leave his workshop and the yard, but is not allowed to make preparations for his departure before the bell rings. Every breach of this rule shall lead to a fine of five silver groschen to the sick fund. Only

From Sidney Pollard and C. Holmes, *Documents of European Economic History*, vol. I: *The Process of Industrialization, 1750–1870* (New York: St. Martin's Press, 1968), 534–36.

those who have obtained special permission by the overseer may stay on in the workshop in order to work. — If a workman has worked beyond the closing bell, he must give his name to the gatekeeper on leaving, on pain of losing his payment for the overtime.

(3) No workman, whether employed by time or piece, may leave before the end of the working day, without having first received permission from the overseer and having given his name to the gatekeeper. Omission of these two actions shall lead to a fine of ten silver groschen payable to the sick fund.

(4) Repeated irregular arrival at work shall lead to dismissal. This shall also apply to those who are found idling by an official or overseer, and refuse to obey their order to resume work.

(5) Entry to the firm's property by any but the designated gateway, and exit by any prohibited route, e.g., by climbing fences or walls, or by crossing the Spree,[1] shall be punished by a fine of fifteen silver groschen to the sick fund for the first offenses, and dismissal for the second.

(6) No worker may leave his place of work otherwise than for reasons connected with his work.

(7) All conversation with fellow-workers is prohibited; if any worker requires information about his work, he must turn to the overseer, or to the particular fellow-worker designated for the purpose.

(8) Smoking in the workshops or in the yard is prohibited during working hours; anyone caught smoking shall be fined five silver groschen for the sick fund for every such offense.

(9) Every worker is responsible for cleaning up his space in the workshop, and if in doubt, he is to turn to his overseer. — All tools must always be kept in good condition, and must be cleaned after use. This applies particularly to the turner, regarding his lathe.

(10) Natural functions must be performed at the appropriate places, and whoever is found soiling walls, fences, squares, etc., and similarly, whoever is found washing his face and hands in the workshop and not in the places assigned for the purpose, shall be fined five silver groschen for the sick fund.

(11) On completion of his piece of work, every workman must hand it over at once to his foreman or superior, in order to receive a fresh piece of work. Pattern makers must on no account hand over their patterns to the foundry without express order of their supervisors. No workman may take over work from his fellow-workman without instruction to that effect by the foreman.

(12) It goes without saying that all overseers and officials of the firm shall be obeyed without question, and shall be treated with due deference. Disobedience will be punished by dismissal.

(13) Immediate dismissal shall also be the fate of anyone found drunk in any of the workshops.

(14) Untrue allegations against superiors or officials of the concern shall lead to stern reprimand, and may lead to dismissal. The same punishment shall be

---

[1]**Spree:** A river in Eastern Germany. [Ed.]

meted out to those who knowingly allow errors to slip through when supervising or stocktaking.

(15) Every workman is obliged to report to his superiors any acts of dishonesty or embezzlement on the part of his fellow workmen. If he omits to do so, and it is shown after subsequent discovery of a misdemeanor that he knew about it at the time, he shall be liable to be taken to court as an accessory after the fact and the wage due to him shall be retained as punishment. Conversely, anyone denouncing a theft in such a way as to allow conviction of the thief shall receive a reward of two Thaler, and, if necessary, his name shall be kept confidential. — Further, the gatekeeper and the watchman, as well as every official, are entitled to search the baskets, parcels, aprons etc., of the women and children who are taking dinners into the works, on their departure, as well as search any worker suspected of stealing any article whatever. . . .

(18) Advances shall be granted only to the older workers, and even to them only in exceptional circumstances. As long as he is working by the piece, the workman is entitled merely to his fixed weekly wage as subsistence pay; the extra earnings shall be paid out only on completion of the whole piece contract. If a workman leaves before his piece contract is completed, either of his own free will, or on being dismissed as punishment, or because of illness, the partly completed work shall be valued by the general manager with the help of two overseers, and he will be paid accordingly. There is no appeal against the decision of these experts.

(19) A free copy of these rules is handed to every workman, but whoever loses it and requires a new one, or cannot produce it on leaving, shall be fined $2\frac{1}{2}$ silver groschen, payable to the sick fund.

■ Discussion Questions

1. As delineated in the rules, what new modes of discipline did factory work require, and why?
2. What was the principal method used to encourage compliance with these rules?
3. Based on this document, how would you describe a typical day in this factory for the workers employed there?

4.
Friedrich Engels
Draft of a Communist Confession of Faith
1847

When Friedrich Engels (1820–1895) composed the following draft of a communist "confession of faith" in 1847, the Industrial Revolution was in full swing in Great Britain and rapidly gaining ground on the continent. Engels observed the impact of

From John E. Toews, ed., *The Communist Manifesto with Related Documents* (Boston: Bedford/St. Martin's, 1999), 99–104.

this process on the working class with a critical eye. Two years earlier, he had joined forces with another critic of industrialization, Karl Marx (1818–1883). Together they launched an ideological revolution with the publication of the Communist Manifesto *in 1848, which set forth a new understanding of industrial society and its problems and proposed a new set of solutions centered on the abolition of capitalist, "private" property. Engels's "confession of faith" illuminates key landmarks on his and Marx's intellectual journey, for it was among the materials Marx used to compose the* manifesto. *The confession was debated and approved in 1847 at the first congress of the Communist League. Although the first six questions reveal Engels's debt to the utopian principle of the community of property, those remaining reflect his and Marx's distinct historical vision.*

DRAFT OF A COMMUNIST CONFESSION OF FAITH

June 9, 1847

QUESTION 1:   *Are you a Communist?*
ANSWER: Yes.
QUESTION 2:   *What is the aim of the Communists?*
ANSWER: To organize society in such a way that every member of it can develop and use all his capabilities and powers in complete freedom and without thereby infringing the basic conditions of this society.
QUESTION 3:   *How do you wish to achieve this aim?*
ANSWER: By the elimination of private property and its replacement by community of property.
QUESTION 4:   *On what do you base your community of property?*
ANSWER: Firstly, on the mass of productive forces and means of subsistence resulting from the development of industry, agriculture, trade and colonization, and on the possibility inherent in machinery, chemical and other resources of their infinite extension.

Secondly, on the fact that in the consciousness or feeling of every individual there exist certain irrefutable basic principles which, being the result of the whole of historical development, require no proof.
QUESTION 5:   *What are such principles?*
ANSWER: For example, every individual strives to be happy. The happiness of the individual is inseparable from the happiness of all, etc.
QUESTION 6:   *How do you wish to prepare the way for your community of property?*
ANSWER: By enlightening and uniting the proletariat.
QUESTION 7:   *What is the proletariat?*
ANSWER: The proletariat is that class of society which lives exclusively by its labor and not on the profit from any kind of capital; that class whose weal and woe, whose life and death, therefore, depend on the alternation of times of good and bad business; in a word, on the fluctuations of competition.
QUESTION 8:   *Then there have not always been proletarians?*

ANSWER: No. There have always been poor and working classes; and those who worked were almost always the poor. But there have not always been proletarians, just as competition has not always been free.

QUESTION 9:   *How did the proletariat arise?*

ANSWER: The proletariat came into being as a result of the introduction of the machines which have been invented since the middle of the last century and the most important of which are: the steam-engine, the spinning machine and the power loom. These machines, which were very expensive and could therefore only be purchased by rich people, supplanted the workers of the time, because by the use of machinery it was possible to produce commodities more quickly and cheaply than could the workers with their imperfect spinning wheels and hand-looms. The machines thus delivered industry entirely into the hands of the big capitalists and rendered the workers' scanty property which consisted mainly of their tools, looms, etc., quite worthless, so that the capitalist was left with everything, the worker with nothing. In this way the factory system was introduced. Once the capitalists saw how advantageous this was for them, they sought to extend it to more and more branches of labor. They divided work more and more between the workers so that workers who formerly had made a whole article now produced only a part of it. Labor simplified in this way produced goods more quickly and therefore more cheaply and only now was it found in almost every branch of labor that here also machines could be used. As soon as any branch of labor went over to factory production it ended up, just as in the case of spinning and weaving, in the hands of the big capitalists, and the workers were deprived of the last remnants of their independence. We have gradually arrived at the position where almost *all* branches of labor are run on a factory basis. This has increasingly brought about the ruin of the previously existing middle class, especially of the small master craftsmen, completely transformed the previous position of the workers, and two new classes which are gradually swallowing up all other classes have come into being, namely:

I. The class of the big capitalists, who in all advanced countries are in almost exclusive possession of the means of subsistence and those means (machines, factories, workshops, etc.) by which these means of subsistence are produced. This is the *bourgeois* class, or the *bourgeoisie.*

II. The class of the completely propertyless, who are compelled to sell their labor to the first class, the bourgeois, simply to obtain from them in return their means of subsistence. Since the parties to this trading in labor are not *equal,* but the bourgeois have the advantage, the propertyless must submit to the bad conditions laid down by the bourgeois. This class, dependent on the bourgeois, is called the class of the *proletarians* or the *proletariat.*

QUESTION 10:   *In what way does the proletarian differ from the slave?*

ANSWER: The slave is sold once and for all, the proletarian has to sell himself by the day and by the hour. The slave is the property of one master and for that very reason has a guaranteed subsistence, however wretched it may be. The proletarian is, so to speak, the slave of the entire bourgeois *class,* not of one master, and therefore has no guaranteed subsistence, since nobody buys his labor if he does not need it. The slave is accounted a *thing* and not a member of civil society. The proletarian is recognized as a *person,* as a member of civil society. The slave *may,* therefore, have a better subsistence than the proletarian but the latter stands at a higher stage of development. The slave frees himself by *becoming a proletarian,* abolishing from the totality of property relationships *only* the relationship of *slavery.* The proletarian can free himself only by abolishing *property in general.*

QUESTION 11:   *In what way does the proletarian differ from the serf?*

ANSWER: The serf has the piece of land, that is, of an instrument of production, in return for handing over a greater or lesser portion of the yield. The proletarian works with instruments of production which belong to someone else who, in return for his labor, hands over to him a portion, determined by competition, of the products. In the case of the serf, the share of the laborer is determined by his own labor, that is, by himself. In the case of the proletarian it is determined by competition, therefore in the first place by the bourgeoisie. The serf has guaranteed subsistence, the proletarian has not. The serf frees himself by driving out his feudal lord and becoming a property owner himself, thus entering into competition and joining for the time being the possessing class, the privileged class. The proletarian frees himself by doing away with property, competition, and all class differences.

QUESTION 12:   *In what way does the proletarian differ from the handicraftsman?*

ANSWER: As opposed to the proletarian, the so-called handicraftsman, who still existed nearly everywhere during the last century and still exists here and there, is at most a *temporary* proletarian. His aim is to acquire capital himself and so to exploit other workers. He can often achieve this aim where the craft guilds still exist or where freedom to follow a trade has not yet led to the organization of handwork on a factory basis and to intense competition. But as soon as the factory system is introduced into handwork and competition is in full swing, this prospect is eliminated and the handicraftsman becomes more and more a proletarian. The handicraftsman therefore frees himself *either* by becoming a bourgeois or in general passing over into the middle class, *or,* by becoming a proletarian as a result of competition (as now happens in most cases) and joining the movement of the proletariat—i.e., the more or less conscious communist movement.

QUESTION 13:   *Then you do not believe that community of property has been possible at any time?*

ANSWER: No. Communism has only arisen since machinery and other inventions made it possible to hold out the prospect of an all-sided development, a happy existence, for all members of society. Communism is the theory of a liberation which was not possible for the slaves, the serfs, or the handicraftsmen, but only for the proletarians and hence it belongs of necessity to the 19th century and was not possible in any earlier period.

QUESTION 14:   *Let us go back to the sixth question. As you wish to prepare for community of property by the enlightening and uniting of the proletariat, then you reject revolution?*

ANSWER: We are convinced not only of the uselessness but even of the harmfulness of all conspiracies. We are also aware that revolutions are not made deliberately and arbitrarily but that everywhere and at all times they are the necessary consequence of circumstances which are not in any way whatever dependent either on the will or on the leadership of individual parties or of whole classes. But we also see that the development of the proletariat in almost all countries of the world is forcibly repressed by the possessing classes and that thus a revolution is being forcibly worked for by the opponents of communism. If, in the end, the oppressed proletariat is thus driven into a revolution, then we will defend the cause of the proletariat just as well by our deeds as now by our words.

QUESTION 15:   *Do you intend to replace the existing social order by community of property at one stroke?*

ANSWER: We have no such intention. The development of the masses cannot be ordered by decree. It is determined by the development of the conditions in which these masses live, and therefore proceeds gradually.

QUESTION 16:   *How do you think the transition from the present situation to community of property is to be effected?*

ANSWER: The first, fundamental condition for the introduction of community of property is the political liberation of the proletariat through a democratic constitution.

QUESTION 17:   *What will be your first measure once you have established democracy?*

ANSWER: Guaranteeing the subsistence of the proletariat.

QUESTION 18:   *How will you do this?*

ANSWER: I. By limiting private property in such a way that it gradually prepares the way for its transformation into social property, e.g., by progressive taxation, limitation of the right of inheritance in favor of the state, etc., etc.

II. By employing workers in national workshops and factories and on national estates.

III. By educating all children at the expense of the state.

QUESTION 19:   *How will you arrange this kind of education during the period of transition?*

ANSWER: All children will be educated in state establishments from the time when they can do without the first maternal care.

QUESTION 20:   *Will not the introduction of community of property be accompanied by the proclamation of the community of women?*

ANSWER: By no means. We will only interfere in the personal relationship between men and women or with the family in general to the extent that the maintenance of the existing institution would disturb the new social order. Besides, we are well aware that the family relationship has been modified in the course of history by the property relationships and by periods of development, and that consequently the ending of private property will also have a most important influence on it.

QUESTION 21:   *Will nationalities continue to exist under communism?*

ANSWER: The nationalities of the peoples who join together according to the principle of community will be just as much compelled by this union to merge with one another and thereby supersede themselves as the various differences between estates and classes disappear through the superseding of their basis—private property.

QUESTION 22:   *Do Communists reject the existing religions?*

ANSWER: All religions which have existed hitherto were expressions of historical stages of development of individual peoples or groups of peoples. But communism is that stage of historical development which makes all existing religions superfluous and supersedes them.

■ Discussion Questions

1. According to Engels's confession, what were the central goals of the communists, and how did they aim to achieve them?

2. How does Engels define the proletariat, and what sets this group apart from other types of workers?

3. How does Engels's confession explicitly link communist ideology to industrialization? What place did revolution have in this ideology?

5.
Sándor Petofi
"National Song" of Hungary
1848

Long under Habsburg control, in the 1830s a growing segment of the Hungarian population advocated for national self-determination. They faced stiff opposition, however, from the absolutist, autocratic court in Vienna, which ultimately erupted into violence there and in another Hungarian city, Pest—part of modern day Budapest. On March 15, 1848, a group of intellectuals gathered in front of the new Hungarian National Museum in Pest to outline their demands for their nation. Among those leaders was the popular radical poet Sándor Petofi (1823–1849), who recited his poem, "National Song," urging bystanders to free Hungary from Habsburg tyranny. Tens of thousands of supporters thronged the city within hours. Although the ensuing revolution was ultimately crushed, in 1991 the National Assembly of Hungary designated March 15 as one of three national days commemorating Hungary's statehood.

RISE, Magyar! is the country's call!
The time has come, say one and all:
Shall we be slaves, shall we be free?

From Eva March Tappan, ed., *Russia, Austria-Hungary, The Balkan States and Turkey: The World's Story. A History of the World in Story, Song, and Art,* vol. VI (Boston: Houghton Mifflin, 1914), 408–10.

This is the question, now agree!
For by the Magyar's God above
     We truly swear,
We truly swear the tyrant's yoke
     No more to bear!

Alas! till now we were but slaves;
Our fathers resting in their graves
Sleep not in freedom's soil. In vain
They fought and died free homes to gain.
But by the Magyar's God above
     We truly swear,
We truly swear the tyrant's yoke
     No more to bear!

A miserable wretch is he
Who fears to die, my land, for thee!
His worthless life who thinks to be
Worth more than thou, sweet liberty!
Now by the Magyar's God above
     We truly swear,
We truly swear the tyrant's yoke
     No more to bear!

The sword is brighter than the chain,
Men cannot nobler gems attain;
And yet the chain we wore, oh, shame!
Unsheath the sword of ancient fame!
For by the Magyar's God above
     We truly swear,
We truly swear the tyrant's yoke
     No more to bear!

The Magyar's name will soon once more
Be honored as it was before!
The shame and dust of ages past
Our valor shall wipe out at last.
For by the Magyar's God above
     We truly swear,
We truly swear the tyrant's yoke
     No more to bear!

And where our graves in verdure rise,
Our children's children to the skies
Shall speak the grateful joy they feel,
And bless our names the while they kneel.

For by the Magyar's God above
　　We truly swear,
We truly swear the tyrant's yoke
　　No more to bear!

■ Discussion Questions

1. Based on this poem, what drove Petofi and his fellow revolutionaries to action, and what did they hope to achieve?

2. Why do you think this poem was so successful in helping to rally people behind the revolution?

3. Despite the revolutionaries' initial successes, ethnic divisions in Hungary ultimately helped to seal the revolution's downfall. In what ways might this poem have contributed to such divisions?

■ Comparative Questions

1. How did the legacy of the French Revolution shape the development of liberalism and nationalism as represented by Macaulay and Mazzini, respectively?

2. Although Macaulay and Engels both recognized the difficulties faced by the working class in the industrial age, how were their responses to this recognition diametrically opposed? What does this suggest about the differences between liberal and communist doctrines?

3. In what ways was Engels reacting against the portrayal of working-class life found in the Berlin factory rules?

4. How is the idea of liberty central to Engels's discussion and to the "National Song" of Hungary?

5. In what ways do these documents offer both competing and complementary visions of a new social order?

Constructing the Nation-State, c. 1850–1880

THE LATE NINETEENTH CENTURY marked a new age in European politics and culture. After the failed revolutions of 1848, politicians, artists, intellectuals, and the general public cast aside the promises of idealists and claimed to see society as it really was: combative, competitive, and inherently disordered. The first two documents explain how European leaders sought to master this unruly scene and strengthen state power from above. The making of the modern nation-state assumed global proportions as governments expanded their empires abroad, the third document highlights the human scope of such efforts in British-controlled India. Politics were not the only force reshaping everyday life, however. Many visual artists likewise abandoned tradition to depict scenes from nature and society as they appeared at any given moment. The fourth document allows us to see this creative process at work through the eyes of the painter Edgar Degas (1834–1917). The biological research of Charles Darwin (1809–1882) reflected the scientific dimensions of the new age, as the final document reveals. To some observers, Darwin's work suggested that just as in politics, only the hardiest survived in the natural world. The social applications of Darwin's theories supported industrial growth and Europe's march toward world dominance.

1.
Rudolf von Ihering
Two Letters
1866

Prussian prime minister Otto von Bismarck (1815–1898) was among the most skilled practitioners of realpolitik in late nineteenth-century Europe. Through his military and diplomatic strategies, Bismarck took advantage of the collapse of the concert of Europe and made the dream of a united Germany a reality. Bismarck had many

From Walter Michael Simon, *Germany in the Age of Bismarck* (London: Allen and Unwin, 1968), 110–13.

detractors, however, including liberals like jurist Rudolf von Ihering (1818–1892). In two letters he wrote in 1866, von Ihering provides a contemporary assessment of realpolitik in action during the war with Austria, a pivotal period in Bismarck's quest for German unification. The war erupted in June 1866, and by early July, Prussia was triumphant. At first, Bismarck's tactics shocked von Ihering. Yet the allure of German unity proved irresistible to him and other liberals, and they soon embraced the sense of military superiority that came to define German nationalism.

(To J. Glaser, Giessen, 1 May.) ... Never, probably, has a war been incited so shamelessly and with such horrifying frivolity as the one that Bismarck is currently trying to start against Austria. My innermost feelings are revolted by this violation of every legal and moral principle. God knows I am no friend of Austria; on the contrary, I have always been regarded as one of her enemies—that is to say of her political system, not of the Austrian people whom I have learned to love ...—; I am devoted to the idea of Prussian influence in north Germany, even though I have little sympathy for the present political system in Prussia. But I would rather cut off my hand than to use it in such a disgusting operation as Prussian policy is now launching against Austria—the common sense of any honest man cannot even comprehend the depths of this perfidy. We ask ourselves in amazement: is it really true that what the whole world knows to be lies can be proclaimed from on high as the truth? Austria is supposed to be mobilizing against Prussia! Any child knows that the opposite is the case. ... The saddest thing about it all is that once the struggle is under way principles of right and wrong must come in absolutely tragic conflict with interests. Whom should we wish victorious, Austria or Prussia? We have no choice, we must come down on the side of the *unjust* cause, because we cannot tolerate the possibility of Austria gaining the upper hand in Germany. Everyone here detests this war, nobody can be comfortable with the idea that it will have the result that we *must* desire—the hegemony of Prussia. That is our situation. Germans taking up arms against Germans, civil war, a plot of three or four Powers against one, with not even an appearance of legality, without popular participation, created by a few diplomats alone, a conspiracy against your poor country, which causes even the enemies of Austria to sympathize with her and in which they would have to desire her victory—if this victory did not mean our own ruin! ... The war would be unthinkable if Austria had not for decades been doing everything to make it impossible even for her friends in Germany to take sides with her and putting the most menacing weapons in the hands of her enemies. ... Everyone agrees on the crying injustice that is being done to Austria, and yet, as I say, thousands here would not lift a finger for her cause, people feel that that would mean turning against one's own cause; for with very few exceptions the general opinion here is that the free development of Germany would be incompatible with Austrian supremacy. This may be wrong, but I am merely stating the fact. There is just as little affection for the German princes: here also one finds the same collision between undoubted historical justice and a total inability to work up any enthusiasm for it. It is sad to be in conflict with one's own feelings—we ought to desire victory for the just cause in this instance too, but we cannot! ...

(To B. Windscheid, Giessen, 19 August.) . . . I think I must be dreaming when I think of how much has happened in the short space of a few weeks; it seems that it must be years. I am only now gradually coming to my senses again; at one time I was quite dizzy from the pace of events. What a surging of emotions—of deep fear, anxious hesitation, joyous exultation, apprehensive suspense, furious indignation, profound pity, and in the end once more a rejoicing of the soul, an ecstasy of happiness such as my heart has never before known! Oh, my dear friend, what enviable luck to be living at this time, to have seen this turning-point in German history with which there has been nothing to compare for a thousand years. For years I have envied the Italians that they succeeded in what seemed for us to lie only in the distant future, I have wished for a German Cavour and Garibaldi as Germany's political messiah. And overnight he has appeared in the person of the much-abused Bismarck. Should we not think we are dreaming if the impossible becomes possible? Like you I was afraid at the prospect of war, I was convinced of the notion that the Austrians, experienced in the practical school of war, would be superior to the Prussians. Has intelligence and moral energy ever in history celebrated such a triumph over crude force? There is something wonderful about this spirit that animates little Prussia, this spirit that lifts us all out of a state of impotence and ignominy and gives to the name of Germany in Europe a lustre and a tone that it has not had for a thousand years. I bow before the genius of Bismarck, who has achieved a masterpiece of political planning and action such as are only rarely to be found in history. How marvelously the man spun all the threads of the great web, how firmly and safely so that none of them broke, how precisely he knew and used all the ways and means—his king, Napoleon, his army, the administration, Austria and her forces—in short, a masterpiece of calculation. I have forgiven the man everything he has done up to now, more, I have convinced myself that it was necessary; what seemed to us, the uninitiated, as criminal arrogance has turned out in the end to have been an indispensable means to the goal. He is one of the greatest men of the century; it is a real revelation to have lived at the same time as such a man; a man of action like that, not heedless action but action inspired and prepared both politically and morally, is worth a hundred men of liberal principles and of powerless honesty!

Nine weeks ago I should not have believed that I would write a paean of praise to Bismarck, but I cannot help myself! I leave it to my stubborn colleagues from Swabia and Bavaria to abuse him, to concentrate everything disgusting they can think of on the name of Bismarck. Incorrigible doctrinaires! For years, they have yelled and drunk themselves hoarse for German unity, and when someone comes on the scene and achieves the impossible by transferring German unity from a book of student songs into reality they cry "crucify him." . . .

■ Discussion Questions

1. What does von Ihering reveal about Bismarck's political methods in these two letters?

2. Why do you think von Ihering was conflicted in his attitudes about these methods?

3. How do von Ihering's opinions change between the time he wrote the first and second letters, and what do you think accounts for this change?

2.

Peter Kropótkin
Memoirs of a Revolutionist
1899

Russia's defeat in the Crimean War (1853–1856) revealed its inability to compete in the rapidly changing industrial world. Among Russia's greatest liabilities was the institution of serfdom—binding the peasant population to the land—which inhibited the growth of a modern labor force and fostered widespread discontent. After years of discussion and debate, Russian Tsar Alexander II (r. 1855–1881) chose a momentous solution to combat these problems: on March 3, 1861, he issued the Emancipation Manifesto officially abolishing serfdom. In the following excerpt from his memoirs, Prince Peter Kropótkin (1842–1921) provides a firsthand glimpse of how people in St. Petersburg reacted to the emancipation decree and of its impact on one of his family estates. At the time, Kropótkin was a student at a select military school in St. Petersburg, the Corps of Pages, and he later gained fame as a revolutionary and anarchist.

. . . I was at the corps, having to take part in the military parade at the riding-school. I was still in bed, when my soldier servant, Ivánoff, dashed in with the tea tray, exclaiming, "Prince, freedom! The manifesto is posted on the Gostínoi Dvor" (the shops opposite the corps).

"Did you see it yourself?"

"Yes. People stand round; one reads, the others listen. It *is* freedom!"

In a couple of minutes I was dressed, and out. A comrade was coming in.

"Kropótkin, freedom!" he shouted. "Here is the manifesto. My uncle learned last night that it would be read at the early mass at the Isaac Cathedral; so we went. There were not many people there; peasants only. The manifesto was read and distributed after the mass. They well understood what it meant. When I came out of the church, two peasants, who stood in the gateway, said to me in such a droll way, 'Well, sir? now—all gone?'" And he mimicked how they had shown him the way out. Years of expectation were in that gesture of sending away the master.

I read and re-read the manifesto. It was written in an elevated style by the old Metropolitan of Moscow, Philarète, but with a useless mixture of Russian and Old Slavonian which obscured the sense. . . . Notwithstanding all this, one thing was evident: serfdom was abolished, and the liberated serfs would get the land and their homesteads. They would have to pay for it, but the old stain of slavery was

From Peter Kropótkin, *Memoirs of a Revolutionist* (New York: Horizon Press, 1968), 133–36.

removed. They would be slaves no more; the reaction had *not* got the upper hand.

We went to the parade; and when all the military performances were over, Alexander II., remaining on horseback, loudly called out, "The officers to me!" They gathered round him, and he began, in a loud voice, a speech about the great event of the day.

"The officers . . . the representatives of the nobility in the army"—these scraps of sentences reached our ears—"an end has been put to centuries of injustice. . . . I expect sacrifices from the nobility . . . the loyal nobility will gather round the throne" . . . and so on. Enthusiastic hurrahs resounded amongst the officers as he ended.

We ran rather than marched back on our way to the corps,—hurrying to be in time for the Italian opera, of which the last performance in the season was to be given that afternoon; some manifestation was sure to take place then. Our military attire was flung off with great haste, and several of us dashed, lightfooted, to the sixth-story gallery. The house was crowded.

During the first entr'acte the smoking-room of the opera filled with excited young men, who all talked to one another, whether acquainted or not. We planned at once to return to the hall, and to sing, with the whole public in a mass choir, the hymn "God Save the Tsar."

However, sounds of music reached our ears, and we all hurried back to the hall. The band of the opera was already playing the hymn, which was drowned immediately in enthusiastic hurrahs coming from all parts of the hall. I saw Bavéri, the conductor of the band, waving his stick, but not a sound could be heard from the powerful band. Then Bavéri stopped, but the hurrahs continued. I saw the stick waved again in the air; I saw the fiddle-bows moving, and musicians blowing the brass instruments, but again the sound of voices overwhelmed the band. Bavéri began conducting the hymn once more, and it was only by the end of that third repetition that isolated sounds of the brass instruments pierced through the clamor of human voices.

The same enthusiasm was in the streets. Crowds of peasants and educated men stood in front of the palace, shouting hurrahs, and the Tsar could not appear without being followed by demonstrative crowds running after his carriage. . . .

Where were the uprisings which had been predicted by the champions of slavery? Conditions more indefinite than those which had been created by the Polozhénie (the emancipation law) could not have been invented. If anything could have provoked revolts, it was precisely the perplexing vagueness of the conditions created by the new law. And yet, except in two places where there were insurrections, and a very few other spots where small disturbances entirely due to misunderstandings and immediately appeased took place, Russia remained quiet, —more quiet than ever. With their usual good sense, the peasants had understood that serfdom was done away with, that "freedom had come," and they accepted the conditions imposed upon them, although these conditions were very heavy.

I was in Nikólskoye in August, 1861, and again in the summer of 1862, and I was struck with the quiet, intelligent way in which the peasants had accepted the new conditions. They knew perfectly well how difficult it would be to pay the re-demption tax for the land, which was in reality an indemnity to the nobles in lieu of the obligations of serfdom. But they so much valued the abolition of their per-sonal enslavement that they accepted the ruinous charges—not without mur-muring, but as a hard necessity—the moment that personal freedom was ob-tained. For the first months they kept two holidays a week, saying that it was a sin to work on Friday; but when the summer came they resumed work with even more energy than before.

When I saw our Nikólskoye peasants, fifteen months after the liberation, I could not but admire them. Their inborn good nature and softness remained with them, but all traces of servility had disappeared. They talked to their masters as equals talk to equals, as if they never had stood in different relations. . . .

■ **Discussion Questions**

1. As described by Kropótkin, how did people react to the emancipation decree?

2. According to Kropótkin, how did the decree challenge traditional social bound-aries?

3. How does Kropótkin describe Alexander II, and what do you think his descrip-tion suggests about the tsar's power at the time?

3.
Krupa Sattianadan
Saguna: A Story of Native Christian Life
1887–1888

Along with strengthening state power at home during the late nineteenth century, European leaders expanded their empires abroad and tightened their control therein. Great Britain's decision to assume direct control of India in 1858 provides a dramatic example of this shift in colonial policy. In her autobiographical novel Saguna, *Krupa Sattianadan (1862–1894) illuminates the everyday dimensions of British imperial-ism. She was born to Christian parents in the Bombay Presidency, an administrative unit of the colonial administration. While in her teens, the death of her beloved brother, Bhasker, gravely affected her physical and emotional health. Sattianadan was sent to a nearby mission school to recover, and she describes her experiences there in the following passage. As she recounts, her white teachers strove to mold her ac-cording to English tastes, morals, and behavior, thereby exposing the racist attitudes underlying British rule. Her book found a ready audience and was published both in English and Tamil, a language widely used in southern India.*

From Susie Tharu and K. Lalita, eds., *Women Writing in India: 600 B.C. to the Present,* vol. I, *600 B.C. to the Early Twentieth Century* (New York: The Feminist Press, 1991), 277–81.

My sister paid a visit to the city, not long after Bhasker's death. She noticed my retired ways and my peculiar moods and took me to her home. One day as I was sitting in the hall, puzzling my head over some books that I found in the study, two ladies were announced, and before I had time to run away, they were in the hall. The first grasped my sister's hand in hers and gave her a hearty kiss. Her appearance at once attracted my notice. She seemed fresh colored, tall, as she looked with a good-humored smile at me over sister's shoulder. There was a twinkle in her eye, as if she wished every one to be a partaker of her high spirits. She was certainly strikingly different from other ladies, I thought, and I listened with great attention to what she had to say. . . . Then she turned round toward me, and, catching hold of both of my hands, put question after question to me in such a way that I could not but answer. She had large light brown eyes, a fine, full long face, a nose rather blunt, and a broad, high forehead. I liked her. Presently she turned toward my sister and talked aside for a few minutes while her companion smiled to me and drew me toward her. But before we could talk much the other turned toward me, and said, "So that's settled; you are to come next month and stay with me. You will learn to your heart's content there, but mind you are to be very free with me and tell me everything. I mean to quarrel with you very often. Ah! you critical thing. Don't I know what you are thinking?" and with a warm, but rather rough hug and a brushing kiss she left me. My sister said I must go and stay with the two ladies for some time. I liked the idea and made up my mind to go. The first thing that I was told on going to Miss Roberts'—for that was the name of the lady who took charge of me—was that I was a little girl; that in England girls of fourteen and fifteen were considered mere chits, and that I was to lay aside all solemnity of manner and behave as a girl. When it came to the lessons I was asked what I was learning.

I said: "History, geography, &c."

"What in history?"

"I have finished *Landmarks of the History of Greece,* and am reading—"

"Greece! Greece! What have you to do with Greece?"

I had loved this little book. It was like a storybook, and I thought that she would have been pleased, but she only murmured, "Well! I will see. I must get something more suited to you. What about English? Can you read fluently?"

Longfellow's poems were put into my hand. The volume opened at "Pleasant it was when woods were green." I read this fast enough.

"Too fast."

"Oh I know it by heart," I exclaimed, anxious to show my cleverness. I shut the book and repeated the whole thing to her. I had once learnt it in a fit of study, and it had given me much pleasure.

"Well! I tell you what," she said, shutting the book, "you know a little too much. When a horse goes too fast, what does his master do?"

I did not know what he did, but I thought the comparison was not a good one, and I exclaimed abruptly, "I am not a horse."

"Well! Well!" she said laughing, "we won't discuss that point. I think you want occupation. You must teach in my little school this afternoon. Now we have done with our lessons for one day."

To my great surprise she shut up the books and put them by. When dinner time came I saw the other lady for the first time. She gave me a smile and pointed to my place by her side, but Miss Roberts never left me alone. She began by saying to her neighbor, "Girls in England never sit at the table with their elders, but of course we shall allow this one." In my sister's house I had learned to some extent how to use spoon and fork, but when I found the lady's eyes fixed on me my fingers trembled, and I thought I was sure to make all kinds of mistakes to her amusement. Already her eyes were twinkling with fun and laughter. I refused many a tempting thing that was offered, while she kept on remarking: "That's right, don't eat if you don't care. Girls in England don't eat these things." At last came curry and rice, of which I took a little, and enjoyed it. . . .

During the day, the school was my delight. This Miss Roberts managed. She instructed me in the art of teaching, in which I found a great delight. I was astonished at the explanations which I was able to give, and the way in which a knowledge of things seemed to spring into existence when it was required. I was in a whirl of delight with the blackboards, the large maps and the pictures, and the new dignity that all these conferred on me. Miss Roberts smiled at my eagerness, and forgot to say that I was only a child. I loved to think myself grown up and important. Miss Roberts used to quarrel with me as impetuously and passionately as if she had been of my own age, and then make it up by giving me a hearty hug and a kiss. She had very peculiar views, and we often had little fights with each other. I can hardly help thinking that she sometimes gave expression to her views for the sole purpose of teasing me. "Oh, Miss D., what made you receive the Bible woman in the drawing room?" she said one day, alluding to a very respectable person, a great friend of our family. "In England we receive them in the kitchen. She is no better than a servant, I assure you."

"In the kitchen?" I said, in amazement and indignation. I was angry, and thought of many grievances that I had heard spoken of. I had also heard that we were the real aristocrats of our country, and that the English ladies who came to India only belonged to the middle class, and I resolved to tell her that, so I boldly added: "What do you think of us? We are real aristocrats of this place." Unfortunately I pronounced the big word wrongly, and she burst out laughing and repeated it again and again, as I had done. "I don't care. Anyhow, you are middle-class people. She is a brahmin, and only takes money from the Mission because she is poor. She is no servant. In your country you are no brahmins. You are sudras." Tears fell from my eyes, and I felt as if I should choke.

"Miss D.," exclaimed the angry lady, now quite beside herself, "do girls ever talk at table like this? I protest against this. I can't have it. I tell you I can't,"—this with so much emphasis that I was quite frightened. Miss D. looked at me and shook her head. The tears that were rolling from my eyes I hastily wiped. "What can I do?" I said, while a shower of words, such as "rude," "bad," "naughty," "disrespectful," &c., fell on my head. Tiffin over, Miss Roberts went with a bounce to her room and I went to mine and began to cry. "Natives," I said to myself, "we are natives. Tomorrow she will say that my mother was a Bible woman too. Oh! I will go away from her," and I began to cry more. About five minutes afterward the door behind me opened, and Miss Roberts rushed in, took hold of me, and kissed me profusely. "Now it is all right," she said smiling and wonderfully changed. "We won't talk about it."

"And you won't send Bible women to the kitchen?" I said.

She shook her head and rushed away from me laughing.

In the evenings we generally sat together in the lobby. It was our free time, and I was told to say anything I liked. I used to sit far back on the deep seat with my hands on my lap, although there was a table in front. I liked to draw my own pictures, with the stars and shadows outside, and often my thoughts were with Bhasker; but I was always disturbed and told to talk. Generally the ladies had some fancy work in their hands; but I never brought any. One day Miss Roberts rebuked me and said: "Why did you not bring some work?"

I felt guilty, but still as I rose I said somehow, "I thought we were expected to be free at this time."

"Yes, but we must not appear so. I hate laziness."

Something in this remark caught my attention. I stood near the table and looked out. All my pictures vanished. I looked into her face and said, "It is only for appearance, is it? What is the good of that? Won't it be acting falsely?"

She flew into a passion, and when I tried to escape to my room, she forced me down. "Falsely! Sit and be lazy," she said, "and let everyone of us put you to shame."

The second lady, however, calmed her, saying, "Really I don't do anything. I had better sit quietly too."

"Sit, sit," said Miss Roberts, who had by this time nearly spent her wrath and was in a little pet.

The other lady had on various occasions whispered to me, "She is Irish and means nothing," and now she looked and smiled at me.

My greatest trials always came through my tongue. I had got into the habit of thinking loudly. Bhasker had encouraged it, and the discussions carried on by my other brothers, in which I often took part, had made me quite an adept in defending my views. I had had to stand up for my rights from my childhood. I had not then learnt the beauty of silence. One day I was sitting in the lobby in my usual half-sleepy, half-dreamy state, when I heard a visitor announced. As soon as Miss Roberts heard the name, she broke out abruptly, "Oh, how disgusting! What a bore she is! and she wants me, that is true enough." So saying she walked out, and an elderly lady met her near the lobby.

"Oh! I am so glad to see you. How do you do?" Miss Roberts said in a hearty tone as she brought in the visitor. Surely this is somebody else, and I am glad that it is a surprise for Miss Roberts, I said to myself. The talk evidently was cheerful and genial, but as soon as it was over, I was rather taken aback to hear Miss Roberts say, "Oh, what a bore to be sure! How glad I am she is gone! We must really not have visitors at this time."

"She! she!" I said, "was not she a surprise to you?"

"What do you mean?" said Miss Roberts, turning abruptly round on me.

"No! I thought the lady was a surprise to you. You said you were so glad to see her."

"Oh! Oh!" she said, lifting her voice and her hands.

"Miss D., I tell you I can't have this imper—"

"You said free speech was allowed here," I answered, interrupting her.

"Free speech, but not to your superiors, not to me," this with a thump on the table. "You naughty girl."

But it was a little overdone, and there was a burst from the other lady in which Miss Roberts found herself heartily joining.

Later on I came to know that they did not mean anything. It was only the custom, and they used the few set phrases that etiquette compelled them to use. But my readers will understand from this what a boor I was. I loved these two ladies and stayed with them for months, and in spite of little quarrels now and then, I lived very happily with them. Not long after I was attacked with fever, and my sister was compelled to take me away.

■ **Discussion Questions**

1. How would you describe the attitudes of Sattianadan's teachers toward her, and vice versa?

2. As described by Sattianadan, how did the mission school further the goals of British colonial policy?

3. What does this passage suggest about the benefits and drawbacks of British colonial policy?

4.
Edgar Degas
Notebooks
1863–1884

Visual artists were not immune to the changes unfolding around them in late nineteenth-century Europe. Beginning in the 1850s, many artists turned away from classical and romantic conventions and portrayed the world in realistic and graphic ways. Some artists pushed the boundaries of tradition further still with a new style called impressionism. Impressionists were equally fascinated with their immediate surroundings but also focused on the light, color, and movement of a single moment. Edgar Degas (1834–1917) embodied this shift in the visual arts. A classically trained draftsman, Degas began his professional career in Paris in 1859, painting portraits and historical subjects. For Degas, the pull of convention was ultimately no match for the novel artistic influences energizing the Parisian art scene at the time, notably Japanese prints, photography, and the fledging impressionist movement. The impact

From Linda Nochlin, ed., *Impressionism and Post-Impressionism, 1874–1904* (Englewood Cliffs: Prentice-Hall, 1966), 61–63.

on Degas was profound. By the late 1860s, he had turned his eye to depicting modern life in motion. The excerpts below from his private notebooks capture his artistic creativity and driving desire to portray local scenes and individuals one moment and one action at a time.

FROM DEGAS' NOTEBOOK: 1863–1867

What is certain is that putting a bit of nature in place and drawing it are two entirely different things.[1]

I don't like to hear people saying like children in front of rosy and glowing flesh: "Oh, what life, what blood!"—the human skin is as varied in appearance, especially among us, as the rest of nature: fields, trees, mountains, water, forests. It is possible to meet with as many resemblances between a face and a pebble as between two pebbles because everyone still wants to see a likeness between two faces. (I am speaking in terms of the question of form, not bringing up that of coloring, since we often find so much connection between a pebble and a fish, a mountain and a dog's head, clouds and horses, etc.)

Therefore, it is not merely instinct which makes us say that we must search for a method of coloring everywhere, for the affinities among what is alive, what is dead and what vegetates. I can, for example, easily recall the color of some hair, because I got the idea that it was hair made out of polished walnutwood, or else flax, or horse-chestnut shells. The rendering of the form will make real hair, with its softness and lightness or its roughness or its weight out of this tone which is almost precisely that of walnutwood, flax, or horse-chestnut shell. And then one paints in such different ways on such different supports that the same tone might be one thing in one place, another in another. . . .

FROM DEGAS' NOTEBOOK: 1878–1884

After having done portraits seen from above, I will do them seen from below— sitting very close to a woman and looking at her from a low viewpoint, I will see her head in the chandelier, surrounded by crystals, etc.; do simple things like draw a profile which would not move, [the painter] himself moving, going up or down, the same for a full face—a piece of furniture, a whole living room; do a series of arm-movements of the dance, or of legs that would not move, himself turning either around or—etc. Finally study a figure or an object, no matter what, from every viewpoint. One could use a looking glass for that, one would not [have to] stir from one's place. Only the looking glass would be lowered or tilted. One

---

[1] According to French poet and Degas admirer Paul Valéry (1871–1945), in this statement Degas "meant to distinguish what he called the *mise en place,* or the conventional representation of objects, from what he called the 'drawing' or the alteration which this exact representation . . . undergoes from a particular artist's way of seeing and working." [Ed.]

would turn about. Studio projects: Set up tiers [a series of benches] all around the room so as to get used to drawing things from above and below. Only let myself paint things seen in a looking glass to get used to hatred of trompe-l'oeil.[1]

For a portrait, make someone pose on the ground floor and work on the first floor to get used to keeping hold of the forms and expressions and never draw or paint *immediately*.

For the Newspaper cut a lot. Of a dancer do either the arms or the legs or the back. Do the shoes—the hands—of the hairdresser—the badly cut coiffure . . . , bare feet in dance, action, etc., etc.

Do every kind of worn object placed, accompanied in such a way that they have the life of the man or the woman; corsets which have just been taken off, for example—and which keep the form of the body, etc., etc.

Series on instruments and instrumentalists, their shapes, twisting of the hands and arms and neck of the violinist, for example, puffing out and hollowing of the cheeks of bassoons, oboes, etc.

Do a series in aquatint on *mourning* (different blacks), black veils of deep mourning (floating on the face), black gloves, carriages in mourning, carriage of the Funeral Company, carriages like Venetian gondolas.

On smoke, smoke of smokers, pipes, cigarettes, cigars, smoke of locomotives, of high chimneys, factories, steamboats, etc. Destruction of smoke under the bridges. Steam.

On the evening. Infinite subjects. In the cafés, different values of the glass-shades reflected in the mirrors.

On the bakery, the bread: series on journeymen bakers, seen in the cellar itself or through the air vents from the street. Colors of pink flour—lovely curves of pie, still lifes on the different breads, large, oval, fluted, round, etc. Experiment, in color, on the yellows, pinks, grey-whites of breads. Perspective views of rows of breads. Charming layout of bakeries. Cakes, the wheat, the mills, the flour, the sacks, the market-porters.

No one has ever done monuments or houses from below, from beneath, up close as one sees them going by in the streets. . . .

■ Discussion Questions

1. What subjects intrigued Degas as an artist? Why was he interested in portraying them from so many different viewpoints and positions?

2. In what ways was this interest typical of impressionism in general?

3. How did the changing economic and social scene in Paris at the time influence Degas's interests and approach?

---

[1]**trompe-l'oeil:** French for "deceive the eye." A style of painting intended to look photographically realistic. [Ed.]

5.

Charles Darwin
The Descent of Man
1871

As Otto von Bismarck (1815–1898) and other realpolitikers were transforming European political views during the late nineteenth century, the English naturalist Charles Darwin (1809–1882) was transforming scientific views. In 1859, Darwin published On the Origin of Species, *in which he argued that animal species evolved over time through a process of natural selection by which the strongest and most well adapted to any given environment survived. The biblical story of creation had no place in Darwin's conclusions, and this incited considerable debate. The debate intensified twelve years later when Darwin applied his theory of evolution directly to humans in* The Descent of Man and Selection in Relation to Sex. *The ramifications of this work extended beyond the field of biology when some people began to use evolutionary principles to understand, justify, and perpetuate the social and political inequalities of the day.*

The main conclusion here arrived at, and now held by many naturalists who are well competent to form a sound judgment, is that man is descended from some less highly organized form. The grounds upon which this conclusion rests will never be shaken, for the close similarity between man and the lower animals in embryonic development, as well as in innumerable points of structure and constitution, both of high and of the most trifling importance, — the rudiments which he retains, and the abnormal reversions to which he is occasionally liable, — are facts which cannot be disputed. They have long been known, but until recently they told us nothing with respect to the origin of man. Now when viewed by the light of our knowledge of the whole organic world, their meaning is unmistakable. The great principle of evolution stands up clear and firm, when these groups of facts are considered in connection with others such as the mutual affinities of the members of the same group, their geographical distribution in past and present times, and their geological succession. It is incredible that all these facts should speak falsely. He who is not content to look, like a savage, at the phenomena of nature as disconnected, cannot any longer believe that man is the work of a separate act of creation. He will be forced to admit that the close resemblance of the embryo of man to that, for instance, of a dog—the construction of his skull, limbs and whole frame on the same plan with that of other mammals, independently of the uses to which the parts may be put—the occasional re-appearance of various structures, for instance of several muscles, which man does not normally possess,

From Charles Darwin, *The Descent of Man and Selection in Relation to Sex* (New York: D. Appleton and Company, 1896), 606–19.

but which are common to the Quadrumana[1]—and a crowd of analogous facts—all point in the plainest manner to the conclusion that man is the co-descendant with other mammals of a common progenitor.

We have seen that man incessantly presents individual differences in all parts of his body and in his mental faculties. These differences or variations seem to be induced by the same general causes, and to obey the same laws as with the lower animals. In both cases similar laws of inheritance prevail. Man tends to increase at a greater rate than his means of subsistence; consequently he is occasionally subjected to a severe struggle for existence, and natural selection will have effected whatever lies within its scope. A succession of strongly-marked variations of a similar nature is by no means requisite; slight fluctuating differences on the individual suffice for the work of natural selection; not that we have any reason to suppose that in the same species, all parts of the organization tend to vary to the same degree. . . .

Through the means just specified, aided perhaps by others as yet undiscovered, man has been raised to his present state. But since he attained to the rank of manhood, he has diverged into distinct races, or as they may be more fitly called, subspecies. Some of these, such as the Negro and European, are so distinct that, if specimens had been brought to a naturalist without any further information, they would undoubtedly have been considered by him as good and true species. Nevertheless all the races agree in so many unimportant details of structure and in so many mental peculiarities, that these can be accounted for only by inheritance from a common progenitor; and a progenitor thus characterized would probably deserve to rank as man.

It must not be supposed that the divergence of each race from the other races, and of all from a common stock, can be traced back to any one pair of progenitors. On the contrary, at every stage in the process of modification, all the individuals which were in any way better fitted for their conditions of life, though in different degrees, would have survived in greater numbers than the less well-fitted. The process would have been like that followed by man, when he does not intentionally select particular individuals, but breeds from all the superior individuals, and neglects the inferior. He thus slowly but surely modifies his stock, and unconsciously forms a new strain. So with respect to modifications acquired independently of selection, and due to variations arising from the nature of the organism and the action of the surrounding conditions, or from changed habits of life, no single pair will have been modified much more than the other pairs inhabiting the same country, for all will have been continually blended through free intercrossing.

By considering the embryological structure of man,—the homologies which he presents with the lower animals,—the rudiments which he retains,—and the reversions to which he is liable, we can partly recall in imagination the former condition of our early progenitors; and can approximately place them in their

---

[1]**Quadrumana:** A division of primates that includes apes and monkeys. [Ed.]

proper place in the zoological series. We thus learn that man is descended from a hairy, tailed quadruped, probably arboreal in its habits, and an inhabitant of the Old World. This creature, if its whole structure had been examined by a naturalist, would have been classed amongst the Quadrumana, as surely as the still more ancient progenitor of the Old and New World monkeys. The Quadrumana and all the higher mammals are probably derived from an ancient marsupial animal, and this through a long line of diversified forms, from some amphibian-like creature, and this again from some fish-like animals. In the dim obscurity of the past we can see that the early progenitor of all the Vertebrata must have been an aquatic animal, provided with branchiae, with the two sexes united in the same individual, and with the most important organs of the body (such as the brain and heart) imperfectly or not at all developed. This animal seems to have been more like the larvae of the existing marine Ascidians than any other known form.

The high standard of our intellectual powers and moral disposition is the greatest difficulty which presents itself, after we have been driven to this conclusion on the origin of man. But every one who admits the principle of evolution, must see that the mental powers of the higher animals, which are the same in kind with those of man, though so different in degree, are capable of advancement. Thus the interval between the mental powers of one of the higher apes and of a fish, or between those of an ant and scale-insect, is immense; yet their development does not offer any special difficulty; for with our domesticated animals, the mental faculties are certainly variable, and the variations are inherited. No one doubts that they are of the utmost importance to animals in a state of nature. Therefore the conditions are favorable for their development through natural selection. The same conclusion may be extended to man; the intellect must have been all-important to him, even at a very remote period, as enabling him to invent and use language, to make weapons, tools, traps, &c., whereby with the aid of his social habits, he long ago became the most dominant of all living creatures. . . .

The development of the moral qualities is a more interesting problem. The foundation lies in the social instincts, including under this term the family ties. These instincts are highly complex, and in the case of the lower animals give special tendencies towards certain definite actions; but the more important elements are love, and the distinct emotion of sympathy. Animals endowed with the social instincts take pleasure in one another's company, warn one another of danger, defend and aid one another in many ways. These instincts do not extend to all the individuals of the species, but only to those of the same community. As they are highly beneficial to the species, they have in all probability been acquired through natural selection. . . .

Social animals are impelled partly by a wish to aid the members of their community in a general manner, but more commonly to perform certain definite actions. Man is impelled by the same general wish to aid his fellows; but has few or no special instincts. He differs also from the lower animals in the power of expressing his desires by words, which thus become a guide to the aid required and bestowed. The motive to give aid is likewise much modified in man: it no longer consists solely of a blind instinctive impulse, but is much influenced by the praise or blame of his fellows. The appreciation and the bestowal of praise and blame both rest on sympathy; and this emotion, as we have seen, is one of the most important elements of the social instincts. Sympathy, though gained as an instinct, is also much strengthened by exercise or habit. As all men desire their own happiness, praise or blame is bestowed on actions and motives, according as they lead to this end; and as happiness is an essential part of the general good, the greatest-happiness principle indirectly serves as a nearly safe standard of right and wrong. As the reasoning powers advance and experience is gained, the remoter effects of certain lines of conduct on the character of the individual, and on the general good, are perceived; and then the self-regarding virtues come within the scope of public opinion, and receive praise, and their opposites blame. But with the less civilized nations reason often errs, and many bad customs and base superstitions come within the same scope, and are then esteemed as high virtues, and their breach as heavy crimes. . . .

The moral nature of man has reached its present standard, partly through the advancement of his reasoning powers and consequently of a just public opinion, but especially from his sympathies having been rendered more tender and widely diffused through the effects of habit, example, instruction, and reflection. It is not improbable that after long practice virtuous tendencies may be inherited. With the more civilized races, the conviction of the existence of an all-seeing Deity has had a potent influence on the advance of morality. Ultimately man does not accept the praise or blame of his fellows as his sole guide, though few escape this influence, but his habitual convictions, controlled by reason, afford him the safest rule. His conscience then becomes the supreme judge and monitor. Nevertheless the first foundation or origin of the moral sense lies in the social instincts, including sympathy; and these instincts no doubt were primarily gained, as in the case of the lower animals, through natural selection. . . .

The belief in God has often been advanced as not only the greatest, but the most complete of all the distinctions between man and the lower animals. It is however impossible, as we have seen, to maintain that this belief is innate or instinctive in man. On the other hand a belief in all-pervading spiritual agencies seems to be universal; and apparently follows from a considerable advance in man's reason, and from a still greater advance in his faculties of imagination, curiosity and wonder. I am aware that the assumed instinctive belief in God has been used by many persons as an argument for His existence. But this is a rash argument, as we should thus be compelled to believe in the existence of many cruel and malignant spirits, only a little more powerful than man; for the belief in them is far more general than in a beneficent Deity. The idea of a universal and beneficent Creator does not seem to arise in the mind of man, until he has been elevated by long-continued culture. . . .

I am aware that the conclusions arrived at in this work will be denounced by some as highly irreligious; but he who denounces them is bound to show why it is more irreligious to explain the origin of man as a distinct species by descent from some lower form, through the laws of variation and natural selection, than to explain the birth of the individual through the laws of ordinary reproduction. The birth both of the species and of the individual are equally parts of that grand sequence of events, which our minds refuse to accept as the result of blind chance. The understanding revolts at such a conclusion, whether or not we are able to believe that every slight variation of structure, — the union of each pair in marriage, — the dissemination of each seed, — and other such events, have all been ordained for some special purpose. . . .

The main conclusion arrived at in this work, namely that man is descended from some lowly organized form, will, I regret to think, be highly distasteful to many. But there can hardly be a doubt that we are descended from barbarians. The astonishment which I felt on first seeing a party of Fuegians[2] on a wild and broken shore will never be forgotten by me, for the reflection at once rushed into my mind — such were our ancestors. These men were absolutely naked and bedaubed with paint, their long hair was tangled, their mouths frothed with excitement, and their expression was wild, startled, and distrustful. They possessed hardly any arts, and like wild animals lived on what they could catch; they had no government, and were merciless to every one not of their own small tribe. He who has seen a savage in his native land will not feel much shame, if forced to acknowledge that the blood of some more humble creature flows in his veins. For my own part I would as soon be descended from that heroic little monkey, who braved his dreaded enemy in order to save the life of his keeper, or from that old baboon, who descending from the mountains, carried away in triumph his young comrade from a crowd of astonished dogs — as from a savage who delights to torture his enemies, offers up bloody sacrifices, practices infanticide without remorse, treats his wives like slaves, knows no decency, and is haunted by the grossest superstitions.

Man may be excused for feeling some pride at having risen, though not through his own exertions, to the very summit of the organic scale; and the fact of his having thus risen, instead of having been aboriginally placed there, may give him hope for a still higher destiny in the distant future. But we are not here concerned with hopes or fears, only with the truth as far as our reason permits us to discover it; and I have given the evidence to the best of my ability. We must, however, acknowledge, as it seems to me, that man with all his noble qualities, with sympathy which feels for the most debased, with benevolence which extends not only to other men but to the humblest living creature, with his god-like intellect which has penetrated into the movements and constitution of the solar system — with all these exalted powers — Man still bears in his bodily frame the indelible stamp of his lowly origin.

■ Discussion Questions

1. What evidence does Darwin supply to support his theory of human evolution?
2. How does this evidence call into question the relationship between religion and science?

---

[2]**Fuegians:** Inhabitants of Tierra del Fuego. [Ed.]

3. According to Darwin, what qualities have contributed to the development of "more civilized races," and why?

4. How does Darwin voice the concern for realism and concrete facts that marked the general mood of his day?

■ Comparative Questions

1. How would you compare the political methods and goals of Bismarck and Alexander II?

2. How does Darwin's picture of nature and man's place within it support the principles of realpolitik?

3. In what ways do you think Darwin's theories might have shaped British attitudes toward colonial peoples as revealed in Sattianadan's story?

4. What do these documents reveal about how European culture, politics, and science built a sense of belonging and national identity?

19

Empire, Modernity, and the Road to War, c. 1880–1914

THE DUAL PHENOMENA of industry and empire transformed Europe and the world in the closing decades of the nineteenth century. With domestic industries booming, European leaders looked abroad for new markets and raw materials. The widespread belief that a nation's imperial holdings were an indication of its strength and racial superiority also fueled the quest for empire. As the first two documents show, this quest was a source of unity and discord on both sides of the Atlantic Ocean. The third document illuminates Germany's especially striking success in melding industrial growth and imperial expansion. As the twentieth century dawned, Europeans surveyed the new landscape with both fear and elation. On the one hand, many enjoyed unprecedented prosperity. On the other, chaos and disorder seemed to lurk around every corner. The fourth document illustrates that women in particular sparked such fears when they took to the streets to demand a political voice. Even what was considered to be "normal" behavior for children was under threat, as the fifth document reveals. Collectively, all five documents demonstrate that the road to modernity was rocky and uncertain, casting a permanent shadow over the Enlightenment's faith in the inevitability of progress.

1.
Jules Ferry
Speech before the French National Assembly
1883

French politician Jules Ferry (1832–1893) fueled his country's quest to compete in the continent's race to conquer foreign territory in the closing decades of the nineteenth century. While serving two terms as premier during the Third Republic, Ferry took the lead in France's colonial expansion in Africa and Asia. Yet not everyone embraced

From Ralph A. Austin, ed., *Modern Imperialism: Western Overseas Expansion and Its Aftermath, 1776–1965* (Lexington: D. C. Heath, 1969), 69–74.

his imperialist policies, including his conservative and socialist colleagues within the government. In the following speech, delivered before the National Assembly in July 1883, Ferry faced his opponents head on, defending not only the political and economic necessity of French expansionism but also its moral justness. At the same time, his critics voice their views, revealing the basis of their anticolonial sentiment.

M. JULES FERRY: Gentlemen, it embarrasses me to make such a prolonged demand upon the gracious attention of the Chamber, but I believe that the duty I am fulfilling upon this platform is not a useless one. It is as strenuous for me as for you, but I believe that there is some benefit in summarizing and condensing, in the form of arguments, the principles, the motives, and the various interests by which a policy of colonial expansion may be justified; it goes without saying that I will try to remain reasonable, moderate, and never lose sight of the major continental interests which are the primary concern of this country. What I wish to say, to support this proposition, is that in fact, just as in word, the policy of colonial expansion is a political and economic system; I wish to say that one can relate this system to three orders of ideas: economic ideas, ideas of civilization in its highest sense, and ideas of politics and patriotism.

In the area of economics, I will allow myself to place before you, with the support of some figures, the considerations which justify a policy of colonial expansion from the point of view of that need, felt more and more strongly by the industrial populations of Europe and particularly those of our own rich and hard working country: the need for export markets. Is this some kind of chimera? Is this a view of the future or is it not rather a pressing need, and, we could say, the cry of our industrial population? I will formulate only in a general way what each of you, in the different parts of France, is in a position to confirm. Yes, what is lacking for our great industry, drawn irrevocably on to the path of exportation by the [free trade] treaties of 1860, what it lacks more and more is export markets. Why? Because next door to us Germany is surrounded by barriers, because beyond the ocean, the United States of America has become protectionist, protectionist in the most extreme sense, because not only have these great markets, I will not say closed but shrunk, and thus become more difficult of access for our industrial products, but also these great states are beginning to pour products not seen heretofore onto our own markets. . . . It is not necessary to pursue this demonstration any farther. Yes, gentlemen, I am speaking to the economists, whose convictions and past services no one appreciates more than I do; I am speaking to the honorable M. Passy, whom I see here and who is one of the most authoritative representatives among us of the old school of economics *[smiles];* I know very well what they will reply to me, what is at the bottom of their thoughts . . . the old school, the great school, gentlemen; one, M. Passy, which your name has embellished, which was led in France by Jean-Baptiste Say and by Adam Smith in England. I do not mean to treat you with any irony, M. Passy, believe me.

I say that I know very well the thoughts of the economists, whom I can call doctrinaires without offending M. Passy. They say to us, "The true export markets are the commercial treaties which furnish and assure them." Gentlemen, I do not look down upon commercial treaties: if we could return to the situation which existed after 1860, if the world had not been subjected to that economic revolution which is the product of the development of science and the speeding up of communications, if this great revolution had not intervened, I would gladly take up the situation which existed after 1860. It is quite true that in that epoch the competition of grain from Odessa did not ruin French agriculture, that the grain of America and of India did not yet offer us any competition; at that moment we were living under the regime of commercial treaties, not only with England, but with the other great powers, with Germany, which had not yet become an industrial power. I do not look down upon them, these treaties; I had the honor of negotiating some of less importance than those of 1860; but gentlemen, in order to make treaties, it is necessary to have two parties: one does not make treaties with the United States; this is the conviction which has grown among those who have attempted to open some sort of negotiations in this quarter, whether officially or officiously.

Gentlemen, there is a second point, a second order of ideas to which I have to give equal attention, but as quickly as possible, believe me; it is the humanitarian and civilizing side of the question. On this point the honorable M. Camille Pellatan has jeered in his own refined and clever manner; he jeers, he condemns, and he says "What is this civilization which you impose with cannonballs? What is it but another form of barbarism? Don't these populations, these inferior races, have the same rights as you? Aren't they masters of their own houses? Have they called upon you? You come to them against their will, you offer them violence, but not civilization." There, gentlemen, is the thesis; I do not hesitate to say that this is not politics, nor is it history: it is political metaphysics. ["Ah, Ah," *on far left*].

. . . Gentlemen, I must speak from a higher and more truthful plane. It must be stated openly that, in effect, superior races have rights over inferior races. *[Movement on many benches on the far left.]*

M. JULES MAIGNE: Oh! You dare to say this in the country which has proclaimed the rights of man!

M. DE GUILLOUTET: This is a justification of slavery and the slave trade!

M. JULES FERRY: If M. Maigne is right, if the declaration of the rights of man was written for the blacks of equatorial Africa, then by what right do you impose regular commerce upon them? They have not called upon you.

M. RAOUL DUVAL: We do not want to impose anything upon them. It is you who wish to do so!

M. JULES MAIGNE: To propose and to impose are two different things!

M. GEORGES PERIN: In any case, you cannot bring about commerce by force.

M. JULES FERRY: I repeat that superior races have a right, because they have a duty. They have the duty to civilize inferior races. . . . *[Approbation from the left. New interruptions from the extreme left and from the right.]*

That is what I have to answer M. Pelletan in regard to the second point upon which he touched.

He then touched upon a third, more delicate, more serious, and upon which I ask your permission to express myself quite frankly. It is the political side of the question. The honorable M. Pelletan, who is a distinguished writer, always comes up with remarkably precise formulations. I will borrow from him the one which he applied the other day to this aspect of colonial policy.

"It is a system," he says, "which consists of seeking out compensations in the Orient with a circumspect and peaceful seclusion which is actually imposed upon us in Europe."

I would like to explain myself in regard to this. I do not like this word, "compensation," and, in effect, not here but elsewhere it has often been used in a treacherous way. If what is being said or insinuated is that any government in this country, any Republican minister could possibly believe that there are in any part of the world compensations for the disasters which we have experienced, an injury is being inflicted . . . and an injury undeserved by that government. *[Applause at the center and left.]* I will ward off this injury with all the force of my patriotism! *[New applause and bravos from the same benches.]*

Gentlemen, there are certain considerations which merit the attention of all patriots. The conditions of naval warfare have been profoundly altered. ["Very true! Very true!"]

At this time, as you know, a warship cannot carry more than fourteen days' worth of coal, no matter how perfectly it is organized, and a ship which is out of coal is a derelict on the surface of the sea, abandoned to the first person who comes along. Thence the necessity of having on the oceans provision stations, shelters, ports for defense and revictualling. *[Applause at the center and left. Various interruptions.]* And it is for this that we needed Tunisia, for this that we needed Saigon and the Mekong Delta, for this that we need Madagascar, that we are at Diégo-Suarez and Vohemar [two Madagascar ports] and will never leave them! *[Applause from a great number of benches.]* Gentlemen, in Europe as it is today, in this competition of so many rivals which we see growing around us, some by perfecting their military or maritime forces, others by the prodigious development of an ever growing population; in a Europe, or rather in a universe of this sort, a policy of peaceful seclusion or abstention is simply the highway to decadence! Nations are great in our times only by means of the activities which they develop; it is not simply "by the peaceful shining forth of institutions" *[Interruptions on the extreme left and right]* that they are great at this hour.

As for me, I am astounded to find the monarchist parties becoming indignant over the fact that the Republic of France is following a policy which does not confine itself to that ideal of modesty, of reserve, and, if you will allow me the expression, of bread and butter *[Interruptions and laughter on the left]* which the representatives of fallen monarchies wish to impose upon France. *[Applause at the center.]*

. . . [The Republican Party] has shown that it is quite aware that one cannot impose upon France a political ideal conforming to that of nations like independent Belgium and the Swiss Republic; that something else is needed for France: that she cannot be merely a free country, that she must also be a great country, exercising all of her rightful influence over the destiny of Europe, that she ought to propagate this influence throughout the world and carry everywhere that she can her language, her customs, her flag, her arms, and her genius. *[Applause at center and left.]*

■ Discussion Questions

1. Why does Ferry consider colonial expansion to be an economic necessity?

2. Aside from its economic benefits, why, according to Ferry, is colonial expansion justified?

3. How does Ferry appeal to nationalist sentiment to defend his imperialist stance, and why?

4. What is the basis of his critics' arguments against imperialism?

2.
Rudyard Kipling
The White Man's Burden
1899

The debate over imperialism was not confined to European shores; it also exploded onto the American scene when the United States gained control of Puerto Rico, Guam, and the Philippines in February 1899 after its victory in the Spanish-American War. Joseph Rudyard Kipling (1865–1936) published the poem "The White Man's Burden" in London and U.S. newspapers in direct response to the United States's fledging status as an imperial power. He urged Americans to share the "burden"—of implanting Western civilization among the "new-caught, sullen peoples" of East Asia—already shouldered by Europe. Born in British India and the son of a civil servant, Kipling was well versed in the ways of empire building and had already made a name for himself as the author of The Jungle Book, *among other works. The poem elicited a swift response across the United States, including the antiimperialist editorial, which appeared in the* San Francisco Call, *that follows the poem.*

Take up the White Man's burden—
    Send forth the best ye breed—
Go bind your sons to exile

From *Rudyard Kipling's Verse: Inclusive Edition (1885–1918)* (New York: Doubleday, 1927), 371–72; "The White Man's Burden." *San Francisco Call* (February 7, 1899). Reprinted at www.boondocksnet.com/ai/, Jim Zwick, ed., *Anti-Imperialism in the United States.*

To serve your captives' need;
To wait in heavy harness,
     On fluttered folk and wild—
Your new-caught, sullen peoples,
     Half-devil and half-child.

Take up the White Man's Burden—
     In patience to abide,
To veil the threat of terror
     And check the show of pride;
By open speech and simple,
     An hundred times made plain,
To seek another's profit,
     And work another's gain.

Take up the White Man's burden—
     The savage wars of peace—
Fill full the mouth of Famine
     And bid the sickness cease;
And when your goal is nearest
     The end for others sought,
Watch Sloth and heathen Folly
     Bring all your hope to nought.

Take up the White Man's burden—
     No tawdry rule of kings,
But toil of serf and sweeper—
     The tale of common things.
The ports ye shall not enter,
     The roads ye shall not tread,
Go make them with your living,
     And mark them with your dead.

Take up the White Man's burden—
     And reap his old reward:
The blame of those ye better,
     The hate of those ye guard—
The cry of hosts ye humor
     (Ah, slowly!) toward the light:—
"Why brought ye us from bondage,
     "Our loved Egyptian night?"

Take up the White Man's burden—
     Ye dare not stoop to less—
Nor call too loud on Freedom

To cloak your weariness;
By all ye cry or whisper,
    By all ye leave or do,
The silent, sullen peoples
    Shall weigh your Gods and you.

Take up the White Man's burden—
    Have done with childish days—
The lightly proffered laurel,
    The easy, ungrudged praise.
Comes now, to search your manhood
    Through all the thankless years,
Cold, edged with dear-bought wisdom,
    The judgment of your peers!

EDITORIAL FROM THE *SAN FRANCISCO CALL*

Rudyard Kipling has joined the ranks of those eminent British jingoes who are trying to induce the United States to help Great Britain in her imperial schemes by taking part in the Oriental imbroglio. Chamberlain and Balfour have enticed us with lofty oratory. Kipling wooes us with a song published in The Call of Sunday.
    The title of the ballad is "The White Man's Burden." Mr. Kipling sings:

Take up the White Man's burden—
    Have done with childish days—
The lightly proffered laurel,
    The easy, ungrudged praise;
Comes now, to search your manhood
    Through all the thankless years,
Cold, edged with dear-bought wisdom,
    The judgment of your peers!

By way of further information as to what we shall have to do when we have done with childish days and set about winning the approving judgment of our peers with their cold, edged, dear-bought wisdom, the poet, drawing an easy lesson from the experience of Great Britain, adds:

Take up the White Man's Burden—
    Send forth the best ye breed—
Go, bind your sons to exile
    To serve your captives' need;
To wait, in heavy harness,
    On fluttered folk and wild—
Your new-caught sullen peoples,
    Half-devil and half-child.

It seems we are to infer from this that if we do not consent to send forth the best we breed to serve in exile amid the jungles of tropic islands for the noble purpose of imposing American law and civilization upon the mongrel races, half devil and half child, we shall lose the esteem of European powers now engaged in that task, and possibly the esteem of Mr. Kipling also. It is a dilemma from which we cannot escape. Fate has ordained it and face it we must.

We might be more willing to enter upon the imperial task if our British cousins were not so outspoken in their eagerness to get us to do so. Their willingness to have us share the glory of civilizing the Orient awakens a suspicion that the glory is not altogether a profitable one. Great Britain evidently has more than she can carry and would like to divide the glory with us.

The invitation to take part is flattering to our pride, but not attractive to our common sense. We have a pretty heavy white man's burden at home and it will take something more than a song even from so strong a singer as Kipling to coax us to go to the Orient in search of an increase.

In all seriousness the eagerness of Chamberlain, Balfour and other British leaders to get the United States involved in the affairs of the Orient and indirectly made a party to all European squabbles, is a significant sign of the times, and ought to be a sufficient warning to all intelligent Americans to avoid imperialism as they would a plague.

The pursuit of imperialism has raised up antagonists to Great Britain in every part of the world; it has imposed upon her people a heavy burden of debt and taxation; it has disturbed her politics by the continual menace of war and thus prevented the accomplishment of many needed reforms at home; and finally it has brought her into a position where without an ally she is confronted by a hostile world and is in danger of having her commerce, and perhaps even her empire, swept away at the first outbreak of war.

Rightly considered the white man's burden is to set and keep his own house in order. It is not required of him to upset the brown man's house under pretense of reform and then whip him into subjugation whenever he revolts at the treatment.

■ Discussion Questions

1. How does Kipling define the "White Man's Burden"? What duties does he think this "burden" entails?

2. What kind of portrait does Kipling paint of non-Western peoples?

3. According to the author of the editorial from the *San Francisco Call*, why should Americans reject Kipling's appeal and avoid imperialism "as they would a plague"?

4. In what ways do these two sources expose the paradoxes of the new imperialism?

3.
Ernest Edwin Williams
Made in Germany
1896

In the closing decades of the nineteenth century, Germany emerged as a new, seemingly unstoppable economic force. It enjoyed astounding industrial growth throughout this period and gained a substantial share of European export markets. Many people in Great Britain observed these events with dismay, seeing Germany as a threat not only to their country's long-standing industrial dominance but also to its national identity as a world power. Journalist Ernest Edwin Williams (1866–1935) fanned the flames of such fears in Made in Germany, *published in 1896. Drawing on a dizzying array of statistics, Williams painted a menacing picture of the omnipresence of German products in his readers' everyday lives. He hoped that his bleak portrait would prompt Parliament to adopt measures to protect and enhance British trade. Although his message went unheeded, it evidently struck a chord, for the book went through six editions in its first year.*

THE DEPARTING GLORY

Preliminary

The Industrial Supremacy of Great Britain has been long an axiomatic commonplace; and it is fast turning into a myth, as inappropriate to fact as the Chinese Emperor's computation of his own status. This is a strong statement. But it is neither wide nor short of the truth. The industrial glory of England is departing, and England does not know it. There are spasmodic outcries against foreign competition, but the impression they leave is fleeting and vague. The phrase, "Made in Germany," is raw material for a jape at the pantomime, or is made the text for a homily by the official guardians of some particular trade, in so far as the matter concerns themselves. British Consuls, too, send words of warning home, and the number of these is increasing with significant frequency. But the nation at large is yet as little alive to the impending danger as to the evil already wrought. The man in the shop or the factory has plenty to say about the Armenian Question[1] and the House of Lords, but about commercial and industrial matters which concern him vitally he is generally much less eloquent. The amount of interest evinced by the amateur politician seems invariably to advance with the remoteness of the matter from his daily bread. It is time to disturb the fatal torpor: even though the moment be, in one sense, unhappily chosen. The pendulum between depression and

---

From Ernest Edwin Williams, *Made in Germany*, 4th ed. (London: William Heinemann, 1896), 1–2, 7–12, 18.

[1]**Armenian Question:** Refers to the topic of the fate of the Armenian people after the breakup of the Ottoman Empire. [Ed.]

prosperity has swung to the latter, and manufacturers and merchants are flushed with the joyful contemplation of their order-books. Slackness has given way to briskness; the lean years have been succeeded by a term of fat ones. The prophet of evil commands his most attentive audiences when the times are with him. When they are good—though the good be fleeting—his words are apt to fall unheeded. . . .

As It Was

There was a time when our industrial empire was unchallenged. It was England which first emerged from the Small-Industry stage. She produced the Industrial Revolution about the middle of the last century, and well-nigh until the middle of this she developed her multitude of mills, and factories, and mines, and warehouses, undisturbed by war at home, and profiting by wars abroad. The great struggles which drained the energies of the Continental nations, sealed her industrial supremacy, and made her absolute mistress of the world-market. Thanks to them, she became the Universal Provider. English machinery, English pottery, English hardware, guns, and cutlery, English rails and bridge-work, English manufactures of well-nigh every kind formed the material of civilization all over the globe. She covered the dry land with a network of railways, and the seas were alive with her own ships freighted with her own merchandise. Between 1793 and 1815 the value of her exports had risen from £17,000,000 to £58,000,000. Her industrial dominion was immense, unquestioned, unprecedented in the history of the human race; and not unnaturally we have come to regard her rule as eternal. But careless self-confidence makes not for Empire. While she was throwing wide her gates to the world at large, her sisters were building barriers of protection against her; and, behind those barriers, and aided often by State subventions, during the middle and later years of the century, they have developed industries of their own. Of course, this was to a certain extent inevitable. England could not hope for an eternal monopoly of the world's manufactures; and industrial growths abroad do not of necessity sound the knell of her greatness. But she must discriminate in her equanimity. And most certainly she must discriminate against Germany. For Germany has entered into a deliberate and deadly rivalry with her, and is battling with might and main for the extinction of her supremacy. . . .

The German Revolution

Up to a couple of decades ago, Germany was an agricultural State. Her manufactures were few and unimportant; her industrial capital was small; her export trade was too insignificant to merit the attention of the official statistician; she imported largely for her own consumption. Now she has changed all that. Her youth has crowded into English houses, has wormed its way into English manufacturing secrets, and has enriched her establishments with the knowledge thus purloined. She has educated her people in a fashion which has made it in some branches of industry the superior, and in most the equal of the English. Her capitalists have been content with a simple style, which has enabled them to dispense with big immediate profits, and to feed their capital. They have toiled at their desks, and made their sons do likewise; they have kept a strict controlling hand on all the strings of their businesses; they have obtained State aid in several ways—as special rates to shipping ports; they have insinuated themselves into every part of the world— civilized, barbarian, savage—learning the languages, and patiently studying the wants and tastes of the several peoples. Not content with reaping the advantages of British colonization—this was accomplished with alarming facility— Germany has "protected" the simple savage on her own account, and the Imperial Eagle now floats on the breezes of the South Sea Islands, and droops in the thick air of the African littoral. Her diplomatists have negotiated innumerable commercial treaties. The population of her cities has been increasing in a manner not unworthy of England in the Thirties and Forties. Like England, too, she is draining her rural districts for the massing of her children in huge factory towns. Her yards (as well as those of England) too, are ringing with the sound of hammers upon ships being builded for the transport of German merchandise. Her agents and travelers swarm through Russia, and wherever else there is a chance of trade on any terms—are even supplying the foreigner with German goods *at a loss,* that they may achieve their purpose in the end. In a word, an industrial development, unparalleled, save in England a century ago, is now her portion. A gigantic commercial State is arising to menace our prosperity, and contend with us for the trade of the world. . . .

Made in Germany

The phrase is fluent in the mouth: how universally appropriate it is, probably no one who has not made a special study of the matter is aware. Take observations, Gentle Reader, in your own surroundings: the mental exercise is recommended as an antidote to that form of self-sufficiency which our candid friends regard as indigenous to the British climate. Your investigations will work out somewhat in this fashion. You will find that the material of some of your own clothes was probably woven in Germany. Still more probably is it that some of your wife's garments are German importations; while it is practically beyond a doubt that the magnificent mantles and jackets wherein her maids array themselves on their Sundays out are German-made and German-sold, for only so could they be done at the figure. Your governess's *fiancé* is a clerk in the City; but he also was made in Germany. The toys, and the dolls, and the fairy books which your children maltreat in the nursery are made in Germany: nay, the material of your favorite (patriotic) newspaper had the same birthplace as like as not. Roam the house over, and the fateful mark will greet you at every turn, from the piano in your drawing-room to the mug on your kitchen dresser, blazoned though it be with the legend, *A Present from Margate.* Descend to your domestic depths, and you shall find your very drain-pipes German made. You pick out of the grate the paper wrappings from a book consignment, and they also are "Made in Germany." You stuff them into the fire, and reflect that the poker in your hand was forged in Germany. As you rise from your hearthrug you knock over an ornament on your mantlepiece; picking up the pieces you read, on the bit that formed the base, "Manufactured in Germany." And you jot your dismal reflections down with a pencil that was made in Germany. At midnight your wife comes home from an opera which was made in Germany, has been here enacted by singers and conductor and players made in Germany, with the aid of instruments and sheets of music made in Germany. You go to bed, and glare wrathfully at a text on the wall; it is illuminated with an English village church, and it was "Printed in Germany." If you are imaginative and dyspeptic, you drop off to sleep only to dream that St. Peter (with a duly stamped halo round his head and a bunch of keys from the Rhineland) has refused you admission into Paradise, because you bear not the Mark of the Beast upon your forehead, and are not of German make. But you console yourself with the thought that it was only a Bierhaus Paradise any way; and you are awakened in the morning by the sonorous brass of a German band.

Is the picture exaggerated? Bear with me, while I tabulate a few figures from the Official Returns of Her Majesty's Custom House, where, at any rate, fancy and exaggeration have no play. In '95 Germany sent us linen manufactures to the value of £91,257; cotton manufactures to the value of £536,471; embroidery and needlework to the value of £11,309; leather gloves to the value of £27,934 (six times the amount imported six years earlier); and woollen manufactures to the value of £1,016,694. Despite the exceeding cheapness of toys, the value of German-made playthings for English nurseries amounted, in '95, to £459,944. In the same year she sent us books to the value of £37,218, and paper to the value of £586,835. For musical instruments we paid her as much as £563,018; for china and earthenware £216,876; for prints, engravings, and photographs, £111,825. This recital of the moneys which *in one year* have come out of John Bull's pocket for the purchase of his German-made household goods is, I submit, disproof enough of any charge of alarmism. For these articles, it must be remembered, are not like oranges and guano. They are not products which we must either import or lack: — *they all belong to the category of English manufactures,* the most important of them, indeed, being articles in the preparation of which Great Britain is held pre-eminent. The total value of manufactured goods imported into the United Kingdom by Germany rose from £16,629,987 in '83 to £21,632,614 in '93: an increase of 30.08 percent. . . .

The Significance of These Facts

These are the sober—to believers in our eternal rule, the sobering—facts. They are picked almost at random from a mass of others of like import, and I think they are sufficient to prove that my general statements are neither untrue nor unduly emphatic. And yet the data needed for the purpose of showing the parlous[2] condition into which our trade is drifting are still largely to seek. Germany is yet in her industrial infancy; and the healthiest infant can do but poor battle against a grown man. England, with her enormous capital, and the sway she has wielded for a cen-

---

[2]**parlous:** Perilous. [Ed.]

tury over the world-market, is as that strong man. Now, to tell a strong man, conscious of his strength to an over-weening degree, that he is in peril from a half-grown youngster, is to invite his derision; and yet if a strong man, as the years advance on him, neglect himself and abuse his strength, he may fall before an energetic stripling. Germany has already put our trade in a bad way; but the worst lies in the future, and it is hard to convince the average Englishman of this. He will admit that Germany's trade has increased, and that at many points it hits our own; but here his robust insularity asserts itself. Germany has not the capital, he will tell you; her workmen are no workmen at all; her capitalists and her managers are poor bureaucratic plodders; the world will soon find out that her products are not of English make, and so forth. And he goes on vocalizing *Rule Britannia* in his best commercial prose.

■ Discussion Questions

1. According to Williams, what are the secrets of Germany's economic "revolution"?

2. Why does he regard Germany's industrial success as a cause for alarm, particularly in Great Britain?

3. What does this excerpt suggest about industrial growth during this period and its impact on international relations?

4.
Emmeline Pankhurst
Speech from the Dock
1908

By granting working-class men the vote in 1884, the British government hoped to make politics more unified and orderly. Yet the realization of such hopes proved elusive, in part because a new political foe had appeared on the scene: the women's suffrage movement. Founder of the Women's Social and Political Union, Emmeline Pankhurst (1858–1928) was among the most influential voices of the movement. Although women in Britain had long been fighting for rights, the expansion of the male electorate further accentuated their political exclusion. In the following speech before a police court judge, Pankhurst defends the WSPU's tactics, which had become increasingly militant since its inception in 1903. She and two colleagues had been arrested for distributing a leaflet encouraging her supporters "to rush the House of Commons," and they faced a prison sentence for refusing to "bind themselves over" — in other words, to promise to behave properly. Pankhurst's speech reflects her belief that the WSPU's struggle was more than a quest for the vote; it was a war against a patriarchical society.

From Emmeline Pankhurst, "Speech from the Dock [Police Court]," in *Votes for Women* (October 29, 1908), 1.

Ever since my girlhood, a period of about 30 years, I have belonged to organizations to secure for women that political power which I have felt was essential to bringing about those reforms which women need. I have tried constitutional methods. I have been womanly. When you spoke to some of my colleagues the day before yesterday about their being unwomanly, I felt that bitterness which I know every one of them felt in their hearts. We have tried to be womanly, we have tried to use feminine influence, and we have seen that it is of no use. Men who have been impatient have invariably got reforms for their impatience. And they have not our excuse for being impatient. . . .

Now, while I share in the feeling of indignation which has been expressed to you by my daughter, I have lived longer in the world than she has. Perhaps I can look round the whole question better than she can, but I want to say here, deliberately, to you, that we are here today because we are driven here. We have taken this action, because as women — and I want you to understand it is as women we have taken this action — it is because we realize that the condition of our sex is so deplorable that it is our duty even to break the law in order to call attention to the reasons why we do so.

I do not want to say anything which may seem disrespectful to you, or in any way give you offense, but I do want to say that I wish, sir, that you could put yourself into the place of women for a moment before you decide upon this case. My daughter referred to the way in which women are huddled into and out of these police-courts without a fair trial. I want you to realize what a poor hunted creature, without the advantages we have had, must feel.

I have been in prison. I was in Holloway Gaol for five weeks. I was in various parts of the prison. I was in the hospital, and in the ordinary part of the prison, and I tell you, sir, with as much sense of responsibility as if I had taken the oath, that there were women there who have broken no law, who are there because they have been able to make no adequate statement.

You know that women have tried to do something to come to the aid of their own sex. Women are brought up for certain crimes, crimes which men do not understand — I am thinking especially of infanticide — they are brought before a man judge, before a jury of men, who are called upon to decide whether some poor, hunted woman is guilty of murder or not. I put it to you, sir, when we see in the papers, as we often do, a case similar to that of Daisy Lord, for whom a great petition was got up in this country, I want you to realize how we women feel, because we are women, because we are not men, we need some legitimate influence to bear upon our law-makers.

Now, we have tried every way. We have presented larger petitions than were ever presented for any other reform; we have succeeded in holding greater public meetings than men have ever had for any reform, in spite of the difficulty which women have in throwing off their natural diffidence, that desire to escape publicity which we have inherited from generations of our foremothers; we have broken through that. We have faced hostile mobs at street corners, because we were told that we could not have that representation for our taxes which men have won unless we converted the whole of the country to our side. Because we have done this, we have been misrepresented, we have been ridiculed, we have had contempt poured upon us. The ignorant mob at the street corner has been incited to offer us violence, which we have faced unarmed and unprotected by the safeguards which Cabinet Ministers have. We know that we need the protection of the vote even more than men have needed it.

I am here to take upon myself now, sir, as I wish the prosecution had put upon me, the full responsibility for this agitation in its present phase. I want to address you as a woman who has performed the duties of a woman, and, in addition, has performed the duties which ordinary men have had to perform, by earning a living for her children, and educating them. In addition to that, I have been a public officer. I enjoyed for 10 years an official post under the Registrar, and I performed those duties to the satisfaction of the head of the department. After my duty of taking the census was over, I was one of the few Registrars who qualified for a special bonus, and was specially praised for the way in which the work was conducted. Well, sir, I stand before you, having resigned that office when I was told that I must either do that or give up working for this movement.

I want to make you realize that it is a point of honor that if you decide—as I hope you will not decide—to bind us over, that we shall not sign any undertaking, as the Member of Parliament did who was before you yesterday. Perhaps his reason for signing that undertaking may have been that the Prime Minister had given some assurance to the people he claimed to represent that something should be done for them. We have no such assurance. Mr. Birrell told the women who questioned him the other day that he could not say that anything would be done to give an assurance to the women that their claims should be conceded. So, sir, if you decide against us today, to prison we must go, because we feel that we should be going back to the hopeless condition this movement was in three years ago if we consented to be bound over to keep the peace which we have never broken, and so, sir, if you decide to bind us over, whether it is for three or six months, we shall submit to the treatment, the degrading treatment, that we have submitted to before.

Although the Government admitted that we are political offenders, and, therefore, ought to be treated as political offenders are invariably treated, we shall be treated as pickpockets and drunkards; we shall be searched. I want you, if you can, as a man, to realize what it means to women like us. We are driven to do this, we are determined to go on with agitation, because we feel in honor bound. Just as it was the duty of your forefathers, it is our duty to make this world a better place for women than it is today. . . .

This is the only way we can get that power which every citizen should have of deciding how the taxes she contributes to should be spent, and how the laws she has to obey should be made, and until we get that power we shall be here—we are here today, and we shall come here over and over again. You must realize how futile it is to settle this question by binding us over to keep the peace. You have tried it; it has failed. Others have tried to do it, and have failed. If you had power to send us to prison, not for six months, but for six years, for 16 years, or for the whole of our lives, the Government must not think that they can stop this agitation. It will go on.

I want to draw your attention to the self-restraint which was shown by our
followers on the night of the 13th, after we had been arrested. It only shows that
our influence over them is very great, because I think that if they had yielded to
their natural impulses, there might have been a breach of the peace on the evening
of the 13th. They were very indignant, but our words have always been, "be patient, exercise self-restraint, show our so-called superiors that the criticism of
women being hysterical is not true; use no violence, offer yourselves to the violence of others." We are going to win. Our women have taken that advice; if we are
in prison they will continue to take that advice.

Well, sir, that is all I have to say to you. We are here not because we are law-
breakers; we are here in our efforts to become law-makers.

■ Discussion Questions

1. How did the WSPU's tactics challenge conventional notions of proper behavior
   for women at the time?

2. According to Pankhurst, why was the WSPU forced to adopt such tactics?

3. Why did she think that women had both a right to and a need for political en-
   franchisement?

5.
Sigmund Freud
Infantile Sexuality
1905

*The fast-paced and conflict-ridden nature of life in industrial Europe undermined
many people's optimism about their own and society's future. Austrian doctor Sigmund
Freud (1856–1939) developed the method of psychoanalysis to tap into and cure such
anxieties. After studying medicine in Vienna, in 1886 Freud opened his own practice to
treat patients with nervous disorders. In the years that followed, he came to attribute
many of his patients' disorders to frustrated sexual desires that they were incapable of
understanding, and of which they were often entirely unaware. Besides his well-known*
The Interpretation of Dreams, *published in 1900, his most influential work was*
Three Essays on the Theory of Sexuality. *The essays first appeared in 1905, but Freud
often returned to these texts, ultimately revising them seven different times over the
course of twenty years. In the second of these three essays, "Infantile Sexuality," Freud
made the revolutionary claim that children have sexual impulses, and that such impulses are natural and normal. This assertion was a crucial element in Freud's practice
of psychoanalysis and remains a widely held view in psychology today.*

From Sigmund Freud, *Three Essays on the Theory of Sexuality,* trans. and ed. James Strachey
(New York: HarperCollins, 1962), 39, 45–49, 63–65.

Neglect of the Infantile Factor

One feature of the popular view of the sexual instinct is that it is absent in childhood and only awakens in the period of life described as puberty. This, however, is not merely a simple error but one that has had grave consequences, for it is mainly to this idea that we owe our present ignorance of the fundamental conditions of sexual life. A thorough study of the sexual manifestations of childhood would probably reveal the essential characters of the sexual instinct and would show us the course of its development and the way in which it is put together from various sources.

It is noticeable that writers who concern themselves with explaining the characteristics and reactions of the adult have devoted much more attention to the primeval period which is comprised in the life of the individual's ancestors—have, that is, ascribed much more influence to heredity—than to the other primeval period, which falls within the lifetime of the individual himself—that is, to childhood. One would surely have supposed that the influence of this latter period would be easier to understand and could claim to be considered before that of heredity. It is true that in the literature of the subject one occasionally comes across remarks upon precocious sexual activity in small children—upon erections, masturbation and even activities resembling coitus. But these are always quoted only as exceptional events, as oddities or as horrifying instances of precocious depravity. So far as I know, not a single author has clearly recognized the regular existence of a sexual instinct in childhood; and in the writings that have become so numerous on the development of children, the chapter of "Sexual Development" is as a rule omitted. . . .

THE MANIFESTATIONS OF INFANTILE SEXUALITY

Thumb-Sucking

For reasons which will appear later, I shall take thumb-sucking (or sensual sucking) as a sample of the sexual manifestations of childhood. . . .

Thumb-sucking appears already in early infancy and may continue into maturity, or even persist all through life. It consists in the rhythmic repetition of a sucking contact by the mouth (or lips). There is no question of the purpose of this procedure being the taking of nourishment. A portion of the lip itself, the tongue, or any other part of the skin within reach—even the big toe—may be taken as the object upon which this sucking is carried out. In this connection a grasping-instinct may appear and may manifest itself as a simultaneous rhythmic tugging at the lobes of the ears or a catching hold of some part of another person (as a rule the ear) for the same purpose. Sensual sucking involves a complete absorption of the attention and leads either to sleep or even to a motor reaction in the nature of an orgasm. It is not infrequently combined with rubbing some sensitive part of the body such as the breast or the external genitalia. Many children proceed by this path from sucking to masturbation. . . .

Auto-Erotism

We are in duty bound to make a thorough examination of this example. It must be insisted that the most striking feature of this sexual activity is that the instinct is not directed towards other people, but obtains satisfaction from the subject's own body, it is "auto-erotic," to call it by a happily chosen term introduced by Havelock Ellis (1910).

Furthermore, it is clear that the behavior of a child who indulges in thumb-sucking is determined by a search for some pleasure which has already been experienced and is now remembered. In the simplest case he proceeds to find this satisfaction by sucking rhythmically at some part of the skin or mucous membrane. It is also easy to guess the occasions on which the child had his first experiences of the pleasure which he is now striving to renew. It was the child's first and most vital activity, his sucking at his mother's breast, or at substitutes for it, that must have familiarized him with this pleasure. The child's lips, in our view, behave like an erotogenic zone, and no doubt stimulation by the warm flow of milk is the cause of the pleasurable sensation. The satisfaction of the erotogenic zone is associated, in the first instance, with the satisfaction of the need for nourishment. To begin with, sexual activity attaches itself to functions serving the purpose of self-preservation and does not become independent of them until later. No one who has seen a baby sinking back satiated from the breast and falling asleep with flushed cheeks and a blissful smile can escape the reflection that this picture persists as a prototype of the expression of sexual satisfaction in later life. The need for repeating the sexual satisfaction now becomes detached from the need for taking nourishment—a separation which becomes inevitable when the teeth appear and food is no longer taken in only by sucking, but is also chewed up. The child does not make use of an extraneous body for his sucking, but prefers a part of his own skin because it is more convenient, because it makes him independent of the external world, which he is not yet able to control, and because in that way he provides himself, as it were, with a second erotogenic zone, though one of an inferior kind. The inferiority of this second region is among the reasons why at a later date he seeks the corresponding part—the lips—of another person. ("It's a pity I can't kiss myself," he seems to be saying.) . . .

The Sexual Aim of Infantile Sexuality

Characteristics of Erotogenic Zones

The example of thumb-sucking shows us still more about what constitutes an erotogenic zone. It is a part of the skin or mucous membrane in which stimuli of a certain sort evoke a feeling of pleasure possessing a particular quality. There can be no doubt that the stimuli which produce the pleasure are governed by special conditions, though we do not know what those are. A rhythmic character must play a part among them and the analogy of tickling is forced upon our notice. It seems less certain whether the character of the pleasurable feeling evoked by the stimulus should be described as a "specific" one—a "specific" quality in which the sexual factor would precisely lie. Psychology is still so much in the dark in questions of pleasure and unpleasure that the most cautious assumption is the one most to be recommended. We may later come upon reasons which seem to support the idea that the pleasurable feeling does in fact possess a specific quality.

The character of erotogenicity can be attached to some parts of the body in a particularly marked way. There are predestined erotogenic zones, as is shown by the example of sucking. The same example, however, also shows us that any other part of the skin or mucous membrane can take over the functions of an erotogenic zone, and must therefore have some aptitude in that direction. Thus the quality of the stimulus has more to do with producing the pleasurable feeling than has the nature of the part of the body concerned. A child who is indulging in sensual sucking searches about his body and chooses some part of it to suck—a part which is afterwards preferred by him from force of habit; if he happens to hit upon one of the predestined regions (such as the nipples or genitals) no doubt it retains the preference.

THE PHASES OF DEVELOPMENT OF THE SEXUAL ORGANIZATION

The characteristics of infantile sexual life which we have hitherto emphasized are the facts that it is essentially autoerotic (i.e., that it finds its object in the infant's own body) and that its individual component instincts are upon the whole disconnected and independent of one another in their search for pleasure. The final outcome of sexual development lies in what is known as the normal sexual life of the adult, in which the pursuit of pleasure comes under the sway of the reproductive function and in which the component instincts, under the primacy of a single erotogenic zone, form a firm organization directed towards a sexual aim attached to some extraneous sexual object.

Pregenital Organizations

The study, with the help of psycho-analysis, of the inhibitions and disturbances of this process of development enables us to recognize abortive beginnings and preliminary stages of a firm organization of the component instincts such as this—preliminary stages which themselves constitute a sexual regime of a sort. These phases of sexual organization are normally passed through smoothly, without giving more than a hint of their existence. It is only in pathological cases that they become active and recognizable to superficial observation.

We shall give the name of "pregenital" to organizations of sexual life in which the genital zones have not yet taken over their predominant part. We have hitherto identified two such organizations, which almost seem as though they were harking back to early animal forms of life.

The first of these is the oral or, as it might be called, cannibalistic pregenital sexual organization. Here sexual activity has not yet been separated from the ingestion of food; nor are opposite currents within the activity differentiated. The *object* of both activities is the same; the sexual *aim* consists in the incorporation of the object—the prototype of a process which, in the form of identification, is later to play such an important psychological part. A relic of this constructed phase of organization, which is forced upon our notice by pathology, may be seen in thumb-sucking, in which the sexual activity, detached from the nutritive activity, has substituted for the extraneous object one situated in the subject's own body.

A second pregenital phase is that of the sadistic-anal organization. Here the opposition between two currents, which runs through all sexual life, is already developed: they cannot yet, however, be described as "masculine" and "feminine," but only as "active" and "passive." The *activity* is put into operation by the instinct for mastery through the agency of the somatic musculature; the organ which, more than any other, represents the *passive* sexual aim is the erotogenic mucous membrane of the anus. Both of these currents have objects, which, however, are not identical. Alongside these, other component instincts operate in an auto-erotic manner. In this phase, therefore, sexual polarity and an extraneous object are already observable. But organization and subordination to the reproductive function are still absent. . . .

■ Discussion Questions

1. How did Freud's theories about the complexities of childhood sexuality differ from those that had come before him?

2. According to Freud, why is it important to study the sexual development of children?

3. What role does pleasure play in Freud's theories of sexuality?

4. In what ways do you think Freud's approach is modern, or scientific? In what ways does his approach seem old-fashioned?

■ Comparative Questions _____

1. According to Ferry and Williams, what factors are key to a nation's strength, and why?

2. What do the views of Ferry and Williams suggest about changes in Europe's place within the world at large?

3. How do you think Kipling would have reacted to Ferry's defense of colonial expansion, and why?

4. What might contemporary readers have found unsettling about the idea that children have normal sexual impulses, or that women should have the right to vote? In what ways did both ideas challenge conventional beliefs and values?

War, Revolution, and Reconstruction, 1914–1929

CONTEMPORARIES DUBBED WORLD WAR I the "Great War" with good reason. Over the course of four years, millions died in battle—victims of advanced military technologies, outdated tactics, wretched leadership, and a desire for total victory. The first document allows us to see these horrors through two soldiers' eyes. The second document reveals that civilians contributed to the staggering death toll, for it was they who manufactured the grenades, rifles, and other weapons used on the front with such devastating effects. Yet the war's legacy did not stop there, as the last three documents attest. Civilian protests against the war unleashed the Russian Revolution, which transformed the world's political landscape. To the west, governments faced their own challenges as they struggled under the weight of postwar reconstruction and popular discontent. Among the people who capitalized on these troubled times were Benito Mussolini (1883–1945) and Adolf Hitler (1889–1945), who ushered in a new age of violent dictatorship in Europe.

1.
Fritz Franke and Siegfried Sassoon
Two Soldiers' Views of the Horrors of War
1914–1918

When the war broke out in August 1914, no one foresaw the years of massive destruction and bloodshed that would follow. By late autumn, the two sides were entrenched along a line that extended from France into Belgium, and so the Western Front was born. Here millions of soldiers like Fritz Franke (1892–1915) and Siegfried Sassoon (1886–1967) faced unspeakable horrors. In the following letter written in the war's first months, Franke, a medical student from Berlin, describes trench warfare as a living hell of shells and corpses. His description also reveals what already had become

From *German Students' War Letters*, trans. A. F. Wedd (New York: E. P. Dutton, 1929), 123–25.

and would remain the war's defining feature in the West: immobility and stalemate. Franke paid the ultimate price for both, as he was killed in May 1915. By contrast, Sassoon, a British officer, survived and became famous for poems like "Counter-Attack," which describes the war's misery and futility.

FRITZ FRANKE

Louve, November 5th, 1914

Yesterday we didn't feel sure that a single one of us would come through alive. You can't possibly picture to yourselves what such a battle-field looks like. It is impossible to describe it, and even now, when it is a day behind us, I myself can hardly believe that such bestial barbarity and unspeakable suffering are possible. Every foot of ground contested; every hundred yards another trench; and everywhere bodies—rows of them! All the trees shot to pieces; the whole ground churned up a yard deep by the heaviest shells; dead animals; houses and churches so utterly destroyed by shell-fire that they can never be of the least use again. And every troop that advances in support must pass through a mile of this chaos, through this gigantic burial-ground and the reek of corpses.

In this way we advanced on Tuesday, marching for three hours, a silent column, in the moonlight, towards the Front and into a trench as Reserve, two to three hundred yards from the English, close behind our own infantry.

There we lay the whole day, a yard and a half to two yards below the level of the ground, crouching in the narrow trench on a thin layer of straw, in an overpowering din which never ceased all day or the greater part of the night—the whole ground trembling and shaking! There is every variety of sound—whistling, whining, ringing, crashing, rolling . . . the beastly things pitch right above one and burst and the fragments buzz in all directions, and the only question one asks is: "Why doesn't one get me?" Often the things land within a hand's breadth and one just looks on. One gets so hardened to it that at the most one ducks one's head a little if a great, big naval-gun shell comes a bit too near and its grey-green stink is a bit too thick. Otherwise one soon just lies there and thinks of other things. And then one pulls out the Field Regulations or an old letter from home, and all at once one has fallen asleep in spite of the row.

Then suddenly comes the order: "Back to the horses. You are relieved!" And one runs for a mile or so, mounts, and is a gay trooper once more; hola, away, through night and mist, in gallop and in trot!

One just lives from one hour to the next. For instance, if one starts to prepare some food, one never knows if one mayn't have to leave it behind within an hour. If you lie down to sleep, you must always be "in Alarm Order." On the road, you have just to ride behind the man in front of you without knowing where you are going, or at the most only the direction for half a day.

All the same, there is a lot that is pleasant in it all. We often go careering through lovely country in beautiful weather. And above all one acquires a knowledge of human nature! We all live so naturally and unconventionally here, every one according to his own instincts. That brings much that is good and much that is ugly to the surface, but in every one there is a large amount of truth, and above all strength — strength developed almost to a mania!

SIEGFRIED SASSOON

Counter-Attack

We'd gained our first objective hours before
While dawn broke like a face with blinking eyes,
Pallid, unshaved and thirsty, blind with smoke.
Things seemed all right at first. We held their line,
With bombers posted, Lewis guns well placed,
And clink of shovels deepening the shallow trench.
    The place was rotten with dead; green clumsy legs
    High-booted, sprawled and grovelled along the saps
    And trunks, face downward, in the sucking mud,
    Wallowed like trodden sand-bags loosely filled;
    And naked sodden buttocks, mats of hair,
    Bulged, clotted heads slept in the plastering slime.
    And then the rain began — the jolly old rain!

A yawning soldier knelt against the bank,
Staring across the morning blear with fog;
He wondered when the Allemands[1] would get busy;
And then, of course, they started with five-nines
Traversing, sure as fate, and never a dud.
Mute in the clamor of shells he watched them burst
Spouting dark earth and wire with gusts from hell,
While posturing giants dissolved in drifts of smoke.
He crouched and flinched, dizzy with galloping fear,
Sick for escape — loathing the strangled horror
And butchered, frantic gestures of the dead.

An officer came blundering down the trench:
"Stand-to and man the fire-step!" On he went . . .
Gasping and bawling, "Fire-step . . . counter-attack!"
    Then the haze lifted. Bombing on the right
    Down the old sap: machine-guns on the left;
    And stumbling figures looming out in front.
    "O Christ, they're coming at us!" Bullets spat,

From Siegfried Sassoon, *Collected Poems* (New York: Viking Press, 1949), 68–69.
[1]**Allemands:** Germans. [Ed.]

And he remembered his rifle . . . rapid fire . . .
And started blazing wildly . . . then a bang
Crumpled and spun him sideways, knocked him out
To grunt and wriggle: none heeded him; he choked
And fought the flapping veils of smothering gloom,
Lost in a blurred confusion of yells and groans . . .
Down, and down, and down, he sank and drowned,
Bleeding to death. The counter-attack had failed.

■ Discussion Questions

1. Although they fought on opposite sides, what attributes did Franke and Sassoon share?

2. Based on Franke's and Sassoon's descriptions of the battlefront, what physical and psychological effects did trench warfare have on soldiers?

3. How does Franke's letter challenge the Allies' propaganda in which German soldiers were depicted as being devoid of humanity?

2.
L. Doriat
Women on the Home Front
1917

The massive mobilization of the homefront made World War I like no other war fought before. Across Europe, thousands of civilians poured into factories to manufacture supplies for the troops. With casualties mounting and more and more men leaving to replenish the armed forces, women became particularly vital to sustaining the wartime labor force. Consequently, new employment opportunities arose for them, especially in traditionally masculine domains such as munitions. The following interview of a French factory worker in the city of Saint-Nazaire in Brittany by journalist L. Doriat puts a human face on this aspect of the war's impact beyond the battlefield. In it, the worker, whom Doriat never identifies, reveals her sense of patriotic duty mingled with her determination not to lose her femininity amid the din and dirt of her job.

The dwelling I enter is tidy, sun lights up the main room and makes the household objects shine; everything speaks of an orderly woman who likes her home. A few flowers in a vase on the table near which she is working prove to me that I was

---

From Margaret R. Higonnet, ed., *Lines of Fire: Women Writers of World War I* (New York: Plume, 1999), 129–31.

right about the woman I've come to see. The factory has not destroyed her feminine sense of delicacy. Without a hat she seems to me younger; she is surprised to
see me, she confesses, because she doubted I would come. Convalescent, she hasn't
worked for a whole month, which is why I am lucky enough to find her.

"The very day after my arrival, I found work, thanks to the foreman of a factory of shells who knew my husband," she hastens to tell me. "There is no comparison between this extremely hard and much more precise work and the little
toy-like petards that I was making. Here it's not sheets of white metal but big 120
shells. You must also pay much more attention, a defect is serious. The factory
never stops, day and night shifts of eight alternate. It's intensive production; no
mawkishness here, we are not women by the arms of the machine. Scarcely any
apprenticeship, one or two days and you're set.

"I am in a workshop for tempering the steel, or rather I was—will they give
me back my place and my machine when I return to the workshop? At the moment of my accident, which I'll tell you about, I was doing the shop-trial of the
steel for the shell, testing or inspecting the casing, of course. Right after the tempering bath, when the steel is still hot and black, the other workers and I had to tap
it with a buffing wheel in order to polish the steel on a small surface of the bottom
and the ogive of the shell. Doing this we handle at least a thousand shells a day,
and as I told you, they are big, very heavy to manipulate. Other workers take these
same pieces and make a light mark on the polished area, which must not etch the
steel further than a certain depth, in a kind of test; they are equipped with a grad-
uated sheet of metal that lets them evaluate the etched lines. If the mark is too
deep, the steel is too soft; if it's too shallow, it is too hard; in either case it can't be
used and goes back to be recast. The inspection requires great attentiveness. A final verification is made by a controller and as we are always required to put our
number on the pieces that pass through our hands, the imperfections, the errors
can be traced to their authors.

"There too you don't talk, you don't even think of it. The deafening noise of
the machines, the enormous heat of the ovens near which you work, the swiftness
of the movements make this precision work into painful labor. When we do it at
night, the glare together with the temperature of the furnace exhausts your
strength and burns your eyes. In the morning when you get home, you throw
yourself on your bed without even the strength to eat a bite. There are also the
lathe workshops, I've never been there; many workers learn quickly to turn a shell
without needing to calibrate it; some turners do piece work; they are always the
ones who hurt themselves. At the job you become very imprudent, as I told you.

"However, you see, I hurt myself too. Forgetting that my buffing machine
does an incalculable number of turns a second, I brushed against it with my arm.
Clothing and flesh were all taken off before I even noticed. They had to scrape the
bone, bandage me every day, I was afraid of an amputation, which luckily was
avoided. Only in the last few days have I been able to go without a sling and use my
arm; next week I go back to the workshop. I don't want them to change my job,
I'm used to my machine and a fresh apprenticeship would not please me at all.

I assure you, the first day I was in this noise, near these enormous blast furnaces, opposite the huge machine at which I had to work for hours, I was afraid. We are all like that, all the more so that we are not given time to reflect. You have to understand and act quickly. Those who lose their heads don't accomplish anything, but they are rare. In general, one week suffices to turn a novice into a skilled worker.

"The foremen scold now and then, but they mustn't count it against us; doesn't everyone know that a man is an apprentice before he becomes a mechanic? But at present, however simplified, however divided up the tasks may be, you become a qualified mechanic right away.

"Yet among us there are women like myself who had never done anything; others who did not know how to sew or embroider; nothing discouraged us. As for me I don't complain, this strained activity pleases me. I can thus forget my loneliness—and not having any children, what else should I do with all my time?

"When the war is over, I will look for a job that corresponds better to my taste. I have enough education to become a cashier in a store. I will then be able to be neater than now, for you can't imagine what care it takes to stay more or less clean if you work in a metallurgy.

"A woman is always a woman; I suffered a lot from remaining for hours with my hands and face dirty with dust and smoke. Everything is a matter of habit; among us there are women who seem fragile and delicate—well! if you saw them at work, you would be stunned: it's a total transformation. As for me, I would never have thought I had so much stamina; when I remember that the least little errand wore me out before, I don't recognize myself. Certainly when the day or the night is over, you go home, the fatigue is great, but we are not more tired than the men are. True, we are more sober because we maintain better hygiene and as a result, our sources of energy are more rational and regular, we don't turn to alcohol for strength.

"Our sense of the present need, of the national peril, of hatred for the enemy, of the courage of our husbands and sons—all this pricks us on, we work with all our heart, with all our strength, with all our soul. It is not necessary to stimulate us, each one is conscious of the task assigned to her and in all simplicity she does it, convinced that she defends her country by forging the arms that will free it. We are very proud of being workers for the national defense."

On that proud phrase, I left this valiant woman, with a warm handshake to thank her and to express my admiration.

■ Discussion Questions

1. What does this account suggest about women's role in the war effort?

2. How do both the interviewer and interviewee cast light on people's fears about the war's effects on traditional gender roles?

3. In what ways does this interview reflect the national consensus supporting the war, as fostered by government-directed propaganda campaigns?

3.

Vladimir Ilych Lenin
Letter to Nikolai Aleksandrovich Rozhkov
January 29, 1919

As World War I dragged on, European governments faced a new foe in civilian protests. The Russian tsar was especially ill equipped for this challenge, which opened the door to revolution. By the fall of 1917, Vladimir Ilych Lenin (1870–1924) had emerged as the leading voice of the Russian Revolution and within a matter of months, he and his Bolshevik Party seized complete control of the government. Their takeover plunged Russia into four years of civil war, further exacerbating the country's desperate economic plight. The following document is Lenin's response to a letter from a colleague that encouraged him to assume "personal dictatorship" as a means of setting Russia on the right course. Lenin dismisses the suggestion and reveals his faith in revolutionary Marxism to effect positive change, not only in Russia but also in western Europe. Ironically, several years after Lenin's death, his self-proclaimed successor, Joseph Stalin (1879–1953), instituted just such a dictatorship.

29 January 1919
Nikolai Aleksandrovich!

I was very glad to get your letter—not because of its contents but because I am hoping for a rapprochement on the general factual basis of soviet work.

The situation is not desperate, only difficult. But now there exists very serious hope of improving the food situation thanks to the victories over the counterrevolution in the south and east.

You should not be thinking of free trade—to an economist, of all people, it should be clear that free trade, given the absolute shortage of essential produce, is equivalent to frenzied, brutal speculation and the triumph of the haves over the have-nots. We should not go backward through free trade but forward through the improvement of the state monopoly, toward socialism. It is a difficult transition, but despair is impermissible and unwise. If, instead of serenading free trade, the nonparty intelligentsia or the intelligentsia close to the party would form emergency groups, small groups, and unions for all-around assistance to the food supply, it would seriously help the cause and lessen hunger.

As for "personal dictatorship," excuse the expression, but it is utter nonsense. The apparatus has already become gigantic—in some places excessively so—and under such conditions a "personal dictatorship" is entirely unrealizable and attempts to realize it would only be harmful.

From Richard Pipes, ed., *The Unknown Lenin: From the Secret Archive* (New Haven: Yale University Press, 1999), 62–63.

A turning point has occurred in the intelligentsia. The civil war in Germany and the struggle precisely along the lines of soviet power against "the universal, direct, equal, and secret ballot, that is, against the counterrevolutionary Constituent Assembly"—this struggle in Germany is breaking through even to the most stubborn intelligentsia minds and will succeed in breaking through. This is more visible from the outside. *Nul n'est prophète en son pays.*[1] At home, in Russia, they regarded this as "merely" the "savagery" of Bolshevism. But now history has shown that it is the worldwide collapse of bourgeois democracy and bourgeois parliamentarism, that you cannot get by anywhere without a civil war *(volentem ducunt fata, nolentem trahunt).*[2] The intelligentsia will have to arrive at the position of helping the workers precisely on a Soviet platform.

Then, I think, circles, organizations, committees, free unions, groups, small groups, and gatherings of the intelligentsia will grow like mushrooms and offer their selfless labor in the most difficult posts in food and transportation work. Then we will shorten and ease the birth pangs by months. Because something amazingly good and viable will be born, no matter how difficult those pangs are.

Greetings, N. Lenin

■ Discussion Questions

1. On what grounds does Lenin reject the idea of personal dictatorship?
2. Why do you think Lenin is optimistic about the future despite Russia's bleak economic situation?
3. In what ways does this letter reflect Lenin's commitment to Marxist principles?

[1]"No one is a prophet in his own country."
[2]"Fate leads the willing and drags the unwilling."

4.
Benito Mussolini
The Doctrine of Fascism
1932

Like millions of his fellow Italians, Benito Mussolini (1883–1945) bitterly resented the outcome of World War I. The Allies had reneged on many of their territorial promises, and Italy's economy was in shambles. Mussolini tapped into this wave of discontent when, in 1919, he founded the Fascist movement, comprising former socialists, war veterans, and others who embraced the radical right as the new symbol of authority and strength. Blaming the parliamentary government for the country's ills, the Fascists marched on Rome in 1922 to take matters into their own hands. Upon the

From Michael Oakeshott, ed. and trans., *The Social and Political Doctrines of Contemporary Europe* (Cambridge: Cambridge University Press, 1947), 164–79.

king's request, Mussolini became prime minister. This marked the beginning of Mussolini's rise to political power. The following excerpt from an article by Mussolini, first published in the Enciclopedia Italiana *in 1932, illuminates the basic ideological contours of Fascism as they had developed during the first decade of his authoritarian rule.*

FUNDAMENTAL IDEAS

7. Against individualism, the Fascist conception is for the State; and it is for the individual in so far as he coincides with the State, which is the conscience and universal will of man in his historical existence. It is opposed to classical Liberalism, which arose from the necessity of reacting against absolutism, and which brought its historical purpose to an end when the State was transformed into the conscience and will of the people. Liberalism denied the State in the interests of the particular individual; Fascism reaffirms the State as the true reality of the individual. And if liberty is to be the attribute of the real man, and not of that abstract puppet envisaged by individualistic Liberalism, Fascism is for liberty. And for the only liberty which can be a real thing, the liberty of the State and of the individual within the State. Therefore, for the Fascist, everything is in the State, and nothing human or spiritual exists, much less has value, outside the State. In this sense Fascism is totalitarian, and the Fascist State, the synthesis and unity of all values, interprets, develops and gives strength to the whole life of the people.

8. Outside the State there can be neither individuals nor groups (political parties, associations, syndicates, classes). Therefore Fascism is opposed to Socialism, which confines the movement of history within the class struggle and ignores the unity of classes established in one economic and moral reality in the State; and analogously it is opposed to class syndicalism. Fascism recognizes the real exigencies for which the socialist and syndicalist movement arose, but while recognizing them wishes to bring them under the control of the State and give them a purpose within the corporative system of interests reconciled within the unity of the State.

9. Individuals form classes according to the similarity of their interests, they form syndicates according to differentiated economic activities within these interests; but they form first, and above all, the State, which is not to be thought of numerically as the sum-total of individuals forming the majority of a nation. And consequently Fascism is opposed to Democracy, which equates the nation to the majority, lowering it to the level of that majority; nevertheless it is the purest form of democracy if the nation is conceived, as it should be, qualitatively and not quantitatively, as the most powerful idea (most powerful because most moral, most coherent, most true) which acts within the nation as the conscience and the will of a few, even of One, which ideal tends to become active within the conscience and the will of all — that is to say, of all those who rightly constitute a nation by reason of nature, history or race, and have set out upon the same line of development and spiritual formation as one conscience and one sole will. . . .

Political and Social Doctrine

Fascism is today clearly defined not only as a regime but as a doctrine. And I mean by this that Fascism today, self-critical as well as critical of other movements, has an unequivocal point of view of its own, a criterion, and hence an aim, in face of all the material and intellectual problems which oppress the people of the world.

3. Above all, Fascism, in so far as it considers and observes the future and the development of humanity quite apart from the political considerations of the moment, believes neither in the possibility nor in the utility of perpetual peace. It thus repudiates the doctrine of Pacifism—born of a renunciation of the struggle and an act of cowardice in the face of sacrifice. War alone brings up to their highest tension all human energies and puts the stamp of nobility upon the peoples who have the courage to meet it. All other trials are substitutes, which never really put a man in front of himself in the alternative of life and death. A doctrine, therefore, which begins with a prejudice in favor of peace is foreign to Fascism; as are foreign to the spirit of Fascism. . . .

5. Such a conception of life makes Fascism the precise negation of that doctrine which formed the basis of the so-called Scientific or Marxian Socialism: the doctrine of historical Materialism, according to which the history of human civilizations can be explained only as the struggle of interest between the different social groups and as arising out of change in the means and instruments of production. That economic improvements—discoveries of raw materials, new methods of work, scientific inventions—should have an importance of their own, no one denies, but that they should suffice to explain human history to the exclusion of all other factors is absurd: Fascism believes, now and always, in holiness and in heroism, that is in acts in which no economic motive—remote or immediate—plays a part. With this negation of historical materialism, according to which men would be only by-products of history, who appear and disappear on the surface of the waves while in the depths the real directive forces are at work, there is also denied the immutable and irreparable "class struggle" which is the natural product of this economic conception of history, and above all it is denied that the class struggle can be the primary agent of social changes. . . .

6. After Socialism, Fascism attacks the whole complex of democratic ideologies and rejects them both in their theoretical premises and in their applications or practical manifestations. Fascism denies that the majority, through the mere fact of being a majority, can rule human societies; it denies that this majority can govern by means of a periodical consultation; it affirms the irremediable, fruitful and beneficent inequality of men, who cannot be levelled by such a mechanical and extrinsic fact as universal suffrage. By democratic regimes we mean those in which from time to time the people is given the illusion of being sovereign, while true effective sovereignty lies in other, perhaps irresponsible and secret, forces. Democracy is a regime without a king, but with very many kings, perhaps more exclusive, tyrannical and violent than one king even though a tyrant. . . .

8. In face of Liberal doctrines, Fascism takes up an attitude of absolute opposition both in the field of politics and in that of economics. It is not necessary to

exaggerate—merely for the purpose of present controversies—the importance of Liberalism in the past century, and to make of that which was one of the numerous doctrines sketched in that century a religion of humanity for all times, present and future. . . . The "Liberal" century, after having accumulated an infinity of Gordian knots, tried to untie them by the hecatomb[1] of the World War. Never before has any religion imposed such a cruel sacrifice. Were the gods of Liberalism thirsty for blood? Now Liberalism is about to close the doors of its deserted temples because the peoples feel that its agnosticism in economics, its indifferentism in politics and in morals, would lead, as they have led, the States to certain ruin. In this way one can understand why all the political experiences of the contemporary world are anti-Liberal, and it is supremely ridiculous to wish on that account to class them outside of history; as if history were a hunting ground reserved to Liberalism and its professors, as if Liberalism were the definitive and no longer surpassable message of civilization. . . .

If it is admitted that the nineteenth century has been the century of Socialism, Liberalism and Democracy, it does not follow that the twentieth must also be the century of Liberalism, Socialism and Democracy. Political doctrines pass; peoples remain. It is to be expected that this century may be that of authority, a century of the "Right," a Fascist century. If the nineteenth was the century of the individual (Liberalism means individualism) it may be expected that this one may be the century of "collectivism" and therefore the century of the State. . . .

10. The keystone of Fascist doctrine is the conception of the State, of its essence, of its tasks, of its ends. For Fascism the State is an absolute before which individuals and groups are relative. Individuals and groups are "thinkable" in so far as they are within the State. The Liberal State does not direct the interplay and the material and spiritual development of the groups, but limits itself to registering the results; the Fascist State has a consciousness of its own, a will of its own, on this account it is called an "ethical" State. In 1929, at the first quinquennial assembly of the regime, I said: "For Fascism, the State is not the night-watchman who is concerned only with the personal security of the citizens; nor is it an organization for purely material ends, such as that of guaranteeing a certain degree of prosperity and a relatively peaceful social order, to achieve which a council of administration would be sufficient, nor is it a creation of mere politics with no contact with the material and complex reality of the lives of individuals and the life of peoples. The State, as conceived by Fascism and as it acts, is a spiritual and moral fact because it makes concrete the political, juridical, economic organization of the nation and such an organization is, in its origin and in its development, a manifestation of the spirit. The State is the guarantor of internal and external security, but it is also the guardian and the transmitter of the spirit of the people as it has been elaborated through the centuries in language, custom, faith. The State is not only present, it is also past, and above all future. It is the State which, transcending the brief limit of individual lives, represents the immanent conscience of the nation.

---

[1]**hecatomb:** Slaughter. [Ed.]

The forms in which States express themselves change, but the necessity of the State remains. It is the State which educates citizens for civic virtue, makes them conscious of their mission, calls them to unity; harmonizes their interests in justice; hands on the achievements of thought in the sciences, the arts, in law, in human solidarity; it carries men from the elementary life of the tribe to the highest human expression of power which is Empire; it entrusts to the ages the names of those who died for its integrity or in obedience to its laws; it puts forward as an example and recommends to the generations that are to come the leaders who increased its territory and the men of genius who gave it glory. When the sense of the State declines and the disintegrating and centrifugal tendencies of individuals and groups prevail, national societies move to their decline."

11. From 1929 up to the present day these doctrinal positions have been strengthened by the whole economico-political evolution of the world. It is the State alone that grows in size, in power. It is the State alone that can solve the dramatic contradictions of capitalism. What is called the crisis cannot be overcome except by the State, within the State. . . . Fascism desires the State to be strong, organic and at the same time founded on a wide popular basis. The Fascist State has also claimed for itself the field of economics and, through the corporative, social and educational institutions which it has created, the meaning of the State reaches out to and includes the farthest off-shoots; and within the State, framed in their respective organizations, there revolve all the political, economic and spiritual forces of the nation. A State founded on millions of individuals who recognize it, feel it, are ready to serve it, is not the tyrannical State of the medieval lord. It has nothing in common with the absolutist States that existed either before or after 1789. In the Fascist State the individual is not suppressed, but rather multiplied, just as in a regiment a soldier is not weakened but multiplied by the number of his comrades. The Fascist State organizes the nation, but it leaves sufficient scope to individuals; it has limited useless or harmful liberties and has preserved those that are essential. It cannot be the individual who decides in this matter, but only the State. . . .

13. The Fascist State is a will to power and to government. In it the tradition of Rome is an idea that has force. In the doctrine of Fascism Empire is not only a territorial, military or mercantile expression, but spiritual or moral. One can think of an empire, that is to say a nation that directly or indirectly leads other nations, without needing to conquer a single square kilometer of territory. For Fascism the tendency to Empire, that is to say, to the expansion of nations, is a manifestation of vitality; its opposite, staying at home, is a sign of decadence: peoples who rise or re-rise are imperialist, peoples who die are denunciatory. Fascism is the doctrine that is most fitted to represent the aims, the states of mind, of a people, like the Italian people, rising again after many centuries of abandonment or slavery to foreigners. But Empire calls for discipline, co-ordination of forces, duty and sacrifice; this explains many aspects of the practical working of the regime and the direction of many of the forces of the State and the necessary severity shown to those who would wish to oppose this spontaneous and destined impulse of the Italy of the twentieth century, to oppose it in the name of the

superseded ideologies of the nineteenth, repudiated wherever great experiments of political and social transformation have been courageously attempted: especially where, as now, peoples thirst for authority, for leadership, for order. If every age has its own doctrine, it is apparent from a thousand signs that the doctrine of the present age is Fascism. That it is a doctrine of life is shown by the fact that it has resuscitated a faith. That this faith has conquered minds is proved by the fact that Fascism has had its dead and its martyrs.

Fascism henceforward has in the world the universality of all those doctrines which, by fulfilling themselves, have significance in the history of the human spirit.

■ Discussion Questions

1. According to Mussolini, how is Fascism opposed to liberalism, democracy, and socialism? How is this opposition rooted in Mussolini's concept of the individual's role in the Fascist state?
2. What does Mussolini mean when he describes Fascism as "totalitarian"?
3. As elaborated here, in what ways were Mussolini's principles rooted in the legacy of World War I?

5.
Adolf Hitler
Mein Kampf
1925

In 1923, Adolf Hitler (1889–1945) was sentenced to five years in prison at Landsberg Castle for his participation in the "Beer Hall Putsch," an attempt by his National Socialist Party to overthrow the German Democratic national government. He was treated well in prison and received many guests as he strolled the castle grounds. When a friend suggested that he write his autobiography to pass the time, Hitler was skeptical; although a gifted orator, he had written very little. After Hitler's fellow inmate, Rudolf Hess (1894–1987), agreed to transcribe it for him, however, Hitler dictated the book. Originally titled Four Years of Struggle Against Lies, Stupidity, and Cowardice, *it was published in 1925 as* My Struggle (Mein Kampf). *In it, Hitler attributed most human achievements to the German race—he called it the "Aryan" race—and argued that it had a duty to dominate the planet. The Jews, conversely, were held responsible for what Hitler viewed as the world's worst problems, including communism, modern art, pornography, prostitution, and Germany's defeat in World War I.*

From Adolf Hitler, *Mein Kampf,* trans. Ralph Manheim (Boston: Houghton Mifflin, 1999), 290, 300, 303, 326, 643, 646, 649, 651–53.

Nation and Race

It is idle to argue which race or races were the original representative of human culture and hence the real founders of all that we sum up under the word "humanity." It is simpler to raise this question with regard to the present, and here an easy, clear answer results. All the human culture, all the results of art, science, and technology that we see before us today, are almost exclusively the creative product of the Aryan. This very fact admits of the not unfounded inference that he alone was the founder of all higher humanity, therefore representing the prototype of all that we understand by the word "man." He is the Prometheus of mankind from whose bright forehead the divine spark of genius has sprung at all times, forever kindling anew that fire of knowledge which illumined the night of silent mysteries and thus caused man to climb the path of mastery over the other beings of this earth. . . .

The mightiest counterpart to the Aryan is represented by the Jew. . . . Not through him does any progress of mankind occur, but in spite of him. . . .

He works systematically for revolutionization in a twofold sense: economic and political.

Around peoples who offer too violent a resistance to attack from within he weaves a net of enemies, thanks to his international influence, incites them to war, and finally, if necessary, plants the flag of revolution on the very battlefields.

In economics he undermines the states until the social enterprises which have become unprofitable are taken from the state and subjected to his financial control.

In the political field he refuses the state the means for its self-preservation, destroys the foundations of all national self-maintenance and defense, destroys faith in the leadership, scoffs at its history and past, and drags everything that is truly great into the gutter.

Culturally he contaminates art, literature, the theater, makes a mockery of natural feeling, overthrows all concepts of beauty and sublimity, of the noble and the good, and instead drags men down into the sphere of his own base nature.

Religion is ridiculed, ethics and morality represented as outmoded, until the last props of a nation in its struggle for existence in this world have fallen. . . .

Eastern Orientation or Eastern Policy

Only an adequately large space on this earth assures a nation of freedom of existence. . . .

The National Socialist movement must strive to eliminate the disproportion between our population and our area — viewing this latter as a source of food as well as a basis for power politics — between our historical past and the hopelessness of our present impotence. And in this it must remain aware that we, as guardians of the highest humanity on this earth, are bound by the highest obligation, and the more it strives to bring the German people to racial awareness so that, in addition to breeding dogs, horses, and cats, they will have mercy on their *own* blood, the more it will be able to meet this obligation.

. . . *The demand for restoration of the frontiers of 1914 is a political absurdity of such proportions and consequences as to make it seem a crime. Quite aside from the fact that the Reich's frontiers in 1914 were anything but logical. For in reality they were neither complete in the sense of embracing the people of German nationality, nor sensible with regard to geo-military expediency. They were not the result of a considered political action, but momentary frontiers in a political struggle that was by no means concluded; partly, in fact, they were the results of chance. . . .*

. . . Moreover, the times have changed since the Congress of Vienna: *Today it is not princes and princes' mistresses who haggle and bargain over state borders; it is the inexorable Jew who struggles for his domination over the nations.* No nation can remove this hand from its throat except by the sword. Only the assembled and concentrated might of a national passion rearing up in its strength can defy the international enslavement of peoples. Such a process is and remains a bloody one.

If, however, we harbor the conviction that the German future, regardless what happens, demands the supreme sacrifice, quite aside from all considerations of political expediency as such, we must set up an aim worthy of this sacrifice and fight for it. . . .

And I must sharply attack those folkish pen-pushers who claim to regard such an acquisition of soil as a "breach of sacred human rights" and attack it as such in their scribblings. One never knows who stands behind these fellows. But one thing is certain, that the confusion they can create is desirable and convenient to our national enemies. By such an attitude they help to weaken and destroy from within our people's will for the only correct way of defending their vital needs. For no people on this earth possesses so much as a square yard of territory on the strength of a higher will or superior right. Just as Germany's frontiers are fortuitous frontiers, momentary frontiers in the current political struggle of any period, so are the boundaries of other nations' living space. And just as the shape of our earth's surface can seem immutable as granite only to the thoughtless softhead, but in reality only represents at each period an apparent pause in a continuous development, created by the mighty forces of Nature in a process of continuous growth, only to be transformed or destroyed tomorrow by greater forces, likewise the boundaries of living spaces in the life of nations.

■ Discussion Questions

1. How do the ideas of race and land acquisition intersect in Hitler's strategy for German domination of the world?

2. In this excerpt, how does Hitler both anticipate and respond to criticism of the genocidal action he prescribes?

3. What does Hitler's response to the "folkish pen-pushers" betray about his attitude toward parliamentary democracy?

■ Comparative Questions

1. In what ways did communist and Fascist ideology offer radically different solutions to similar problems?

2. What do Franke, Sassoon, and the French factory worker reveal about the role of technology in World War I?

3. What specific facets of liberal ideology did Lenin, Mussolini, and Hitler reject, and why?

4. Compare and contrast Mussolini's conception of "vitality" with Hitler's ideas of "race." What does this suggest about the similarities and differences between German and Italian Fascism?

An Age of Catastrophes, 1929–1945

T HE GREAT DEPRESSION of the 1930s ushered in an age of unprecedented violence and suffering around the globe. Millions were out of work, hungry, and
disillusioned. Authoritarian leaders capitalized on the downhearted, gaining
widespread support with their promises to revive the economy and to restore national glory. As the first document vividly shows, the Nazi Party, led by Adolf
Hilter (1889–1945), was one of the most menacing of these new political forces.
Western democracies responded cautiously to the Nazis, hoping to contain
Hitler's ambition through a policy of appeasement rather than military might.
The second document illustrates this policy in action at a critical juncture in
Hitler's march toward war. Not everyone passively accepted the Fascists' rise to
power, however. For example, European and North American citizens formed international brigades in Spain to fight the threat of Fascism there, as the third document illustrates. Although the ensuing civil war was dreadful in its destruction,
no one was truly prepared for the horrors of World War II. The last two documents reveal that the combination of ideology and advanced technology that fueled the war was especially cruel to the civilian population, setting a dangerous
precedent for the future.

1.
Joseph Goebbels
Nazi Propaganda Pamphlet
1930

*Perhaps no one better personifies the power of authoritarian rulers to manipulate the
minds of millions in the 1930s than Adolf Hitler (1889–1945). Among the secrets of
Hitler's success was his propaganda chief Joseph Goebbels (1895–1945). A member of
the National Socialist Party since 1922, Goebbels shared Hitler's belief that the masses*

From Louis L. Snyder, ed., *Documents of German History* (New Brunswick: Rutgers University Press, 1958), 414–16.

were easily managed if the message directed to them was simple and repetitive. To this end, Goebbels wrote pamphlets, such as the one that follows, in support of the Nazi cause. In it, he reveals the virulent anti-Semitism that shaped the Nazis' political program and set them apart from other totalitarian regimes. Goebbels's tactics helped propel Hitler to national leadership in 1933.

WHY ARE WE NATIONALISTS?

We are NATIONALISTS because we see in the NATION the only possibility for the protection and the furtherance of our existence.

The NATION is the organic bond of a people for the protection and defense of their lives. He is nationally minded who understands this IN WORD AND IN DEED.

Today, in GERMANY, NATIONALISM has degenerated into BOURGEOIS PATRIOTISM, and its power exhausts itself in tilting at windmills. It says GERMANY and means MONARCHY. It proclaims FREEDOM and means BLACK-WHITE-RED.

Young nationalism has its unconditional demands. BELIEF IN THE NATION is a matter of all the people, not for individuals of rank, a class, or an industrial clique. The eternal must be separated from the contemporary. The maintenance of a rotten industrial system has nothing to do with nationalism. I can love Germany and hate capitalism; not only CAN I do it, I also MUST do it. The germ of the rebirth of our people LIES ONLY IN THE DESTRUCTION OF THE SYSTEM OF PLUNDERING THE HEALTHY POWER OF THE PEOPLE.

WE ARE NATIONALISTS BECAUSE WE, AS GERMANS, LOVE GERMANY. And because we love Germany, we demand the protection of its national spirit and we battle against its destroyers.

WHY ARE WE SOCIALISTS?

We are SOCIALISTS because we see in SOCIALISM the only possibility for maintaining our racial existence and through it the reconquest of our political freedom and the rebirth of the German state. SOCIALISM has its peculiar form first of all through its comradeship in arms with the forward-driving energy of a newly awakened nationalism. Without nationalism it is nothing, a phantom, a theory, a vision of air, a book. With it, it is everything, THE FUTURE, FREEDOM, FATHERLAND!

It was a sin of the liberal bourgeoisie to overlook THE STATE-BUILDING POWER OF SOCIALISM. It was the sin of MARXISM to degrade SOCIALISM to a system of MONEY AND STOMACH.

We are SOCIALISTS because for us THE SOCIAL QUESTION IS A MATTER OF NECESSITY AND JUSTICE, and even beyond that A MATTER FOR THE VERY EXISTENCE OF OUR PEOPLE.

SOCIALISM IS POSSIBLE ONLY IN A STATE WHICH IS FREE INSIDE AND OUTSIDE.

DOWN WITH POLITICAL BOURGEOIS SENTIMENT: FOR REAL NATIONALISM!

DOWN WITH MARXISM: FOR TRUE SOCIALISM!

UP WITH THE STAMP OF THE FIRST GERMAN NATIONAL SOCIALIST STATE!

AT THE FRONT THE NATIONAL SOCIALIST GERMAN WORKERS PARTY! . . .

WHY DO WE OPPOSE THE JEWS?

We are ENEMIES OF THE JEWS, because we are fighters for the freedom of the German people. THE JEW IS THE CAUSE AND THE BENEFICIARY OF OUR MISERY. He has used the social difficulties of the broad masses of our people to deepen the unholy split between Right and Left among our people. He has made two halves of Germany. He is the real cause for our loss of the Great War.

The Jew has no interest in the solution of Germany's fateful problems. He CANNOT have any. FOR HE LIVES ON THE FACT THAT THERE HAS BEEN NO SOLUTION. If we would make the German people a unified community and give them freedom before the world, then the Jew can have no place among us. He has the best trumps in his hands when a people lives in inner and outer slavery. THE JEW IS RESPONSIBLE FOR OUR MISERY AND HE LIVES ON IT.

That is the reason why we, AS NATIONALISTS and AS SOCIALISTS, oppose the Jew. HE HAS CORRUPTED OUR RACE, FOULED OUR MORALS, UNDER-MINED OUR CUSTOMS, AND BROKEN OUR POWER.

THE JEW IS THE PLASTIC DEMON OF THE DECLINE OF MANKIND.

THE JEW IS UNCREATIVE. He produces nothing. HE ONLY HANDLES PRODUCTS. As long as he struggles against the state, HE IS A REVOLUTION-ARY; as soon as he has power, he preaches QUIET AND ORDER, so that he can consume his plunder at his convenience.

ANTI-SEMITISM IS UN-CHRISTIAN. That means, then, that he is a Christian who looks on while the Jew sews straps around our necks. TO BE A CHRISTIAN MEANS: LOVE THY NEIGHBOR AS THYSELF! MY NEIGHBOR IS ONE WHO IS TIED TO ME BY HIS BLOOD. IF I LOVE HIM, THEN I MUST HATE HIS EN-EMIES. HE WHO THINKS GERMAN MUST DESPISE THE JEWS. The one thing makes the other necessary.

WE ARE ENEMIES OF THE JEWS BECAUSE WE BELONG TO THE GERMAN PEOPLE. THE JEW IS OUR GREATEST MISFORTUNE.

It is not true that we eat a Jew every morning at breakfast.

It is true, however, that he SLOWLY BUT SURELY ROBS US OF EVERY-THING WE OWN.

THAT WILL STOP, AS SURELY AS WE ARE GERMANS.

■ Discussion Questions

1. According to this pamphlet, what do the terms *nationalist* and *socialist* mean within the context of the Nazi Party?

2. Why do you think the pamphlet targets Jews as enemies of the German people?

3. What does the pamphlet suggest about the link between the Nazis' racial views and their goals for Germany's future?

2.
Neville Chamberlain
Speech on the Munich Crisis
1938

During the troubled 1930s, many Europeans' deep longing for peace clouded their ability to see the true nature of the Nazi threat. The British politician Neville Chamberlain (1869–1940) was no exception. He became prime minister in 1937 when Hitler's preparations for war were well under way. After annexing Austria in March 1938, Hitler turned to his next target, Czechoslovakia. Chamberlain, Benito Mussolini (1883–1945), and French premier Edouard Daladier (1884–1970) met with Hitler in Munich in September 1938 to defuse the situation; their meeting resulted in an agreement that accepted Germany's territorial claims. In his closing speech, delivered during a debate on the agreement in the House of Commons, Chamberlain defended his policy of appeasement toward Hitler as the key to peace. Tragically, it was instead a prelude to war.

War today—this has been said before, and I say it again—is a different thing not only in degree, but in kind from what it used to be. We no longer think of war as it was in the days of Marlborough or the days of Napoleon or even in the days of 1914. When war starts today, in the very first hour, before any professional soldier, sailor or airman has been touched, it will strike the workman, the clerk, the man-in-the-street or in the 'bus, and his wife and children in their homes. As I listened I could not help being moved, as I am sure everybody was who heard the hon. Member for Bridgeton (Mr. Maxton) when he began to paint the picture which he himself had seen and realized what it would mean in war—people burrowing underground, trying to escape from poison gas, knowing that at any hour of the day or night death or mutilation was ready to come upon them. Remembering that the dread of what might happen to them or to those dear to them might remain with fathers and mothers for year after year—when you think of these things you cannot ask people to accept a prospect of that kind; you cannot force them into a position that they have got to accept it; unless you feel yourself, and can make them feel, that the cause for which they are going to fight is a vital cause—a cause that transcends all the human values, a cause to which you can point, if some day you win the victory, and say, "That cause is safe."

Since I first went to Berchtesgaden more than 20,000 letters and telegrams have come to No. 10, Downing Street. Of course, I have only been able to look at a tiny fraction of them, but I have seen enough to know that the people who wrote did not feel that they had such a cause for which to fight, if they were asked to go to war in order that the Sudeten Germans might not join the Reich. That is how

From *Parliamentary Debates,* Fifth Series, Vol. 339, *House of Commons Official Report* (London, 1938), 544–52.

they are feeling. That is my answer to those who say that we should have told Germany weeks ago that, if her army crossed the border of Czechoslovakia, we should be at war with her. We had no treaty obligations and no legal obligations to Czechoslovakia and if we had said that, we feel that we should have received no support from the people of this country. . . .

As regards future policy, it seems to me that there are really only two possible alternatives. One of them is to base yourself upon the view that any sort of friendly relations, or possible relations, shall I say, with totalitarian States are impossible, that the assurances which have been given to me personally are worthless, that they have sinister designs and that they are bent upon the domination of Europe and the gradual destruction of democracies. Of course, on that hypothesis, war has got to come, and that is the view—a perfectly intelligible view—of a certain number of hon. and right hon. Gentlemen in this House. I am not sure that it is not the view of some Members of the party opposite. [An HON. MEMBER: "Yes."] Not all of them. They certainly have never put it in so many words, but it is illustrated by the observations of the hon. Member for Derby (Mr. Noel-Baker), who spoke this afternoon, and who had examined the Agreement signed by the German Chancellor and myself, which he described as a pact designed by Herr Hitler to induce us to relinquish our present obligations. That shows how far prejudice can carry a man. The Agreement, as anyone can see, is not a pact at all. So far as the question of "never going to war again" is concerned, it is not even an expression of the opinion of the two who signed the paper, except that it is their opinion of the desire of their respective peoples. I do not know whether the hon. Member will believe me or attribute to me also sinister designs when I tell him that it was a document not drawn up by Herr Hitler but by the humble individual who now addresses this House.

If the view which I have been describing is the one to be taken, I think we must inevitably proceed to the next stage—that war is coming, broadly speaking the democracies against the totalitarian States—that certainly we must arm ourselves to the teeth, that clearly we must make military alliances with any other Powers whom we can get to work with us, and that we must hope that we shall be allowed to start the war at the moment that suits us and not at the moment that suits the other side. That is what some right hon. and hon. Gentlemen call collective security. Some hon. Members opposite will walk into any trap if it is only baited with a familiar catchword and they do it when this system is called collective security. But that is not the collective security we are thinking of or did think of when talking about the system of the League of Nations. That was a sort of universal collective security in which all nations were to take their part. This plan may give you security; it certainly is not collective in any sense. It appears to me to contain all the things which the party opposite used to denounce before the War—entangling alliances, balance of power and power politics. If I reject it, as I do, it is not because I give it a label; it is because, to my mind, it is a policy of utter despair.

If that is hon. Members' conviction, there is no future hope for civilization or for any of the things that make life worth living. Does the experience of the Great War and of the years that followed it give us reasonable hope that if some new war started that would end war any more than the last one did? No. I do not believe that war is inevitable. . . . It seems to me that the strongest argument against the inevitability of war is to be found in something that everyone has recognized or that has been recognized in every part of the House. That is the universal aversion from war of the people, their hatred of the notion of starting to kill one another again. . . .

What is the alternative to this bleak and barren policy of the inevitability of war? In my view it is that we should seek by all means in our power to avoid war, by analyzing possible causes, by trying to remove them, by discussion in a spirit of collaboration and good will. I cannot believe that such a program would be rejected by the people of this country, even if it does mean the establishment of personal contact with dictators, and of talks man to man on the basis that each, while maintaining his own ideas of the internal government of his country, is willing to allow that other systems may suit better other peoples. The party opposite surely have the same idea in mind even if they put it in a different way. They want a world conference. Well, I have had some experience of conferences, and one thing I do feel certain of is that it is better to have no conference at all than a conference which is a failure. The corollary to that is that before you enter a conference you must have laid out very clearly the lines on which you are going to proceed, if you are at least to have in front of you a reasonable prospect that you may obtain success. I am not saying that a conference would not have its place in due course. But I say it is no use to call a conference of the world, including these totalitarian Powers, until you are sure that they are going to attend, and not only that they are going to attend, but that they are going to attend with the intention of aiding you in the policy on which you have set your heart.

I am told that the policy which I have tried to describe is inconsistent with the continuance, and much more inconsistent with the acceleration of our present program of arms. I am asked how I can reconcile an appeal to the country to support the continuance of this program with the words which I used when I came back from Munich the other day and spoke of my belief that we might have peace for our time. I hope hon. Members will not be disposed to read into words used in a moment of some emotion, after a long and exhausting day, after I had driven through miles of excited, enthusiastic, cheering people — I hope they will not read into those words more than they were intended to convey. I do indeed believe that we may yet secure peace for our time, but I never meant to suggest that we should do that by disarmament, until we can induce others to disarm too. Our past experience has shown us only too clearly that weakness in armed strength means weakness in diplomacy, and if we want to secure a lasting peace, I realize that diplomacy cannot be effective unless the consciousness exists, not here alone, but elsewhere, that behind the diplomacy is the strength to give effect to it.

One good thing, at any rate, has come out of this emergency through which we have passed. It has thrown a vivid light upon our preparations for defense, on their strength and on their weakness. I should not think we were doing our duty if we had not already ordered that a prompt and thorough inquiry should be made to cover the whole of our preparations, military and civil, in order to see, in the light of what has happened during these hectic days, what further steps may be necessary to make good our deficiencies in the shortest possible time. There have been references in the course of the Debate to other measures which hon. Members have suggested should be taken. I would not like to commit myself now, until I have had a little time for reflection, as to what further it may seem good to ask the nation to do, but I think nobody could fail to have been impressed by the fact that the emergency brought out that the whole of the people of this country, whatever their class, whatever their station, were ready to do their duty, however disagreeable, however hard, however dangerous it may have been.

I cannot help feeling that if, after all, war had come upon us, the people of this country would have lost their spiritual faith altogether. As it turned out the other way, I think we have all seen something like a new spiritual revival, and I know that everywhere there is a strong desire among the people to record their readiness to serve their country, wherever or however their services could be most useful. I would like to take advantage of that strong feeling if it is possible, and although I must frankly say that at this moment I do not myself clearly see my way to any particular scheme, yet I want also to say that I am ready to consider any suggestions that may be made to me, in a very sympathetic spirit.

Finally, I would like to repeat what my right hon. Friend the Chancellor of the Exchequer said yesterday in his great speech. Our policy of appeasement does not mean that we are going to seek new friends at the expense of old ones, or, indeed, at the expense of any other nations at all. I do not think that at any time there has been a more complete identity of views between the French Government and ourselves than there is at the present time. Their objective is the same as ours — to obtain the collaboration of all nations, not excluding the totalitarian States, in building up a lasting peace for Europe. . . .

■ Discussion Questions

1. How did Chamberlain justify his policy of appeasement?

2. According to Chamberlain, why did some people oppose a policy of appeasement?

3. What does Chamberlain's defense indicate about popular attitudes toward war and peace?

3.
Isidora Dolores Ibárruri Gómez
La Pasionaria's Farewell Address
November 1, 1938

Isidora Dolores Ibárruri Gómez (1895–1989) was born into a poor family of miners, the eighth of eleven children. At twenty-one, she married a miner who was also a

From Online Journal and Multimedia Companion to Cary Nelson, ed., *Anthology of Modern American Poetry* (www.english.uiuc.edu/maps/scw/farewell.htm).

trade union activist. His imprisonment in 1916 led her to become active in politics, and by 1920 she was an elected member of the Basque Communist Party, which was based in northeast Spain. Under the pseudonym "La Pasionaria" ("the Passion Flower"), she published articles in the miners' newspaper, rallying them to the communist cause. She soon rose to the top of the communist leadership and attended meetings of the Comintern as part of the Spanish delegation. A vocal opponent of Fascism, she was a passionate orator for the Republicans during the Spanish Civil War, and is probably best remembered for her rallying cry—"It is better to die on your feet than to live on your knees." In the speech that follows, given on November 1, 1938, before a crowd of 15,000 in Barcelona, she praised the efforts of the antifascist International Brigades—60,000 volunteers who had come from across Europe and North America to fight alongside the Spanish Republicans. The International Brigades were dissolved for diplomatic reasons in late 1938, and many volunteers were arrested on their return home, particularly those from Great Britain because the British government had formally forbidden its citizens to participate in the Spanish Civil War.

It is very difficult to say a few words in farewell to the heroes of the International Brigades, because of what they are and what they represent. A feeling of sorrow, an infinite grief catches our throat—sorrow for those who are going away, for the soldiers of the highest ideal of human redemption, exiles from their countries, persecuted by the tyrants of all peoples—grief for those who will stay here forever mingled with the Spanish soil, in the very depth of our heart, hallowed by our feeling of eternal gratitude.

From all peoples, from all races, you came to us like brothers, like sons of immortal Spain; and in the hardest days of the war, when the capital of the Spanish Republic was threatened, it was you, gallant comrades of the International Brigades, who helped save the city with your fighting enthusiasm, your heroism and your spirit of sacrifice. — And Jarama and Guadalajara, Brunete and Belchite, Levante and the Ebro, in immortal verses sing of the courage, the sacrifice, the daring, the discipline of the men of the International Brigades.

For the first time in the history of the peoples' struggles, there was the spectacle, breathtaking in its grandeur, of the formation of International Brigades to help save a threatened country's freedom and independence—the freedom and independence of our Spanish land.

Communists, Socialists, Anarchists, Republicans—men of different colors, differing ideology, antagonistic religions—yet all profoundly loving liberty and justice, they came and offered themselves to us unconditionally.

They gave us everything—their youth or their maturity; their science or their experience; their blood and their lives; their hopes and aspirations—and they asked us for nothing. But yes, it must be said, they did want a post in battle, they aspired to the honor of dying for us.

Banners of Spain! Salute these many heroes! Be lowered to honor so many martyrs!

Mothers! Women! When the years pass by and the wounds of war are stanched; when the memory of the sad and bloody days dissipates in a present of liberty, of peace and of well-being; when the rancors have died out and pride in a free country is felt equally by all Spaniards, speak to your children. Tell them of these men of the International Brigades.

Recount for them how, coming over seas and mountains, crossing frontiers bristling with bayonets, sought by raving dogs thirsting to tear their flesh, these men reached our country as crusaders for freedom, to fight and die for Spain's liberty and independence threatened by German and Italian fascism. They gave up everything—their loves, their countries, home and fortune, fathers, mothers, wives, brothers, sisters and children—and they came and said to us: "We are here. Your cause, Spain's cause, is ours. It is the cause of all advanced and progressive mankind."

Today many are departing. Thousands remain, shrouded in Spanish earth, profoundly remembered by all Spaniards. Comrades of the International Brigades: Political reasons, reasons of state, the welfare of that very cause for which you offered your blood with boundless generosity, are sending you back, some to your own countries and others to forced exile. You can go proudly. You are history. You are legend. You are the heroic example of democracy's solidarity and universality in the face of the vile and accommodating spirit of those who interpret democratic principles with their eyes on hoards of wealth or corporate shares which they want to safeguard from all risk.

We shall not forget you; and, when the olive tree of peace is in flower, entwined with the victory laurels of the Republic of Spain—return!

Return to our side for here you will find a homeland—those who have no country or friends, who must live deprived of friendship—all, all will have the affection and gratitude of the Spanish people who today and tomorrow will shout with enthusiasm—

Long live the heroes of the International Brigades!

■ Discussion Questions

1. How does Ibárruri Gómez's speech reflect the international character of her communist ideology?

2. According to Ibárruri Gómez, why did the volunteers of the International Brigades come to fight in Spain?

3. What role does Ibárruri Gómez think women should play in keeping the memory of the International Brigades' heroism alive, and why is national memory of the International Brigades important?

4. In this speech, Ibárruri Gómez uses the rhetoric of both nationalism and international unity. Is she successful in her effort, or are these ideologies mutually exclusive?

4.
Sam Bankhalter and Hinda Kibort
Memories of the Holocaust
1938–1945

When Neville Chamberlain (1869–1940) detailed the horrors that modern warfare would inflict on civilians, not even he knew how true his words would prove to be. Once the war erupted, one segment of the civilian population in particular was the target of Hitler's fury: Jews. The result was the Final Solution, a technologically and bureaucratically sophisticated system of camps for incarcerating or exterminating European Jews that the Germans put into place between 1941 and 1942. Either inmates were killed on their arrival or spared to endure a different kind of death: starvation, abuse, and overwork. The two interviews that follow allow us to see the Holocaust through the eyes of its victims. The first is that of Sam Bankhalter, who was captured by the Nazis in his native Poland and sent to Auschwitz at age fourteen. The second voice is that of Hinda Kibort, a Lithuanian who was nineteen when the Nazis began their assault on the local Jewish population. In 1944, she was deported to Stutthof, a labor camp in northern Poland.

SAM BANKHALTER

Lodz, Poland

There was always anti-Semitism in Poland. The slogan even before Hitler was "Jew, get out of here and go to Palestine." As Hitler came to power, there was not a day at school I was not spit on or beaten up.

I was at camp when the Germans invaded Poland. The camp directors told us to find our own way home. We walked many miles with airplanes over our heads, dead people on the streets. At home there were blackouts. I was just a kid, tickled to death when I was issued a flashlight and gas mask. The Polish army was equipped with buggies and horses, the Germans were all on trucks and tanks. The war was over in ten days.

The Ghetto   The German occupation was humiliation from day 1. If Jewish people were wearing the beard and sidecurls, the Germans were cutting the beard, cutting the sidecurls, laughing at you, beating you up a little bit. Then the Germans took part of Lodz and put on barbed wire, and all the Jews had to assemble in this ghetto area. You had to leave in five or ten minutes or half an hour, so you couldn't take much stuff with you. . . .

Auschwitz   We were the first ones in Auschwitz. We built it. What you got for clothing was striped pants and the striped jacket, no underwear, no socks. In win-

From Rhoda G. Lewin, *Witnesses to the Holocaust: An Oral History* (Boston: Twayne Publishers, 1990), 5–8, 50–55.

tertime you put paper in your shoes, and we used to take empty cement sacks and put a string in the top, put two together, one in back and one in front, to keep warm.

If they told you to do something, you went to do it. There was no yes or no, no choices. I worked in the crematorium for about eleven months. I saw Dr. Mengele's experiments on children, I knew the kids that became vegetables. Later in Buchenwald I saw Ilse Koch with a hose and regulator, trying to get pressure to make a hole in a woman's stomach. I saw them cutting Greek people in pieces. I was in Flossenburg for two weeks, and they shot 25,000 Russian soldiers, and we put them down on wooden logs and burned them. Every day the killing, the hanging, the shooting, the crematorium smell, the ovens, and the smoke going out.

I knew everybody, knew every trick to survive. I was one of the youngest in Auschwitz, and I was like "adopted" by a lot of the older people, especially the fathers. Whole families came into Auschwitz together, and you got to Dr. Mengele, who was saying "right, left, left, right," and you knew, right there, who is going to the gas chamber and who is not. Most of the men broke down when they knew their wives and their kids—three-, five-, nine-year-olds—went into the gas chambers. In fact, one of my brothers committed suicide in Auschwitz because he couldn't live with knowing his wife and children are dead.

I was able to see my family when they came into Auschwitz in 1944. I had a sister, she had a little boy a year old. Everybody that carried a child went automatically to the gas chamber, so my mother took the child. My sister survived, but she still suffers, feels she was a part of killing my mother. . . .

Looking Back   Once you start fighting for your life, all the ethics are gone. You live by circumstances. There is no pity. You physically draw down to the point where you cannot think any more, where the only thing is survival, and maybe a little hope that if I survive, I'm gonna be with my grandchildren and tell them the story.

In the camps, death actually became a luxury. We used to say, "Look at how lucky he is. He doesn't have to suffer any more."

I was a lucky guy. I survived, and I felt pretty good about it. But then you feel guilty living! My children—our friends are their "aunts" and "uncles." They don't know what is a grandfather, a grandmother, a cousin, a holiday sitting as a family.

As you grow older, you think about it, certain faces come back to you. You remember your home, your brothers, children that went to the crematorium. You wonder, how did your mother and father feel when they were in the gas chamber? Many nights I hear voices screaming in those first few minutes in the gas chamber, and I don't sleep.

I talk to a lot of people, born Americans, and they don't relate. They can't understand, and I don't blame them. Sometimes it's hard even for me to understand the truth of this whole thing. Did it really happen? But I saw it.

The majority of the people here live fairly good. I don't think there's a country in the world that can offer as much freedom as this country can offer. But the Nazi Party exists here, now. This country is supplying anti-Semitic material to the whole world, printing it here and shipping it all over, and our leaders are silent, just as the world was silent when the Jews were being taken to the camps. How quick we forget.

When I sit in a plane, I see 65 percent of the people will pick up the sports page of the newspaper. They don't care what is on the front page! And this is where the danger lies. All you need is the economy to turn a little sour and have one person give out the propaganda. With 65 percent of the population the propaganda works, and then the other 35 percent is powerless to do anything about it.

HINDA KIBORT

Kovno, Lithuania

When the Germans marched in in July 1941, school had let out for the summer, so our whole family was together, including my brother who was in the university and my little sister who was in tenth grade. We tried to leave the city, but it was just like you see in the documentaries—people with their little suitcases walking along highways and jumping into ditches because German planes were strafing, coming down very low, and people killed, and all this terror. German tanks overtook us, and we returned home.

The Occupation   We did not have time like the German Jews did, from '33 until the war broke out in '39, for step-by-step adjustments. For us, one day we were human, the next day we're subhuman. We had to wear yellow stars. Everybody could command us to do whatever they wanted. They would make you hop around in the middle of the street, or they made you lie down and stepped on you, or spit on you, or they tore at beards of devout Jews. And there was always an audience around to laugh. . . .

The Ghetto   In September all the Jews were enclosed in a ghetto. We lived together in little huts, sometimes two families to a room. There were no schools, no newspapers, no concerts, no theater. Officially, we didn't have any radios or books, but people brought in many books and they circulated. We also had a couple of radios and we could hear the BBC, so we were very much aware of what was going on with the war.

As long as we were strong and useful, we would survive. Everybody had to go to work except children under twelve and the elderly. There were workshops in the ghetto where they made earmuffs for the army, for instance, but mostly people went out to work in groups, with guards. A few tried to escape, but were caught.

We did not know yet about concentration camps.

In 1943 the war turned, and we could feel a terrible tension from the guards and from Germans we worked with on the outside. We could exchange clothing or jewelry for food, but this was extremely dangerous because every time a column came back from work, we were all searched. A baker, they found some bread and a few cigarettes in his pocket. He was hanged publicly, on a Sunday. There was a little orchard in the ghetto, a public place, and we Jews had to build a gallows there and a Jew had to hang him. We were all driven out by the guards and had to stand and watch this man being hanged.

November 5, 1943, was the day all the children were taken away. They brought in Romanian and Ukrainian S.S. to do it. All five of us in our family were employed in a factory adjacent to the ghetto, so we could see through the window what was happening. They took everybody out who stayed in the ghetto—all the children, all the elderly. When we came back after work we were a totally childless society! You can imagine parents coming home to—nothing. Everybody was absolutely shattered.

People were looking for answers, for omens. They turned to seances or to heaven to look for signs. And this was the day when we heard for the first time the word *Auschwitz*. There was a rumor that the children were taken there, but we didn't know the name so we translated it as *Der Schweiz*—Switzerland. We hoped that the trains were going to Switzerland, that the children would be hostages there.

The Transport   On July 16, 1944, the rest of the ghetto were put on cattle trains, with only what we could carry. We had no bathrooms. There was a pail on one side that very soon was full. We were very crowded. The stench and the lack of water and the fear, the whole experience, is just beyond explanation.

At one time, when we were in open country, a guard opened the door and we sat on the side and let our feet down and got some fresh air. We even tried to sing. But then they closed it up, and we were all inside again.

Labor Camp   When we arrived at Stutthof our family was separated—the men to one side of the camp, women to the other. My mother and sister and I had to undress. There were S.S. guards around, men and women. In the middle of the room was a table and an S.S. man in a white coat. We came in in batches, totally naked.

I cannot describe how you feel in a situation like this. We were searched, totally, for jewelry, gold, even family pictures. We had to stand spread-eagle and spread out our fingers. They looked through the hair, they looked into the mouth, they looked in the ears, and then we had to lie down. They looked into every orifice of the body, right in front of everybody. We were in total shock.

From this room we were rushed through a room that said above the door "shower room." There were little openings in the ceiling and water was trickling through. In the next room were piles of clothing, rags, on the floor. You had to grab a skirt, a blouse, a dress, and exchange among yourselves to find what fit. The same thing with shoes. Some women got big men's shoes. I ended up with brown suede pumps with high heels and used a rock to break off the heels, so I could march and stand in line on roll calls.

After this we went into registration and they took down your profession, scholastic background, everything. We got black numbers on a white piece of cloth that had to be sewn on the sleeve. My mother and sister and I had numbers in the 54,000s. People from all over Europe—Hungarian women and Germans, Czechoslovakia, Belgium, you name it—they were there. Children, of course, were not there. When families came with children, the children were taken right away.

As prisoners of Stutthof we were taken to outside work camps. A thousand of us women were taken to dig antitank ditches, a very deep V-shaped ditch that went for miles and miles. The Germans had the idea that Russian tanks would fall into those ditches and not be able to come up again!

When we were done, 400 of us were taken by train deeper into Germany. We ended up in tents, fifty women to a tent. We had no water for washing and not even a latrine. If at night you wanted to go, you had to call a guard who would escort you to this little field, stand there watching while you were crouching down, and then escort you back.

We were covered with lice, and we became very sick and weak. But Frau Schmidt taught us to survive. She was a chemist, and she taught us what roots or grasses we could eat that weren't poisonous. She also said that to survive we have to keep our minds occupied and not think about the hunger and cold. She made us study every day! . . .

By the middle of December we had to stop working because the snow was very deep and everything was frozen. January 20, 1945, they made a selection. The strong women that could still work would be marched out, and the sick, those who couldn't walk or who had bent backs, or who were just skeletons and too weak to work, would be left behind. My mother was selected and my sister and I decided to stay behind with her.

We were left without food, with two armed guards. We thought the guards will burn the tents, with us in them. Then we heard there was a factory where they boiled people's bodies to manufacture soap. But the next day the guards put us in formation and marched us down the highway until we came to a small town.

We were put in the jail there. There we were, ninety-six women standing in a small jail cell, with no bathroom, pressed so close together we couldn't sit down, couldn't bend down. Pretty soon everybody was hysterical, screaming. Then slowly we quieted down.

In the morning when they opened the doors, we really spilled outside! They had recruited a bunch of Polish guards and they surrounded us totally, as if in a box. So there we were, ninety-six weak, emaciated women, marching down the highway with all these guards with rifles.

Then the German guards told us to run into the woods. The snow was so deep, up to our knees, and most of us were barefoot, frozen, our feet were blistered. We couldn't really run, but we spread out in a long line, with my mother and sister and I at the very end. I was near one guard, and all of a sudden I heard the sound of his rifle going "click." I still remember the feeling in the back of my spine, very strange and very scary. Then the guards began to shoot.

There was a terrible panic, screams. People went really crazy. The three of us always hand-held with my mother in the middle, but now she let go of us and ran toward the guards, screaming not to shoot her children. They shot her, and my sister and I grabbed each other by the hand and ran into the woods.

We could hear screaming and shooting, and then it got very quiet. We were afraid to move. The guards wore those awesome-looking black uniforms with the skull and crossbones insignia, and every tree looked like another guard! A few women came out from behind the trees, and eventually, ten of us made it out to the highway.

With our last strength, we made it to a small Polish village about a mile away. We knocked on doors, but they didn't let us in, and they started to throw things at us. We went to the church, and the priest said he couldn't help us because the Germans were in charge.

We were so weak we just sat there on the church steps, and late in the evening the priest came with a man who told us to go hide in a barn that was empty. We did not get any other help, whatsoever, from that whole Polish village — not medical help, not a rag to cover ourselves, not even water. Nothing.

Liberation   The next morning there was a terrible battle right in front of the barn. We were so afraid. Then it got very quiet. We opened the door, and we saw Russian tanks. We were free!

The Russians put us into an empty farmhouse. They gave us Vaseline and some rags, all they had, to cover our wounds. Then they put us on trucks and took us to a town where we found a freight train and just jumped on it.

At the border Russian police took us off the train. They grilled us. "How did you survive? You must have cooperated with the Germans." It was terrible. But finally we got identity cards — in Russia, you are nobody without some kind of I.D. — and my sister and I decided to go to the small town where we had lived. We thought somebody might have survived. . . .

Looking Back   I was a prisoner from age nineteen to twenty-three. I lost my mother and twenty-eight aunts, uncles and cousins — all killed. To be a survivor has meant to me to be a witness because being quiet would not be fair to the ones that did not survive.

There are people writing and saying the Holocaust never happened, it's a hoax, it's Jewish propaganda. We should keep talking about it, so the next generation won't grow up not knowing how a human being can turn into a beast, not knowing the danger in keeping quiet when you see something brewing. The onlooker, the bystander, is as much at fault as the perpetrator because he lets it happen. That is why I have this fear of what is called the "silent majority."

So when a non-Jewish friend or a student asks, "What can I do?" I say, when you see something anti-Semitic happen, get up and say, "This is wrong" or "I protest." Send a letter to the newspaper saying, "This should not happen in my community," and sign your name. Then maybe somebody else will be brave enough to come forward and say that he protests, too.

■ **Discussion Questions**

1. According to these accounts, what role did the ghettos play in the Final Solution?
2. Based on these interviews, what was the principal difference between camps like Auschwitz and those like Stutthof?

3. What do these accounts reveal about conditions in the camps and the inmates' strategies for survival?

4. What lessons does the Holocaust hold for the future?

5.
Harry S. Truman
Truman Announces the Dropping of the Atom Bomb on Hiroshima
1945

Although World War II began in Europe, in 1941 the conflict engulfed the world as Japan and the United States entered the war on opposite camps. Despite initial successes, within a year the Japanese began to lose ground to the Allies' formidable forces. Even so, they fought on, unwilling to surrender no matter what the material and human costs. This strategy prompted Allied leaders to make a fateful decision. On August 6, 1945, an American plane dropped an atomic bomb on the Japanese city of Hiroshima, adding tens of thousands to the war's civilian death toll. That same day, the president of the United States, Harry S. Truman (1884–1972), made the following public announcement regarding the event. He described the Allies' successful race to develop the bomb before the Germans, and he proclaimed that the result was a marvel of modern science that would bring the war to an end. Although right on both counts, Truman did not foresee that, with the dawning of the atomic age, a potentially more deadly conflict was about to begin: the cold war.

STATEMENT BY THE PRESIDENT OF THE UNITED STATES
AUGUST 6, 1945

The White House, Washington, D.C.

Sixteen hours ago an American airplane dropped one bomb on Hiroshima, an important Japanese Army base. That bomb had more power than 20,000 tons of T.N.T. It had more than two thousand times the blast power of the British "Grand Slam" which is the largest bomb ever yet used in the history of warfare.

The Japanese began the war from the air at Pearl Harbor. They have been repaid many fold. And the end is not yet. With this bomb we have now added a new and revolutionary increase in destruction to supplement the growing power of our armed forces. In their present form these bombs are now in production and even more powerful forms are in development.

From Department of State, *The International Control of Atomic Energy: Growth of a Policy* (Washington, DC: U.S. Government Printing Office, 1946), 95–97.

It is an atomic bomb. It is a harnessing of the basic power of the universe. The force from which the sun draws its power has been loosed against those who brought war to the Far East.

Before 1939, it was the accepted belief of scientists that it was theoretically possible to release atomic energy. But no one knew any practical method of doing it. By 1942, however, we knew that the Germans were working feverishly to find a way to add atomic energy to the other engines of war with which they hoped to enslave the world. But they failed. We may be grateful to Providence that the Germans got the V-1's and the V-2's late and in limited quantities and even more grateful that they did not get the atomic bomb at all.

The battle of the laboratories held fateful risks for us as well as the battles of the air, land, and sea, and we have now won the battle of the laboratories as we have won the other battles.

Beginning in 1940, before Pearl Harbor, scientific knowledge useful in war was pooled between the United States and Great Britain, and many priceless helps to our victories have come from that arrangement. Under that general policy the research on the atomic bomb was begun. With American and British scientists working together we entered the race of discovery against the Germans.

The United States had available the large number of scientists of distinction in the many needed areas of knowledge. It had the tremendous industrial and financial resources necessary for the project and they could be devoted to it without undue impairment of other vital war work. In the United States the laboratory work and the production plants, on which a substantial start had already been made, would be out of reach of enemy bombing, while at that time Britain was exposed to constant air attack and was still threatened with the possibility of invasion. For these reasons Prime Minister Churchill and President Roosevelt agreed that it was wise to carry on the project here. We now have two great plants and many lesser works devoted to the production of atomic power. Employment during peak construction numbered 125,000 and over 65,000 individuals are even now engaged in operating the plants. Many have worked there for two and a half years. Few know what they have been producing. They see great quantities of material going in and they see nothing coming out of these plants, for the physical size of the explosive charge is exceedingly small. We have spent two billion dollars on the greatest scientific gamble in history—and won.

But the greatest marvel is not the size of the enterprise, its secrecy, nor its cost, but the achievement of scientific brains in putting together infinitely complex pieces of knowledge held by many men in different fields of science into a workable plan. And hardly less marvelous has been the capacity of industry to design, and of labor to operate, the machines and methods to do things never done before so that the brain child of many minds came forth in physical shape and performed as it was supposed to do. Both science and industry worked under the direction of the United States Army, which achieved a unique success in managing so diverse a problem in the advancement of knowledge in an amazingly short time. It is doubtful if such another combination could be got together in the world. What has been done is the greatest achievement of organized science in history. It was done under high pressure and without failure.

We are now prepared to obliterate more rapidly and completely every productive enterprise the Japanese have above ground in any city. We shall destroy their docks, their factories, and their communications. Let there be no mistakes; we shall completely destroy Japan's power to make war.

It was to spare the Japanese people from utter destruction that the ultimatum of July 26 was issued at Potsdam. Their leaders promptly rejected that ultimatum. If they do not now accept our terms they may expect a rain of ruin from the air, the like of which has never been seen on this earth. Behind this air attack will follow sea and land forces in such numbers and power as they have not yet seen and with the fighting skill of which they are already well aware.

The Secretary of War, who has kept in personal touch with all phases of the project, will immediately make public a statement giving further details.

His statement will give facts concerning the sites at Oak Ridge near Knoxville, Tennessee, and at Richland near Pasco, Washington, and an installation near Santa Fe, New Mexico. Although the workers at the sites have been making materials to be used in producing the greatest destructive force in history they have not themselves been in danger beyond that of many other occupations, for the utmost care has been taken of their safety.

The fact that we can release atomic energy ushers in a new era in man's understanding of nature's forces. Atomic energy may in the future supplement the power that now comes from coal, oil, and falling water, but at present it cannot be produced on a basis to compete with them commercially. Before that comes there must be a long period of intensive research.

It has never been the habit of the scientists of this country or the policy of this Government to withhold from the world scientific knowledge. Normally, therefore, everything about the work with atomic energy would be made public.

But under present circumstances it is not intended to divulge the technical processes of production or all the military applications, pending further examination of possible methods of protecting us and the rest of the world from the danger of sudden destruction.

I shall recommend that the Congress of the United States consider promptly the establishment of an appropriate commission to control the production and use of atomic power within the United States. I shall give further consideration and make further recommendations to the Congress as to how atomic power can become a powerful and forceful influence towards the maintenance of world peace.

■ Discussion Questions

1. Why, according to Truman, was the development and use of the atomic bomb necessary?

2. How did the bomb's development reflect the general wartime trend of increasing government involvement in industrial production?

3. What future potential uses did Truman see for atomic power?

■ Comparative Questions

1. In what ways was the central message of Goebbels's pamphlet a reality for Bankhalter and Kibort?

2. How would you compare the views of Chamberlain, Ibárruri Gómez, and Truman on the use of military power as an instrument of peace?

3. How might the Spanish Civil War have represented a rehearsal for World War II? How was it different from this later conflict?

4. How did the use of the atomic bomb and the implementation of the Final Solution set World War II apart from World War I?

22

Remaking Europe in the Shadow of Cold War, c. 1945–1965

D ESPITE WIDESPREAD FEELINGS of relief and joy when World War II at last came
to an end, an uncertain path lay ahead for the world. With Europe in shambles, two new superpowers emerged from the rubble: the United States and the
Soviet Union. Their rivalry, known as the *cold war,* would shape international affairs for decades to come. The first two documents expose the ideological and political roots of U.S. and Soviet cold war policies. The bipolarization of world politics was not the only sign of Europe's diminished international identity, as the
third document shows. War-weary and bitter, colonial peoples from Asia to Africa
successfully battled for independence from European rule. Campaigns for freedom also appeared on the horizon closer to home. As societal and governmental
pressures reasserted traditional boundaries between men and women, the fourth
document reveals that some women called for change, setting the stage for the
women's liberation movement during the 1960s. The fifth document highlights an
additional struggle for change, as eastern Europeans risked imprisonment and
even death to challenge Soviet rule.

1.
The Formation of the Communist Information Bureau (Cominform)
1947

*Despite his instrumental role in defeating Fascism, the head of the Soviet Union,
Joseph Stalin (1879–1953), deeply mistrusted his Western allies. Convinced that
their ultimate goal was to destroy communism, Stalin moved rapidly to establish a*

From United States Senate, 81st Congress, 1st Session, Document No. 48, *North Atlantic
Treaty: Documents Relating to the North Atlantic Treaty* (Washington, DC: U.S. Government
Printing Office, 1949), 117–20.

buffer zone of satellite states in eastern Europe. At a meeting in September 1947, communist leaders consolidated the Soviets' hold in the East by establishing a centralized association of communist parties—the Communist Information Bureau (Cominform). As the following document justifying their actions reveals, the Cominform embodied Stalin's belief that only by coordinating their efforts could the Soviet Union and its clients defeat the "imperialist" threat. Stalin's Western rivals worked to put their own counterstrategies in place, thus hardening the battle lines of the cold war.

The representatives of the Communist Party of Yugoslavia, the Bulgarian Workers' Party (Communists), the Communist Party of Rumania, the Hungarian Communist Party, the Polish Workers' Party, the Communist Party of the Soviet Union (Bolsheviks), the Communist Party of France, the Communist Party of Czechoslovakia and the Communist Party of Italy, having exchanged views on the international situation, have agreed upon the following declaration.

Fundamental changes have taken place in the international situation as a result of the Second World War and in the post-war period.

These changes are characterized by a new disposition of the basic political forces operating in the world arena, by a change in the relations among the victor states in the Second World War, and their realignment.

While the war was on, the Allied States in the War against Germany and Japan went together and comprised one camp. However, already during the war there were differences in the Allied camp as regards the definition of both war aims and the tasks of the post-war peace settlement. The Soviet Union and the other democratic countries regarded as their basic war aims the restoration and consolidation of democratic order in Europe, the eradication of fascism and the prevention of the possibility of new aggression on the part of Germany, and the establishment of a lasting all-round cooperation among the nations of Europe. The United States of America, and Britain in agreement with them, set themselves another aim in the war: to rid themselves of competitors on the markets (Germany and Japan) and to establish their dominant position. This difference in the definition of war aims and the tasks of the post-war settlement grew more profound after the war. Two diametrically opposed political lines took shape: on the one side the policy of the USSR and the other democratic countries directed at undermining imperialism and consolidating democracy, and on the other side, the policy of the United States and Britain directed at strengthening imperialism and stifling democracy. Inasmuch as the USSR and the countries of the new democracy became obstacles to the realization of the imperialist plans of struggle for world domination and smashing of democratic movements, a crusade was proclaimed against the USSR and the countries of the new democracy, bolstered also by threats of a new war on the part of the most zealous imperialist politicians in the United States of America and Britain.

Thus two camps were formed—the imperialist and anti-democratic camp having as its basic aim the establishment of world domination of American imperialism and the smashing of democracy, and the anti-imperialist and democratic camp having as its basic aim the undermining of imperialism, the consolidation of democracy, and the eradication of the remnants of fascism.

The struggle between the two diametrically opposed camps—the imperialist camp and the anti-imperialist camp—is taking place in a situation marked by a further aggravation of the general crisis of capitalism, the weakening of the forces of capitalism and the strengthening of the forces of Socialism and democracy.

Hence the imperialist camp and its leading force, the United States, are displaying particularly aggressive activity. This activity is being developed simultaneously along all lines—the lines of strategic military measures, economic expansion and ideological struggle. The Truman-Marshall Plan is only a constituent part, the European sub-section, of the general plan for the policy of global expansion pursued by the United States in all parts of the World. The plan for the economic and political enslavement of Europe by American imperialism is being supplemented by plans for the economic and political enslavement of China, Indonesia, the South American countries. Yesterday's aggressors—the capitalist magnates of Germany and Japan—are being groomed by the United States of America for a new role, that of instruments of the imperialist policy of the United States in Europe and Asia.

The arsenal of tactical weapons used by the imperialist camp is highly diversified. It combines direct threats of violence, blackmail and extortion, every means of political and economic pressure, bribery, and utilization of internal contradictions and strife in order to strengthen its own positions, and all this is concealed behind a liberal-pacifist mask designed to deceive and trap the politically inexperienced. . . .

Under these circumstances it is necessary that the anti-imperialist, democratic camp should close its ranks, draw up an agreed program of actions and work out its own tactics against the main forces of the imperialist camp, against American imperialism and its British and French allies, against the right-wing Socialists, primarily in Britain and France.

To frustrate the plan of imperialist aggression the efforts of all the democratic anti-imperialist forces of Europe are necessary. The right-wing Socialists are traitors to this cause. With the exception of those countries of the new democracy where the bloc of the Communists and the Socialists with other democratic, progressive parties forms the basis of the resistance of these countries to the imperialist plans, the Socialists in the majority of other countries, and primarily the French Socialists and the British Labourites . . . by their servility and sycophancy are helping American capital to achieve its aims, provoking it to resort to extortion and impelling their own countries on to the path of vassal-like dependence on the United States of America.

This imposes a special task on the Communist Parties. They must take into their hands the banner of defense of the national independence and sovereignty of their countries. If the Communist Parties stick firmly to their positions, if they do not let themselves be intimidated and blackmailed, if they courageously safeguard democracy and the national sovereignty, liberty and independence of their countries, if in their struggle against attempts to enslave their countries economically and politically they be able to take the lead of all the forces that are ready to fight for honor and national independence, no plans for the enslavement of the countries of Europe and Asia can be carried into effect.

This is now one of the principal tasks of the Communist Parties.

It is essential to bear in mind that there is a vast difference between the desire of the imperialists to unleash a new war and the possibility of organizing such a war. The nations of the world do not want war. The forces standing for peace are so large and so strong that if these forces be staunch and firm in defending the peace, if they display stamina and resolution, the plans of the aggressors will meet with utter failure. It should not be forgotten that the war danger hullabaloo raised by the imperialist agents is intended to frighten the nervous and unstable elements and by blackmail to win concessions for the aggressor.

The principal danger for the working class today lies in underestimating their own strength and overestimating the strength of the imperialist camp. Just as the Munich policy untied the hands of Hitlerite aggression in the past, so yielding to the new line in the policy of the United States and that of the imperialist camp is bound to make its inspirers still more arrogant and aggressive. Therefore, the Communist Parties must take the lead in resisting the plans of imperialist expansion and aggression in all spheres—state, political, economic and ideological; they must close their ranks, unite their efforts on the basis of a common anti-imperialist and democratic platform and rally around themselves all the democratic and patriotic forces of the nation.

RESOLUTION ON INTERCHANGE OF EXPERIENCE AND COORDINATION OF ACTIVITIES OF THE PARTIES REPRESENTED AT THE CONFERENCE

The Conference states that the absence of contacts among the Communist Parties participating at this Conference is a serious shortcoming in the present situation. Experience has shown that such lack of contacts among the Communist Parties is wrong and harmful. The need for interchange of experience and voluntary coordination of action of the various Parties is particularly keenly felt at the present time in view of the growing complication of the post-war international situation, a situation in which the lack of connections among the Communist Parties may prove detrimental to the working class.

In view of this, the participants in the Conference have agreed on the following:

1. To set up an Information Bureau consisting of representatives of the Communist Party of Yugoslavia, the Bulgarian Workers' Party (Communists), the Communist Party of Rumania, the Hungarian Communist Party, the Polish Workers' Party, the Communist Party of the Soviet Union (Bolsheviks), the Communist Party of France, the Communist Party of Czechoslovakia and the Communist Party of Italy.

2. To charge the Information Bureau with the organization of interchange of experience, and if need be, coordination of the activities of the Communist Parties on the basis of mutual agreement.

3. The Information Bureau is to consist of two representatives from each Central Committee, the delegations of the Central Committees to be appointed and replaced by the Central Committees.

4. The Information Bureau is to have a printed organ—a fortnightly and subsequently, a weekly. The organ is to be published in French and Russian, and when possible, in other languages as well.

5. The Information Bureau is to be located in the city of Belgrad [sic].

■ **Discussion Questions**

1. According to the document, how did the relationship between the Soviet Union and its Western allies change during the postwar period, and why?

2. What does the document mean when it describes the United States as an "imperialist" power?

3. What course of action does the document set forth to undermine this power, and to what end?

4. How does this document distort the reality of Soviet actions in eastern Europe?

2.
National Security Council
Paper Number 68
1950

Although he had helped to end World War II, U.S. President Harry S. Truman (president, 1945–1953) had little time to celebrate. Daunting challenges still lay ahead as the fragile wartime alliance between the United States and the Soviet Union collapsed. By 1949, the Soviet bloc in eastern Europe was firmly in place, and the threat of international communism loomed large with the triumph of Mao Zedong (1893–1976) in China. In response, Truman set out to devise a coherent strategy for combating the expansion of Soviet power. To this end, he commissioned the U.S. Departments of State and Defense to compile a report on the subject, which was compiled in 1950 on the eve of the outbreak of the Korean War. The classified report, excerpted here, elucidates not only the basis of U.S. cold war tactics but also the fears and perceptions underlying them.

Within the past thirty-five years the world has experienced two global wars of tremendous violence.... During the span of one generation, the international distribution of power has been fundamentally altered. For several centuries it had

From National Security Council, Paper Number 68, *Foreign Relations of the United States* (Washington, DC: U.S. Government Printing Office, 1977), 235–92.

proved impossible for any one nation to gain such preponderant strength that a coalition of other nations could not in time face it with greater strength. The international scene was marked by recurring periods of violence and war, but a system of sovereign and independent states was maintained, over which no state was able to achieve hegemony.

Two complex sets of factors have now basically altered this historical distribution of power. First, the defeat of Germany and Japan and the decline of the British and French Empires have interacted with the development of the United States and the Soviet Union in such a way that power has increasingly gravitated to these two centers. Second, the Soviet Union, unlike previous aspirants to hegemony, is animated by a new fanatic faith, antithetical to our own, and seeks to impose its absolute authority over the rest of the world. Conflict has, therefore, become endemic and is waged, on the part of the Soviet Union, by violent or non-violent methods in accordance with the dictates of expediency. . . .

On the one hand, the people of the world yearn for relief from the anxiety arising from the risk of atomic war. On the other hand, any substantial further extension of the area under the domination of the Kremlin would raise the possibility that no coalition adequate to confront the Kremlin with greater strength could be assembled. It is in this context that this Republic and its citizens in the ascendancy of their strength stand in their deepest peril.

The issues that face us are momentous, involving the fulfillment or destruction not only of this Republic but of civilization itself. They are issues which will not await our deliberations. With conscience and resolution this Government and the people it represents must now take new and fateful decisions. . . .

Our overall policy at the present time may be described as one designed to foster a world environment in which the American system can survive and flourish. It therefore rejects the concept of isolation and affirms the necessity of our positive participation in the world community.

This broad intention embraces two subsidiary policies. One is a policy which we would probably pursue even if there were no Soviet threat. It is a policy of attempting to develop a healthy international community. The other is the policy of "containing" the Soviet system. . . .

As for the policy of "containment," it is one which seeks by all means short of war to (1) block further expansion of Soviet power, (2) expose the falsities of Soviet pretensions, (3) induce a retraction of the Kremlin's control and influence and (4) in general, so foster the seeds of destruction within the Soviet system that the Kremlin is brought at least to the point of modifying its behavior to conform to generally accepted international standards.

It was and continues to be cardinal in this policy that we possess superior overall power in ourselves or in dependable combination with other like-minded nations. One of the most important ingredients of power is military strength. In the concept of "containment," the maintenance of a strong military posture is deemed to be essential for two reasons: (1) as an ultimate guarantee of our national security and (2) as an indispensable backdrop to the conduct of the policy of "containment." . . .

At the same time, it is essential to the successful conduct of a policy of "containment" that we always leave open the possibility of negotiation with the U.S.S.R. A diplomatic freeze—and we are in one now—tends to defeat the very purposes of "containment" because it raises tensions at the same time that it makes Soviet retractions and adjustments in the direction of moderated behavior more difficult. It also tends to inhibit our initiative and deprives us of opportunities for maintaining a moral ascendancy in our struggle with the Soviet system. . . .

It is quite clear from Soviet theory and practice that the Kremlin seeks to bring the free world under its dominion by the methods of the cold war. The preferred technique is to subvert by infiltration and intimidation. Every institution of our society is an instrument which it has sought to stultify and turn against our purposes. Those that touch most closely our material and moral strength are obviously the prime targets, labor unions, civil enterprises, schools, churches, and all media for influencing opinion. The effort is not so much to make them serve obvious Soviet ends as to prevent them from serving our ends, and thus to make them sources of confusion in our economy, our culture, and our body politic. The doubts and diversities that in terms of our values are part of the merit of a free system, the weaknesses and the problems that are peculiar to it, the rights and privileges that free men enjoy, and the disorganization and destruction left in the wake of the last attack in our freedoms, all are but opportunities for the Kremlin to do its evil work. Every advantage is taken of the fact that our means of prevention and retaliation are limited by those principles and scruples which are precisely the ones that give our freedom and democracy its meaning for us. None of our scruples deter those whose only code is, "morality is that which serves the revolution."

At the same time the Soviet Union is seeking to create overwhelming military force, in order to back up infiltration with intimidation. In the only terms in which it understands strength, it is seeking to demonstrate to the free world that force and the will to use it are on the side of the Kremlin, that those who lack it are decadent and doomed. In local incidents it threatens and encroaches both for the sake of local gains and to increase anxiety and defeatism in all the free world. . . .

Our position as the center of power in the free world places a heavy responsibility upon the United States for leadership. We must organize and enlist the energies and resources of the free world in a positive program for peace which will frustrate the Kremlin design for world domination by creating a situation in the free world to which the Kremlin will be compelled to adjust. Without such a cooperative effort, led by the United States, we will have to make gradual withdrawals under pressure until we discover one day that we have sacrificed positions of vital interest. . . .

In summary, we must, by means of a rapid and sustained build-up of the political, economic, and military strength of the free world, and by means of an affirmative program intended to wrest the initiative from the Soviet Union, confront it with convincing evidence of the determination and ability of the free world to frustrate the Kremlin to the new situation. Failing that, the unwillingness of the determination and ability of the free world to the Kremlin design of a world dominated by its will *[sic]*. Such evidence is the only means short of war which eventually may force the Kremlin to abandon its present course of action and to negotiate acceptable agreements on issues of major importance.

The whole success of the proposed program hangs ultimately on recognition by this Government, the American people, and all free peoples, that the cold war is in fact a real war in which the survival of the free world is at stake. Essential prerequisites to success are consultations with Congressional leaders designed to make the program the object of nonpartisan legislative support, and a presentation to the public of a full explanation of the facts and implications of the present international situation. The prosecution of the program will require of us all the ingenuity, sacrifice, and unity demanded by the vital importance of the issue and the tenacity to persevere until our national objectives have been attained.

■ Discussion Questions

1. As described in the report, how did World War II transform the international distribution of power?

2. According to the report, in what ways did the Soviet Union pose a danger to Americans and all "free peoples"?

3. What solutions does the document set forth to counter this danger?

4. Why does the report describe the cold war as a "real" war?

3.
Ho Chi Minh
Declaration of Independence of the Republic of Vietnam
1945

The devastation wrought by World War II encompassed more than the countless bombed buildings and millions of dead. The war had also fatally weakened the European powers' grip on their empires, as colonial peoples around the globe rose up against imperialist rule. A small nationalist organization—Viet Minh—had formed in French Indochina in 1939 and achieved new prominence in the wake of World War II when the French sought to reassert their control in the region. Less than a month after Japan's surrender, the Viet Minh declared Vietnam's independence from France, as noted in the following document. It was signed by "President Ho Chi Minh" (1890–1969)—one of the organization's original leaders—who had lived in Paris, Moscow, and China. The document explicitly draws on the language of the French Enlightenment to further the Viet Minh's cause and condemn that of France.

From Allan B. Cole, ed., *Conflict in Indo-China and International Repercussions: A Documentary History, 1945–1955* (Ithaca: Cornell University Press, 1956), 20–21.

"All men are created equal. They are endowed by their Creator with certain un-alienable rights, among these are Life, Liberty and the pursuit of happiness."

This immortal statement was made in the Declaration of Independence of the United States of America in 1776. Now if we enlarge the sphere of our thoughts, this statement conveys another meaning: All the peoples on the earth are equal from birth, all the peoples have a right to live, be happy and free.

The Declaration of the Rights of Man and of the Citizen of the French Revolution in 1791 also states: "All men are born free and with equal rights, and must always be free and have equal rights."

BEFORE THE OUTBREAK OF WAR

Those are undeniable truths.

Nevertheless, for more than eighty years, the French imperialists deceitfully raising the standard of Liberty, Equality and Fraternity, have violated our Fatherland and oppressed our fellow-citizens. They have acted contrarily to the ideals of humanity and justice.

In the province of politics, they have deprived our people of every liberty.

They have enforced inhuman laws; to ruin our unity and national consciousness, they have carried out three different policies in the North, the Center and the South of Vietnam.

They have founded more prisons than schools. They have mercilessly slain our patriots; they have deluged our revolutionary areas with innocent blood. They have fettered public opinion; they have promoted illiteracy.

To weaken our race they have forced us to use their manufactured opium and alcohol.

In the province of economics, they have stripped our fellow-citizens of everything they possessed, impoverishing the individual and devastating the land.

They have robbed us of our rice fields, our mines, our forests, our raw materials. They have monopolized the printing of bank-notes, the import and export trade; they have invented numbers of unlawful taxes, reducing our people, especially our countryfolk, to a state of extreme poverty.

They have stood in the way of our businessmen and stifled all their undertakings; they have extorted our working classes in a most savage way.

In the Autumn of the year 1940, when the Japanese fascists violated Indochina's territory to get one more foothold in their fight against the Allies, the French imperialists fell on their knees and surrendered, handing over our country to the Japanese, adding Japanese fetters to the French ones. From that day on the Vietnamese people suffered hardships yet unknown in the history of mankind. The result of this double oppression was terrific: from Quangtri to the Northern border two million people were starved to death in the early months of 1945.

On the 9th of March 1945 the French troops were disarmed by the Japanese. Once more the French either fled, or surrendered unconditionally, showing thus that not only they were incapable of "protecting" us, but that they twice sold us to the Japanese.

Yet, many times before the month of March, the Vietminh had urged the French to ally with them against the Japanese. The French colonists never answered. On the contrary they intensified their terrorizing policy. Before taking their flight they even killed a great number of our patriots who had been imprisoned at Yenbay and Caobang.

DEMOCRATIC REPUBLIC OF VIETNAM

Nevertheless, towards the French people our fellow-citizens have always manifested an attitude pervaded with toleration and humanity. Even after the Japanese putsch of March 1945 the Vietminh have helped many Frenchmen to reach the frontier, have delivered some of them from the Japanese jails, and never failed to protect their lives and properties.

The truth is that since the Autumn of 1940 our country had ceased to be a French colony and had become a Japanese outpost. After the Japanese had surrendered to the Allies our whole people rose to conquer political power and institute the Republic of Vietnam.

The truth is that we have wrested our independence from the Japanese and not from the French. The French have fled, the Japanese have capitulated, Emperor Bao Dai has abdicated, our people has broken the fetters which for over a century have tied us down; our people has at the same time overthrown the monarchic constitution that had reigned supreme for so many centuries and instead has established the present Republican Government.

For these reasons, we, members of the provisional Government, representing the whole population of Vietnam, have declared and renew here our declaration that we break off all relations with the French people and abolish all the special rights the French have unlawfully acquired on our Fatherland.

The whole population of Vietnam is united in a common allegiance to the Republican Government and is linked by a common will which is to annihilate the dark aims of the French imperialists.

We are convinced that the Allied nations which have acknowledged at Teheran and San Francisco the principles of self determination and equality of status will not refuse to acknowledge the independence of Vietnam.

A people that has courageously opposed French domination for more than eighty years, a people that has fought by the Allies' side these last years against the fascists, such a people must be free, such a people must be independent.

For these reasons we, members of the Provisional Government of Vietnam, declare to the world that Vietnam has the right to be free and independent, and has in fact become a free and independent country. We also declare that the Vietnamese people is determined to make the heaviest sacrifices to maintain its independence and its Liberty.

■ Discussion Questions

1. How does the document characterize the actions of the French in Vietnam, and why?

2. In what ways did World War II further the cause of the Viet Minh?

3. Why did the Viet Minh believe that the Vietnamese people had an undeniable right to independence?

4.
Simone de Beauvoir
The Second Sex
1949

Like Ho Chi Minh, Simone de Beauvoir (1908–1986) challenged traditional power structures in the postwar era. However, although she watched the growing independence movement in French Indochina with interest, her battle did not center on the plight of the colonized people. Rather, she dedicated herself to examining the condition of modern women, which, she argued, was similarly marked by injustice and discrimination. She presented her views to the world in her book The Second Sex, *published in 1949. In the following excerpt, Beauvoir outlines the fundamental premise of her work that, throughout history, women's identities have been defined by men and thus subjugated to them. Beauvoir believed that women could break free from their subservience only by taking charge of their own lives. Her views would help galvanize the women's liberation movement in the United States and Europe during the 1960s.*

A man would never get the notion of writing a book on the peculiar situation of the human male. But if I wish to define myself, I must first of all say: "I am a woman"; on this truth must be based all further discussion. A man never begins by presenting himself as an individual of a certain sex; it goes without saying that he is a man. The terms *masculine* and *feminine* are used symmetrically only as a matter of form, as on legal papers. In actuality the relation of the two sexes is not quite like that of two electrical poles, for man represents both the positive and the neutral, as is indicated by the common use of *man* to designate human beings in general; whereas woman represents only the negative, defined by limiting criteria, without reciprocity. In the midst of an abstract discussion it is vexing to hear a man say: "You think thus and so because you are a woman"; but I know that my only defense is to reply: "I think thus and so because it is true," thereby removing my subjective self from the argument. It would be out of the question to reply: "And you think the contrary because you are a man," for it is understood that the fact of being a man is no peculiarity. A man is in the right in being a man; it is the woman who is in the wrong. It amounts to this: just as for the ancients there was an absolute vertical with reference to which the oblique was defined, so there is an

From Simone de Beauvoir, *The Second Sex*, trans. and ed. H. M. Parshley (New York: Knopf, 1953), xvi–xx.

absolute human type, the masculine. Woman has ovaries, a uterus; these peculiarities imprison her in her subjectivity, circumscribe her within the limits of her own nature. It is often said that she thinks with her glands. Man superbly ignores the fact that his anatomy also includes glands, such as the testicles, and that they secrete hormones. He thinks of his body as a direct and normal connection with the world, which he believes he apprehends objectively, whereas he regards the body of woman as a hindrance, a prison, weighed down by everything peculiar to it. . . . And she is simply what man decrees; thus she is called "the sex," by which is meant that she appears essentially to the male as a sexual being. For him she is sex—absolute sex, no less. She is defined and differentiated with reference to man and not he with reference to her; she is the incidental, the inessential as opposed to the essential. He is the Subject, he is the Absolute—she is the Other. . . .

Thus it is that no group ever sets itself up as the One without at once setting up the Other over against itself. If three travelers chance to occupy the same compartment, that is enough to make vaguely hostile "others" out of all the rest of the passengers on the train. In small-town eyes all persons not belonging to the village are "strangers" and suspect; to the native of a country all who inhabit other countries are "foreigners"; Jews are "different" for the anti-Semite, Negroes are "inferior" for American racists, aborigines are "natives" for colonists, proletarians are the "lower class" for the privileged. . . .

No subject will readily volunteer to become the object, the inessential; it is not the Other who, in defining himself as the Other, establishes the One. The Other is posed as such by the One in defining himself as the One. But if the Other is not to regain the status of being the One, he must be submissive enough to accept this alien point of view. Whence comes this submission in the case of woman?

There are, to be sure, other cases in which a certain category has been able to dominate another completely for a time. Very often this privilege depends upon inequality of numbers—the majority imposes its rule upon the minority or persecutes it. But women are not a minority, like the American Negroes or the Jews; there are as many women as men on earth. Again, the two groups concerned have often been originally independent; they may have been formerly unaware of each other's existence, or perhaps they recognized each other's autonomy. But a historical event has resulted in the subjugation of the weaker by the stronger. The scattering of the Jews, the introduction of slavery into America, the conquests of imperialism are examples in point. In these cases the oppressed retained at least the memory of former days; they possessed in common a past, a tradition, sometimes a religion or a culture.

The parallel drawn . . . between women and the proletariat is valid in that neither ever formed a minority or a separate collective unit of mankind. And instead of a single historical event it is in both cases a historical development that explains their status as a class and accounts for the membership of *particular individuals* in that class. But proletarians have not always existed, whereas there have always been women. They are women in virtue of their anatomy and physiology. Throughout history they have always been subordinated to men, and hence their dependency is not the result of a historical event or a social change—

it was not something that *occurred*. The reason why otherness in this case seems to be an absolute is in part that it lacks the contingent or incidental nature of historical facts. A condition brought about at a certain time can be abolished at some other time, as the Negroes of Haiti and others have proved; but it might seem that a natural condition is beyond the possibility of change. In truth, however, the nature of things is no more immutably given, once for all, than is historical reality. If woman seems to be the inessential which never becomes the essential, it is because she herself fails to bring about this change. Proletarians say "We"; Negroes also. Regarding themselves as subjects, they transform the bourgeois, the whites, into "others." But women do not say "We," except at some congress of feminists or similar formal demonstration; men say "women," and women use the same word in referring to themselves. They do not authentically assume a subjective attitude. The proletarians have accomplished the revolution in Russia, the Negroes in Haiti, the Indo-Chinese are battling for it in Indo-China; but the women's effort has never been anything more than a symbolic agitation. They have gained only what men have been willing to grant; they have taken nothing, they have only received.

The reason for this is that women lack concrete means for organizing themselves into a unit which can stand face to face with the correlative unit. They have no past, no history, no religion of their own; and they have no such solidarity of work and interest as that of the proletariat. They are not even promiscuously herded together in the way that creates community feeling among the American Negroes, the ghetto Jews, the workers of Saint-Denis, or the factory hands of Rennault. They live dispersed among the males, attached through residence, housework, economic condition, and social standing to certain men — fathers or husbands — more firmly than they are to other women. If they belong to the bourgeoisie, they feel solidarity with men of that class, not with proletarian women; if they are white, their allegiance is to white men, not to Negro women. The proletariat can propose to massacre the ruling class, and a sufficiently fanatical Jew or Negro might dream of getting sole possession of the atomic bomb and making humanity wholly Jewish or black; but woman cannot even dream of exterminating the males. The bond that unites her to her oppressors is not comparable to any other. The division of the sexes is a biological fact, not an event in human history. . . . The couple is a fundamental unity with its two halves riveted together, and the cleavage of society along the line of sex is impossible. Here is to be found the basic trait of woman: she is the Other in a totality of which the two components are necessary to one another.

■ Discussion Questions

1. What does Beauvoir mean when she describes women as the "Other"?

2. According to Beauvoir, how does women's status both resemble and differ from that of other oppressed groups such as colonized peoples?

3. Why, unlike some of these groups, have women been unable to change their status?

5.
Béla Lipták
Birth of MEFESZ
1956

After Stalin's death in 1953, a climate of uncertainty enveloped communist parties around the world. The new leader of the Soviet Union, Nikita Khrushchev (1894–1971), attacked Stalinism and opened the door for the possibility of reform. In 1956, tens of thousands of people in Eastern Europe sought to take advantage of the change in mood by protesting against Soviet rule. The Hungarian uprising in October was among the most daring and heroic of these rebellions; university students and factory workers joined together to advocate for free speech and personal liberty. This excerpt from A Testament of Revolution *was written by Béla Lipták, a student in Budapest at the time of the uprising and ultimately one of the rebellion's leaders. Lipták describes the first spontaneous act of protest that led to the formation of an anticommunist student group at Budapest's Technical University. Although the protesters were brutally suppressed, they came to symbolize anticommunist courage against draconian oppression. In 1956, instead of choosing an individual person,* Time *magazine named "the Hungarian Freedom Fighter" as Man of the Year.*

Attila and I settled down in the gallery of the aula, the large assembly hall of the Technical University....

That day there must have been a couple of thousand students in the aula, but none of us was really paying much attention to what was going on. One could hear this constant murmur in the hall. It was like any other meeting in the Communist world. They talked *at* us, and our only defense against that was to not listen.

Below our gallery, on the main floor of the aula, the two rectors of the dual university, László Gillemot and Tibor Cholnoky, were at the microphone. With them were some professors, the Communist Party secretary, lesser Party officials, and the leaders of the Communist Youth Organization, the DISZ. It was the DISZ that had convened the meeting. In their uniform of blue jackets, white shirts, and red neckties, the leaders of the DISZ looked like a special breed of penguins or booby birds. Their purpose for calling the meeting was to preempt the spread of MEFESZ, the new non-Communist student association. Since the recent formation of MEFESZ in the city of Szeged, suddenly the DISZ seemed to care a lot about us. They talked about special train passes for students, cheaper textbooks, and better food and housing. We did not speak up. We never did. It was their show, and we let them do all the talking.

And talk they did. I was scraping the corrosion off my "gold" ring, which had cost me thirty-six forints and must have had some copper in its heritage, because

---

From Béla Lipták, *A Testament of Revolution* (College Station: Texas A&M University Press, 2001), 25–29.

it was turning green. I was spitting on it, rubbing it, and was just beginning to make some progress when I felt Attila's elbow in my side. He was pointing down to the speakers' platform, where there was some commotion. The murmur in the aula stopped. Now there was total silence. In startled curiosity the dozing students were beginning to wake up. We were sitting up and starting to pay attention. Now you could hear a pin drop. Then, from the middle of the tumult at the microphone, a voice rose: "I represent the MEFESZ of Szeged! I want to speak!"

It was unprecedented! Extraordinary! The air was thick with tension. We did not know who had spoken, did not understand what was happening. All we could see was that the DISZ penguins were shoving a small fellow away from the microphone. He was a student like us, and he was talking, gesticulating, but we heard nothing—the blue-jacketed DISZ had pushed him all the way to the wall.

Then the Party secretary, Mrs. Orbán, came to the microphone and admonished us, "You have only one duty! Your duty is to study!" She was almost screaming. "You don't want the MEFESZ of Szeged! You don't want any ideas from Szeged!" I could not imagine why Szeged was suddenly such a bad place. I did not particularly care what she was saying but I was hypnotized by this minihero, this crazy little guy from Szeged.

My mind raced on: I do not understand him. I do not understand what he wants. Is he out of his mind? Does he not know that he will be kicked out of the university? Not only that, he will also be thrown in jail—that is, right after they beat the shit out of him. Does he not understand that we are nobodies, that our collective name is "Shut Up"? Does he not understand that he is nothing, that I am nothing, that we have no say in anything? Does he not understand that the microphone is only for the Party collaborators and nobody, but nobody, else talks into it? Does he not know that even the penguins dare only read their prepared statements? And that even then they wait until they are told that it is their turn to read?

Attila muttered my own racing thoughts when he said, "I just don't get it!"

Then we saw the members of the military department, the only people who possessed arms at the university, marching onto the speaker's platform, and we got very quiet. My throat was dry, my breath bated. All eyes were on the officers. Then suddenly, from a distance, we heard a voice. It was that of a fifth-year architecture student, a blond, very tall young man by the name of Jancsi Danner. He yelled, "Let him speak!"

My heart stopped. Nothing like this had ever happened since the Red Army had occupied Hungary. I stared at Jancsi. His ears were red, his mouth was trembling, but he did not blink; he faced the bewildered and frightened stares of two thousand students.

"God, he has lost his marbles!" I said.

In the meantime a new and angry sort of murmur was building up, replacing the previously astonished silence, and now, a few rows in front of us, Laci Zsindely, a classmate of mine, hesitantly started to clap. It was then that the miracle occurred.

First one, then two, then four or five students joined in, and suddenly this sparse clapping turned into a hurricane, a burst of thunderous applause the likes of which I had never heard. I saw Attila clapping like a madman as he shouted to me, "Applaud or I will never speak to you again!"

I had never seen anything like it. As some of the students stood up, the ovation continued, and the Party officials around the microphone became nervous, surprised, angry—and just a bit uncertain. I had never seen them uncertain. That was something new. My flesh was creeping, and I was clapping as though my life depended on it, as if I were out of my mind. And during all this my mind was racing. Is this possible? Can we actually have a say? Can we contradict them like this, directly to their faces? Is it possible that I matter, that what I think matters? Is it possible that I do not have to hold my tongue all the time? Is it possible that I am not alone?

Now, it was total chaos. The Party secretary ran to the telephone. The rest of her penguins were white as sheets. The hands of the officers of the military department had moved to the guns on their belts while the chief of DISZ kept screaming into the microphone. And then, through all the pandemonium and over the thunderous applause, we heard his voice once more: "I represent the MEFESZ of Szeged! Allow me to speak!"

Now I really felt hypnotized. I stood up and began walking toward that voice and saw Attila doing the same thing. From other directions, another twenty, then thirty, students were also starting to move toward the voice. This was all completely spontaneous. We walked without knowing who was walking with us. We were drawn toward the speaker's stand, toward the angry but scared penguins, who had encircled the boy from MEFESZ. The circle thinned as we got closer and we just started pushing the whole group toward the microphone. I saw my hand rise, reaching for one of the fat penguins. . . . But then I saw the microphone. Five more meters and we would have it! I pushed with all my might. The DISZ resistance faltered. Now, Jancsi Danner grabbed the microphone and proclaimed, "I ask the representative of the students of Szeged to speak!"

There was a deafening ovation that took quite a while to taper off until there was total silence. I saw the six-foot-four Jancsi Danner reaching down to his waist as he gave the microphone to the diminutive delegate from Szeged. I just stood in the protective ring around him, and my eyes filled with tears as he started to speak in a strong voice: "Fellow students! Hungarians!"

I saw the flash of cameras. I saw strangers rushing to the telephones. Floodlights started to glare and film cameras begun to buzz. And the little fellow from Szeged was oblivious to it all as he started to speak: "Once again, the wind of freedom is blowing in from Poland. The Polish exchange students at our university are asking for our support. Russian troops are surrounding Warsaw, but the Polish army is also encircling the Russians. The city of Poznan is also free, but surrounded. Poland is showing the way and is asking for our solidarity. We will not let them down! We, the students of Szeged, have decided to follow the Poles in establishing our independent student organization, the MEFESZ. Please join us. Please do not believe the lies. Please form your own MEFESZ!"

At that point he seemed confused. His voice faltered. And then, haltingly, without a tune, he started to mumble the words of our forbidden hymn, the hymn most hated by the Communists: our national anthem. This anthem had not been heard in public for nearly a decade; one could sing it only in church, after the mass. This anthem that stood for the things the Communists most despised: God, country, and liberty. The anthem that we call our national prayer, the anthem that a Hungarian can sing only while standing at attention.

The great chandelier of the aula trembled and the windows shook as we sang our hearts out. As we finished we were all weeping. And during those couple of minutes of singing, a miracle occurred in that great hall. We were not the same people we had been a few minutes earlier. We, these tearful kids still standing at attention in that great hall, we had been reborn. We had stopped being scared. And therefore we were free! . . .

■ Discussion Questions

1. Why do you think the microphone had such central importance to this event?

2. What does this passage reveal about the norms of everyday life under Soviet communism?

3. How did Lipták's sense of freedom and confidence challenge the communist mentality?

4. Although this protest occurred in the presence of armed guards, not a shot was fired. Why do you think the guards refrained from using their weapons? What does this suggest about the power of words over weaponry?

■ Comparative Questions

1. How does the Cominform's vision of communism in the abstract compare with Béla Lipták's view of communism in practice?

2. Based on the Cominform declaration and National Security Council paper, what similarities do you see between Soviet and American cold war attitudes and corresponding policies?

3. How would you compare the struggles of Ho Chi Minh, Simone de Beauvoir, and Béla Lipták against rigid power structures during the postwar era?

4. How does a deep sense of anxiety permeate the documents? What was the source of such anxiety, and where does it surface in the documents?

23

Postindustrial Society and the End of the Cold War Order, 1965–1989

T HE 1960S AND 1970S were filled with turmoil fueled by feelings of both opti-mism and despair. During these years, millions of people took to the streets to challenge cold war politics and society. As the first document illustrates, for a few brief months in 1968, people in Czechoslovakia challenged Soviet communism and implemented a liberal government. A wave of public demonstrations swept across Europe and into the United States, where students protested against the war in Vietnam and for a more open political discourse. The second document cap-tures some of their voices while the third—a photograph of Vietnamese children burned by napalm, which appeared in newspapers worldwide—puts human faces on the tragedy of war. At the same time, a new threat to world stability emerged, as the fourth document illustrates. In 1973, Arab countries attacked Israel and united to restrict the West's access to crude oil. No one could have foreseen that the politi-cal landscape would dramatically shift in the late 1980s when the Soviet Empire disintegrated. The final document pulls back the curtain on this drama, revealing how government-sponsored state reforms set the stage not for brutal repression, as they had in Prague twenty years earlier, but rather for the end of the cold war.

1.
Josef Smrkovský
What Lies Ahead
February 9, 1968

In the immediate aftermath of World War II, the Soviet Union created a buffer of satellite states in eastern Europe, including Czechoslovakia. By 1957, when the presi-dency there passed to Antonín Novotný (1904–1975), a politician committed to

---

From Jaromir Navrátil, ed., *The Prague Spring 1968: A National Security Archive Documents Reader* (New York: Central European Press, 1998), 45–50.

communist unity with the Soviet Union, Czechoslovakia had become an authoritarian state with collectivized property and suppressed civil liberties. However, a group led by Josef Smrkovský (1911–1974) and Alexander Dubček (1921–1992) calling for more political and social openness secretly gathered strength in the highest ranks of the Czechoslovakian Communist Party. In January 1968, Dubček succeeded Novotný as the head of the party, and he initiated a broad range of reforms, including free speech, an independent press, the right to assemble, and religious freedom. The following newspaper article excerpt, written by Smrkovský a month after Dubček gained power, became the new government's most important manifesto. In it, Smrkovský emphasized a break with the "old" party, while calling for all the people of Czechoslovakia to build a "new," liberal Communist Party. The reforms were not to last. In August 1968, Soviet dominance returned after Soviet and Warsaw Pact troops invaded Czechoslovakia, killed more than one hundred people, and arrested Dubček and his allies.

ON THE CONCLUSIONS OF THE JANUARY PLENUM OF THE CPCz CC[1]

The questions that the Central Committee of the party considered and resolved in December and January have set the entire party in motion, and the public at large has been paying great attention to them. This is so even though we failed to ensure the prompt and sufficient release of information. We must put this right, and that is precisely what we are doing, since there must be no discrepancy between our statements of Leninist principles and democratic traditions, on the one hand, and our future practical activities, on the other.

We can already say that in general the last Central Committee session has met with a favorable response in politically active sections of society. As more information has become available, discussions have been gaining momentum, and this in turn has generated greater enthusiasm for political activity. Yet even sincere persons who in the past have often been disappointed still show signs of skepticism. Old practices are still embedded in the activities of many of our organs and in the minds of people working in them. This creates doubts and insecurity. People are demanding guarantees. . . .

A COMMON REPUBLIC

Still, the common interest in truly maintaining the republic's internal unity demands that we rely on proven traditions, stemming from the joint anti-fascist liberation struggle, and that we come to grips with the issue of our relations in the interest of a modern socialist community. . . . For the first time in the history of the CPCz, a Slovak communist has been placed at the helm of the party. Cde. Dubček has become first secretary as an honest and experienced communist. At

---

[1]The Central Committee of the Czechoslovakian Communist Party.

the CPCz CC session it was not at all a question of a "power seizure by the Slovaks" as we sometimes hear because of a lack of information in Czech circles.

CONFIDENCE IN THE INTELLIGENTSIA

By the same token, no one has threatened the working-class nature of the party. Those who spoke in the discussion could not be divided into intellectuals and workers, as is claimed erroneously in certain quarters. The open and passionate debate included intellectuals as well as workers and peasants, who were motivated by the same sincere concern for the cause of the republic, the interests of the people, and the improvement and consolidation of socialism. As a workers' official, which I consider myself to be, this is something I wish to emphasize. . . . The present era of the scientific-technical revolution—in which, unfortunately, we are badly lagging behind—demands more than ever that the creative forces of the working class, the peasantry, and the intelligentsia combine their efforts. . . .

Even further from the truth is the suggestion that what happened at the recent sessions of the CPCz CC was no more than a personal quarrel and a rotation of individuals. Of course, no one finds it easy to set aside his personal biases, not even at sessions of the party's Central Committee. Nevertheless, the personnel changes were in fact motivated by considerations that are of far greater urgency and importance to the party: the imperative to remove the obstacles that for some time have been obstructing the party's progressive efforts, and the need to remove everything . . . that inhibits the activation of all healthy forces in the party and among the people. . . . It is also essential to eliminate everything that has been distorting socialism, damaging people's spirits, causing pain, and depriving people of their faith and enthusiasm. This means we must do whatever is necessary to rehabilitate communists and other citizens who were unjustly sentenced in political trials so that we, as communists, can look ourselves in the face without shame. . . .

The CC session attempted to find the cause of the passivity and indifference in our country, things which we can no longer conceal. There is a conviction growing that everything we have achieved in transforming the structure of the society will facilitate—indeed will absolutely necessitate—a basic change of course. Such a change must be aimed at the democratization of the party and the society as a whole, and must be brought about consistently and honestly; it also must be backed by realistic guarantees that are understood by the majority to ensure that it will not be undermined by hedging and reservations. . . .

. . . What, then, lies ahead? We shall find no ready-made solutions. It is up to us, both Czechs and Slovaks, to launch out courageously into unexplored territory and search for a Czechoslovak road to socialism. . . .

THE EXAMPLE OF THE CENTRAL COMMITTEE

The first task is to inform the party, the whole party, of the content of the discussion at the CC session. . . . Scope must be given to a sincere and frank exchange of views from top to bottom, with priority to be given to the cogency of the arguments rather than to the power of the voice or the office. Priority also will be given to action instead of to indifference and passive submission. All truly progressive and responsible trends must be given a chance, and their chance must be given boldly and judiciously, sooner rather than later.

No mistake would be greater than to start carrying out these tasks on the basis of obsolete procedures, in the form of a one-off campaign that would, as usual, pay lip-service and then wither and die a few months later....

The whole set of tasks and problems that are accumulating today before us can best be characterized as a steady process of democratization within both the party and the state. This process is the main precondition for a truly mature and thus voluntary form of discipline, without which the party would lose its capacity to act. Although we must cure and revive the whole party organism, we cannot do so through some "back-door" method. Nor can we compensate by relying on even the most hard-working apparatus. The entire party and each of its members must be convinced that the party as a whole is responsible not only for the implementation of tasks, but also for their conceptualization—that is, for the formulation of party policy, in which each communist must participate so that they can then regard it as their very own.

No doubt, we must "clear the table"—a phrase one often hears among comrades nowadays—but this must be done peacefully and in a businesslike manner so that we can prudently return to our former work and can reaffirm and develop whatever has been successful in the past, while rectifying shortcomings and mistakes in a just and sincere manner. Let us give to the past what it deserves—truth, purity, and justice. Let us do this without further delay and without scandals and recriminations, and let us do it consistently so we can then fully concentrate on what has always been the main interest of all communists: the future....

The Position of the Party

... Let us not have any illusions. Nothing will happen on its own, without a struggle, or without some effort. Nothing will fall into our laps, and no one should expect charitable donations. There must be a sense of responsibility both "at the top" and "at the bottom."

People have emerged from various quarters who talk about a shake-up and turbulence; more such people will emerge, and the talk will continue. This eventful session, where people spoke frankly, openly, courageously, critically, and self-critically, may appear turbulent to some. But there are different types of turbulence. I think it will be a good thing if the December and January plenary sessions bring a real shake-up—a shake-up that is beneficial in releasing and reviving new and fresh forces that can move our society and our socialist republic forward into a new phase. All this is fully within the power of the party and within the power of our 1.5 million communists, who can count on the total help and support of broad masses of the population who want the same things that we do.

■ Discussion Questions

1. Why do you think Smrkovský devoted so much of his newspaper article to dispelling the skepticism, doubt, and insecurity of his readers?

2. How did the practices of the Czechoslovakian Communist Party compare to the new proposals?

3. How do you think this article was received when it was first published? What aspects do you think were most controversial then, and what aspects seem most revolutionary to you today?

2.
Student Voices of Protest
1968

College campuses were hotbeds of social activism during the 1960s, and they exploded into action with unprecedented force in the spring of 1968. The year was beset with tragedies, from the mounting number of casualties in the Vietnam War to the assassination of Robert Kennedy and the American civil rights leader Martin Luther King Jr. Students from New York to Paris to Berlin rose up in protest, particularly over racial and antiwar issues. They demonstrated, occupied buildings, shut down classes, and went on strike. The following excerpts bring these students to life in their own words, which convey not only frustration and despair but also a desire to bring about lasting change.

My most vivid memory of May '68? The new-found ability for everyone to *speak*—to speak of anything with anyone. In that month of talking during May you learnt more than in the whole of your five years of studying. It was really another world—a dream world perhaps—but that's what I'll always remember: the need and the right for everyone to speak.—René Bourrigaud, student at the École Supérieure d'Agriculture, Angers, France

People were learning through doing things themselves, learning self-confidence. It was magic, there were all these kids from nice middle-class homes who'd never done or said anything and were now suddenly speaking. It was democracy of the public space in the market place, a discourse where nobody was privileged. If anything encapsulated what we were trying to do and why, it was that. . . .—Pete Latarche, leader of the university occupation at Hull, England, 1968

From Ronald Fraser et al., *1968: A Student Generation in Revolt* (New York: Pantheon Books, 1988), 9–12.

It's a moment I shall never forget. Suddenly, spontaneously, barricades were being thrown up in the streets. People were building up the cobblestones because they wanted — many of them for the first time — to throw themselves into a collective, spontaneous activity. People were releasing all their repressed feelings, expressing them in a festive spirit. Thousands felt the need to communicate with each other, to love one another. That night has forever made me optimistic about history. Having lived through it, I can't ever say, "It will never happen." . . . — Dany Cohn-Bendit, student leader at Nanterre University, on the night of the Paris barricades, 10/11 May 1968

The unthinkable happened! Everything I had ever dreamt of since childhood, knowing that it would never happen, now began to become real. People were saying, fuck hierarchy, authority, this society with its cold rational elitist logic! Fuck all the petty bosses and the mandarins at the top! Fuck this immutable society that refuses to consider the misery, poverty, inequality and injustice it creates, that divides people according to their origins and skills! Suddenly, the French were showing they understood that they had to refuse the state's authority because it was malevolent, evil, just as I'd always thought as a child. Suddenly they realized that they had to find a new sort of solidarity. And it was happening in front of my eyes. That was what May '68 meant to me! . . . — Nelly Finkielsztejn, student at Nanterre University, Paris

My world had been very staid, very traditional, very frightened, very middle-class and respectable. And here I was doing these things that six months before I would have thought were just horrible. But I was in the midst of an enormous tide of people. There was so much constant collective reaffirmation of it. The ecstasy was stepping out of time, out of traditional personal time. The usual rules of the game in capitalist society had been set aside. It was phenomenally liberating. . . . At the same time it was a political struggle. It wasn't just Columbia. There *was* a fucking war on in Vietnam, and the civil rights movement. These were profound forces that transcend that moment. 1968 just cracked the universe open for me. And the fact of getting involved meant that never again was I going to look at something outside with the kind of reflex condemnation or fear. Yes, it was the making of me — or the unmaking. — Mike Wallace, occupation of Columbia University, New York, April 1968

We'd been brought up to believe in our hearts that America fought on the side of justice. The Second World War was very much ingrained in us, my father had volunteered. So, along with the absolute horror of the war in Vietnam, there was also a feeling of personal betrayal. I remember crying by myself late at night in my room listening to the reports of the war, the first reports of the bombing. Vietnam was the catalyst. . . . — John Levin, student leader at San Francisco State College

I was outraged, what shocked me most was that a highly developed country, the super-modern American army, should fall on these Vietnamese peasants — fall on them like the conquistadores on South America, or the white settlers on the North American Indians. In my mind's eye, I always saw those bull-necked fat pigs—like in Georg Grosz's pictures—attacking the small, child-like Vietnamese. — Michael von Engelhardt, German student

The resistance of the Vietnamese people showed that it could be done—a fight back was possible. If poor peasants could do it well why not people in Western Europe? That was the importance of Vietnam, it destroyed the myth that we just had to hold on to what we had because the whole world could be blown up if the Americans were "provoked." The Vietnamese showed that if you were attacked you fought back, and then it depended on the internal balance of power whether you won or not. . . . — Tariq Ali, a British Vietnam Solidarity Campaign leader

So we started to be political in a totally new way, making the connection between our student condition and the larger international issues. A low mark in mathematics could become the focal point of an occupation by students who linked the professor's arbitrary and authoritarian behavior to the wider issues, like Vietnam. Acting on your immediate problems made you understand better the bigger issues. If it hadn't been for that, perhaps the latter would have remained alien, you'd have said "OK, but what can *I* do?" — Agnese Gatti, student at Trento Institute of Social Sciences, Italy

Creating a confrontation with the university administration you could significantly expose the interlocking network of imperialism as it was played out on the campuses. You could prove that they were working hand-in-hand with the military and the CIA, and that ultimately, when you pushed them, they would call upon all the oppressive apparatus to defend their position from their own students. . . . — Jeff Jones, Students for a Democratic Society (SDS), New York regional organizer

Everybody was terribly young and didn't know what was going on. One had a sort of megalomaniac attitude that by sheer protest and revolt things would be changed. It was true of the music, of the hallucinogenics, of politics, it was true across the board—people threw themselves into activity without experience. The desire to do something became tremendously intense and the capacity to do it diminished by the very way one was rejecting the procedures by which things could be done. It led to all sorts of crazy ideas. —Anthony Barnett, sociology student, Leicester University, England

■ Discussion Questions

1. What were some of the students' principal targets for criticism, and why?

2. In what ways did the events of 1968 personally transform some of these students?

3. Some historians argue that the student protests of 1968 made governments less inviolable and sacred. What evidence can you find here to support this assertion?

3.
Nick Ut
Children Fleeing from a Napalm Attack in South Vietnam
June 8, 1972

Although the cold war dominated the European landscape during the 1950s and 1960s, it also loomed large in Asia. Responding to years of resistance against French colonial rule led by the founder of the Indochinese Communist Party, Ho Chi Minh (1890–1969), the Geneva Convention divided Vietnam into North and South in 1954. Ho Chi Minh and his followers were ordered to retreat to the North. U.S. leaders feared that the communist presence there would spread elsewhere in the region, and gradually their commitment to a noncommunist South Vietnam escalated to all-out war. By 1966, the United States had more than a half million soldiers in South Vietnam. One of the most compelling images of the Vietnam War is that of children running down a dusty road, screaming in terror and pain after a napalm attack on their village. The photograph, taken by Associated Press photographer Nick Ut, appeared on the front pages of newspapers around the world and helped turn public opinion against the war. Although South Vietnamese aircraft executed the attack, it had been ordered by the U.S. Army — a fact that shocked much of the American public. In the years following its publication, the North Vietnamese government used the photograph as evidence of American atrocities.

From Associated Press Photo Archive. AP Photo/Nick Ut.

■ Discussion Questions

1. Why do you think this image had such a powerful impact on the public at the time?

2. What does the image of the young girl in the center of the photograph, with her clothes having been burned off and her skin on fire, reveal about the technology of war and its human costs?

3. How might the photograph's effect on U.S. public opinion have been different had the perpetrators of the napalm attack been the North Vietnamese army rather than the South Vietnamese and the Americans?

4. What do you think the political impact of this photograph was in North Vietnam after its publication?

4.
U.S. Embassy, Saudi Arabia
Saudi Ban on Oil Shipments to the United States
October 23, 1973

In a show of pan-Arabian unity and nationalism, military forces from Egypt and Syria invaded Israel on October 6, 1973. The United States quickly offered extensive financial aid to Israel. As punishment for U.S. support of Israel, the Organization of the Petroleum Exporting Countries (OPEC) banned its members from exporting oil to the United States and raised the price of oil for the U.S. allies in western Europe. Overnight, the price of a barrel rose from $3 to $5.11, and by January 1974, it had risen to $11.65, resulting in widespread fuel shortages across the West. The actions of OPEC, which were infused with Arab nationalism, shocked citizens in Europe and the United States, who were not accustomed to being at the mercy of nations they once dominated. In this confidential cable, which was only declassified in September 2003, an unidentified writer from the U.S. Embassy in Saudi Arabia offers an inside view of the Saudis' strategy in their decision to participate in the OPEC ban on exporting oil to the United States.

23 OCTOBER 1973
FROM: AMERICAN EMBASSY IN SAUDI ARABIA
TO: THE SECRETARY OF STATE, WASHINGTON D.C.
SUBJECT: SAUDI BAN ON OIL SHIPMENTS TO U.S.

SUMMARY: SAUDI DECISION TO CUT OFF OIL SHIPMENTS TO U.S. ATTRIBUTABLE TO KING'S OWN DECISION: KING ANGRY AT AN-

From U.S. Embassy in Saudi Arabia, Cable 4663 to U.S. State Department, "Saudi Ban on Oil Shipments to U.S." (Washington, DC: National Security Archive, 1973).

NOUNCEMENT OF LARGE U.S. MILITARY GRANT PROGRAMS TO ISRAEL AND PROBABLY FELT THAT ANY LESSER RESPONSE WOULD LEAVE SAUDI ARABIA UNCOMFORTABLY ISOLATED IN ARAB WORLD. U.S. MISSION CONTACTS WITH HIGH-LEVEL SAG [the Government of Saudi Arabia] OFFICIALS, HOWEVER, INDICATE SAG WISHES TO MINIMIZE DAMAGE THAT PRESENT CRISIS MAY DO TO U.S.-SAG RELATIONS. JOINT U.S.-USSR RESOLUTION IN SECURITY COUNCIL, POTENTIALLY A RADICALLY POSITIVE STEP, BUT IF IT DOES NOT SUCCEED, SAG MAY FEEL COMPELLED TO INCREASE PRESSURE ON U.S. INTERESTS IN MILITARY, COMMERCIAL, ENERGY AND FINANCIAL AREAS. EMBASSY IS STRESSING WITH SAG NEED THAT CHANNELS OF COMMUNICATION REMAIN OPEN, AND THAT EACH SIDE GIVE [each] OTHER MAXIMUM ADVANCE NOTICE OF ANY MEASURES IT IS CONTEMPLATING. END SUMMARY.

1. THERE IS LITTLE DOUBT THAT SAG DECISION TO BAN PETROLEUM EXPORTS TO U.S. STEMMED FROM KING FAISAL HIMSELF. DISCUSSION BETWEEN HIGH-RANKING SAG OFFICIALS AND AMBASSADOR IN 24 HOURS PREVIOUS HAD NOT INDICATED SAG ON VERGE OF TAKING SUCH BIG STEP.

2. SOURCES IN ROYAL DIWAN OCT 21 HAVE CONFIRMED TO EMBASSY THAT DECISION [was] TAKEN BY KING, AND WAS PRINCIPALLY MOTIVATED BY U.S. PROPOSAL TO PROVIDE ISRAEL WITH 2.2 MILLION DOLLARS OF GRANT [money for] MILITARY AID. WAS TOLD BY CHIEF OF ROYAL DIWAN, AHMAD ABDUL WAHAB (A WELL-ADJUSTED PRO-AMERICAN FIGURE) THAT KING WAS AS FURIOUS AS HE HAD EVER SEEN HIM AND THAT HE TOOK PARTICULAR UMBRAGE AT WHAT HE CONSIDERED TO BE DIFFERENCE BETWEEN REASSURING TONE OF VARIOUS COMMUNICATIONS HE HAD RECEIVED FROM USG [the United States Government] AND U.S. ANNOUNCEMENT OF "INCREDIBLE" AMOUNT OF AID TO GOI [the Government of Israel]. KING'S SUBSEQUENT CALL FOR JIHAD CAN ALSO BE ASCRIBED TO KING'S DISPLEASURE. KING'S MOOD EMPHATICALLY REFLECTED ALSO BY ABLE, NATIONALIST MINISTER HISHAM NAZER, HEAD OF CENTRAL PLANNING ORGANIZATION.

3. WE SHOULD NOT, HOWEVER, OVERSTRESS THE CAUSATIVE EFFECT OF PURE EMOTION IN KING'S DECISION TO CUT BACK OIL SHIPMENTS TO U.S. A NUMBER OF ARAB COUNTRIES HAD ALREADY TAKEN STEP OF BANNING SUCH SHIPMENTS, AND [Sheikh Zaki] YAMANI [the official in charge of Saudi oil policy in 1973] HAD INFORMED AMBASSADOR THAT OTHERS WOULD PROBABLY FOLLOW. AS IMPACT OF U.S. AID DECISION MADE ITSELF FELT IN ARAB WORLD, KING MAY HAVE FELT THAT SAG WOULD OCCUPY EXPOSED SALIENT IF IT—

ALONE AMONG ARAB OIL PRODUCERS—CONTINUED TO PROVIDE OIL TO U.S.

4. EMBASSY CONTACTS ELSEWHERE IN SAG, MOREOVER, TEND TO CONFIRM OUR ASSESSMENT THAT SAG WISHES [to] MINIMIZE DAMAGE THAT PRESENT CRISIS COULD CAUSE TO U.S.-SAUDI RELATIONS. . . . DURING MEETING OCT 21 BETWEEN CHIEF OF U.S. MILITARY TRAINING MISSION (USMTM), GENERAL HILL, DEPUTY MUDA, AND KING'S BROTHER PRINCE TURKI, PRINCE STATED "WE HAVE HAD TO TAKE CERTAIN POLITICAL DECISIONS DURING THE WAR JUST AS YOU HAVE, BUT THAT MUST BE KEPT ENTIRELY SEPA-RATE FROM RELATIONSHIPS BETWEEN MUDA AND USMTM." PRINCE IN SOMBER MOOD, BUT WAS AT ALL TIMES COURTEOUS AND FRIENDLY TO GENERAL HILL AND HIS STAFF. . . .

6. SAG ACTION COULD ALSO DELIVER A SETBACK TO IMPORTANT U.S. COMMERCIAL AND MILITARY SALES: SAG HAS GROWN TO BE ONE OF LARGEST MARKETS FOR AMERICAN PRODUCTS . . . WITH SALES RUN-NING AT MORE THAN A THIRD OF A BILLION DOLLARS THIS YEAR. OUR MILITARY SALES PROGRAMS MOREOVER HAVE . . . IN THE PAST THREE YEARS EXCEEDED 500 MILLION DOLLARS, AND THERE ARE GOOD PROSPECTS FOR CASH SALES OF A SIMILAR ORDER TO BE CON-CLUDED WITHIN THE NEXT TWO YEARS. WE SHOULD REMEMBER THAT EUROPE, PARTICULARLY FRENCH AND BRITISH SOURCES, ARE MORE THAN PREPARED TO PICK UP THE FALLOUT FROM THE AMER-ICAN DILEMMA IN THE MIDDLE EAST CONFLICT.

7. IN THE MEANTIME, AMBASSADOR HAS PASSED WORD TO CHIEF OF ROYAL DIWAN THAT IT IS ESSENTIAL FOR CHANNELS OF COMMUNI-CATION BETWEEN HIM AND SAG TO REMAIN OPEN AT ALL TIMES. . . .

8. FINALLY, WITH REGARD TO SAUDI ACTIONS AGAINST U.S. OIL AND OTHER INTERESTS, WE SHOULD AVOID ACRIMONIOUS COMMENTS, SINCE THESE TEND TO KEEP AN UNHELPFUL DIALOGUE GOING.

■ Discussion Questions

1. What do you think the writer's main concern was in sending this cable to the U.S. State Department?

2. How would you characterize the writer's attitude toward Saudi Arabian govern-ment officials?

3. How were European countries directly affected by U.S. policies toward Saudi Arabia and other OPEC countries? Where do you see direct references to this in the telegram?

5.
Glasnost *and the Soviet Press*
1988

When Mikhail Gorbachev (b. 1931) became the general secretary of the Soviet Communist Party in 1985, the nation's economy was in ruins, and people struggled to meet even their most basic needs. Gorbachev implemented revolutionary policies of economic restructuring (perestroika) and "openness" (glasnost) to confront the crisis. The two articles excerpted here illuminate the crucial role of the Soviet press in this process as a forum for public debate. Never before had Soviet citizens experienced such freedom of speech and expression. Written by Nina Andreyeva, the first article appeared as a letter to the editor on the front page of the prestigious newspaper Sovetskaya Rossiya *in March 1988. Politically conservative, Andreyeva attacked Gorbachev's reforms as a violation of socialist ideology. Gorbachev and his supporters countered her assault in an article of their own, published three weeks later in* Pravda, *defending* glasnost *and* perestroika *as the path to a better future.*

POLEMICS: I CANNOT WAIVE PRINCIPLES

Nina Andreyeva

I decided to write this letter after lengthy deliberation. I am a chemist, and I lecture at Leningrad's Lensovet Technology Institute. Like many others, I also look after a student group. Students nowadays, following the period of social apathy and intellectual dependence, are gradually becoming charged with the energy of revolutionary changes. Naturally, discussions develop about the ways of restructuring and its economic and ideological aspects. *Glasnost,* openness, the disappearance of zones where criticism is taboo, and the emotional heat of mass consciousness (especially among young people) often result in the raising of problems that are, to a greater or lesser extent, "prompted" either by Western radio voices or by those of our compatriots who are shaky in their conceptions of the essence of socialism. And what a variety of topics that are being discussed! A multiparty system, freedom of religious propaganda, emigration to live abroad, the right to broad discussion of sexual problems in the press, the need to decentralize the leadership of culture, abolition of compulsory military service. There are particularly numerous arguments among students about the country's past. . . .

In the numerous discussions now taking place on literally all questions of the social sciences, as a college lecturer I am primarily interested in the questions that have a direct effect on young people's ideological and political education, their moral health, and their social optimism. Conversing with students and deliberating with them on controversial problems, I cannot help concluding that our coun-

From Isaac J. Tarasulo, ed., *Gorbachev and Glasnost: Viewpoints from the Soviet Press* (Wilmington: SR Books, 1989), 277–78, 281–85, 290–95, 299–302.

try has accumulated quite a few anomalies and one-sided interpretations that clearly need to be corrected. I would like to dwell on some of them in particular.

Take, for example the question of Joseph Stalin's place in our country's history. The whole obsession with critical attacks is linked with his name, and in my opinion this obsession centers not so much on the historical individual himself as on the entire highly complex epoch of transition, an epoch linked with unprecedented feats by a whole generation of Soviet people who are today gradually withdrawing from active participation in political and social work. The industrialization, collectivization, and cultural revolution which brought our country to the ranks of the great world powers are being forcibly squeezed into the "personality cult" formula. All of this is being questioned. Matters have gone so far that persistent demands for "repentance" are being made of "Stalinists" (and this category can be taken to include anyone you like). There is rapturous praise for novels and movies that lynch the epoch of "storms and onslaught," which is presented as a "tragedy of the peoples." . . .

I support the party's call to uphold the honor and dignity of the trailblazers of socialism. I think that these are the party-class positions from which we must assess the historical role of all leaders of the party and the country, including Stalin. In this case, matters cannot be reduced to their "court" aspect or to abstract moralizing by persons far removed both from those stormy times and from the people who had to live and work in those times, and to work in such a fashion as to still be an inspiring example for us today. . . .

I think that, no matter how controversial and complex a figure in Soviet history Stalin may be, his genuine role in the building and defense of socialism will sooner or later be given an objective and unambiguous assessment. Of course, unambiguous does not mean an assessment that is one-sided, that whitewashes, or that eclectically sums up contradictory phenomena making it possible subjectively (albeit with slight reservations) "to forgive or not forgive," "to reject or retain." Unambiguous means primarily a specific historical assessment detached from short-term considerations which would demonstrate—according to historical results!—the dialectics of the correlation between the individual's actions and the basic laws governing society's development. In our country these laws were also linked with the answer to the question "Who will defeat whom?" in its domestic as well as international aspects. If we are to adhere to the Marxist-Leninist methodology of historical analysis then, in Mikhail Gorbachev's words, we must primarily and vividly show how the millions of people lived, how they worked, and what they believed in, as well as the coupling of victories and failures, discoveries and errors, the bright and the tragic, the revolutionary enthusiasm of the masses and the violations of socialist legality and even crimes at times. . . .

It seems to me that the question of the role and position of socialist ideology is extremely acute today. The authors of timeserving articles circulating under the guise of moral and spiritual "cleansing" erode the dividing lines and criteria of scientific ideology, manipulate *glasnost,* and foster nonsocialist pluralism, which applies the brakes on *perestroika* in the public conscience. This has a particularly painful effect on young people which, I repeat, is clearly sensed by us, the college lecturers, schoolteachers, and all who have to deal with young people's problems. As Mikhail Gorbachev said at the CPSU Central Committee February *plenum,* "our actions in the spiritual sphere—and maybe primarily and precisely there— must be guided by our Marxist-Leninist principles. Principles comrades, must not be compromised on any pretext whatever."

This is what we stand for now, and this is what we will continue to stand for. Principles were not given to us as a gift, we have fought for them at crucial turning points in the fatherland's history.

PRINCIPLES OF PERESTROIKA: THE REVOLUTIONARY NATURE OF THINKING AND ACTING

Pravda Editorial

The CPSU Central Committee February *plenum* solidified the party's new tasks in restructuring all spheres of life at the present stage. The *plenum* speech of Mikhail Gorbachev, general secretary of the CPSU Central Committee ("Revolutionary *Perestroika* Requires Ideology of Renewal") made a clear analysis of today's problems and set forth a program of ideological support for *perestroika.* People want to be better aware of the nature of the changes that have begun in society, to see the essence and significance of the proposed solutions, and to know what is meant by the new quality of society we want to achieve. The struggle for *perestroika* is being waged both in production and in the spiritual sphere. And even though this struggle does not take the form of class antagonisms, it is proceeding sharply. The emergence of something new always excites attitudes toward and judgments about the new thing.

The debate itself and its nature and thrust attest to the democratization of our society. The diversity of judgments, assessments, and positions is one of the most important signs of the times and attests to the socialist pluralism of opinions which really exists now.

But it is impossible not to notice one very specific dimension of this debate. It occasionally declares itself not in a desire to interpret what is happening and to investigate it nor in a wish to advance the cause but, on the contrary, in attempts to slow it down by shouting the usual incantations: "They are betraying ideals!" "Abandoning principles!" "Undermining foundations!" . . .

The long article "I Cannot Waive Principles" [pp. 220–22] that appeared in the newspaper *Sovetskaya Rossiya* on March 13 was a reflection of such feelings. . . .

Whether the author wanted it or not, primarily the article artificially sets off certain categories of Soviet people against one another. And this at precisely the moment when the unity of creative forces, despite all the shades of opinion, is more necessary than ever and when such unity is the prime requirement of *perestroika* and an absolute necessity simply for normal life, work, and the constructive renewal of society. Herein resides the fundamental feature of *perestroika,* which is designed to unite the maximum number of like-minded people in the struggle against phenomena impeding our life. Precisely and principally against all of these phenomena, not only or simply against certain incorrigible proponents of bureaucracy, corruption, abuse, and so forth.

In addition, the article is unconstructive. In an extensive, pretentiously titled article essentially no space was found to work out a single problem of *perestroika*. Whatever it discussed — *glasnost*, openness, the disappearance of areas free from criticism, youth — these processes and *perestroika* itself were linked only with difficulties and adverse consequences. . . .

There are, in point of fact, two basic theses running throughout the article: Why all of this *perestroika*, and haven't we gone too far with democratization and *glasnost?* The article urges us to amend and adjust *perestroika;* otherwise, it is alleged, "people in authority" will have to rescue socialism.

It is evident that not everyone has realized clearly yet the dramatic nature of the situation the country found itself in by April 1985, a situation which today we rightfully describe as precrisis. It is evident that not everyone is fully aware yet that administrative edict methods are totally obsolete. It is time that anyone who still places hopes in these methods or in their modification understands that all of this has already been tried, tried repeatedly, and it has failed to produce the desired results. Any ideas about the simplicity and effectiveness of these methods are nothing but illusions without any historical justification.

So, how is socialism to be "saved" today?

Should authoritarian methods, the practice of blind obedience, and the stifling of initiative be retained? Should we retain the system in which bureaucratism, lack of control, corruption, bribery, and petty bourgeois degeneration flourished lavishly?

Or should we revert to Leninist principles, whose essence is democratism, social justice, economic accountability, and respect for the individual's honor, life, and dignity? Do we have the right, in the face of the real difficulties and unsatisfied needs of the people, to adhere to the same old approaches that prevailed in the 1930s and 1940s? Has not the time come to clearly differentiate between the essence of socialism and the historically restricted forms of its implementation? Has not the time come for a scientifically critical investigation of our history, primarily in order to change the world in which we live and to learn harsh lessons for the future?

Almost half of the article is devoted to an assessment of our distant and recent history. The last few years have provided graphic proof of the growing interest in the past shown by the broadest strata of the population. The principles of scientific historicism and truth are increasingly the basis on which the people's historical awareness is taking shape. At the same time, there are instances of people playing on the idea of patriotism. Those who loudly scream about alleged "internal threats" to socialism, those who join certain political extremists and look everywhere for internal enemies, "counterrevolutionary nations," and so on, those are not patriots. The patriots are those who act in the country's interests and for the people's benefit, without fearing any difficulties. We do not need contemplative or verbal patriotism, we need creative patriotism. Not nostalgic and backward-looking patriotism, but the patriotism of socialist transformations. Patriotism based not only on love for the area of your birth, but also imbued with pride in the accomplishments of the great motherland of socialism.

Past experience is vitally necessary for the present, for solving the tasks of *perestroika*. Life's demand — "More socialism!" — makes it incumbent upon us to investigate what we did yesterday and how we did it, what has to be rejected and what has to be retained. Which principles and values ought to be considered really socialist? And if today we are taking a critical look at our history, we are doing so only because we want a better and more complete idea of our path into the future. . . .

The best teacher of *perestroika* — the one to whom we should constantly listen — is life, and life is dialectical. We should constantly remember the words of [Friedrich] Engels to the effect that nothing has been unconditionally established once and for all as sacrosanct. It is this continual motion and the constant renewal of nature, society, and our thinking that is the point of departure for and the initial, most cardinal principle in our thinking.

Let us return to the question: What has been done already? How are the party's course and the decisions of the 27th Party Congress and Central Committee plenums being implemented? What positive changes are taking place in people's lives?

We have really got down to tackling the most pressing, highest priority problems: housing, food, and the supply of goods and services to the population. A turn toward accelerated development of the social sphere has begun. Concrete decisions about restructuring education and health care have been adopted. Radical economic reform, our main lever for implementing large-scale transformations, is being put into practice. "That is the main political result of the last three years," M. Gorbachev said at the 4th All-Union Congress of *kolkhoz*[1] members.

The voice of the intelligentsia and of all the working people has begun to make itself heard powerfully and strongly in society's spiritual life. This is one of the first gains accomplished by *perestroika*. Democratism is impossible without freedom of thought and speech, without the open, broad clash of opinions, without keeping a critical eye on our life. . . .

There are no prohibited topics today. Journals, publishing houses, and studios decide for themselves what to publish. But the appearance of the article "I Cannot Waive Principles" is part of an attempt little by little to revise party decisions. It has been said repeatedly at meetings in the party Central Committee that the Soviet press is not a private concern, that Communists writing for the press and editors should have a sense of responsibility for articles and publications. In this case the newspaper *Sovetskaya Rossiya*, which, let us be frank, has done much for *perestroika*, departed from this principle.

Debates, discussions, and polemics are, of course, necessary. They lie in store for us in our future, too. There are also many pitfalls in store for us, traps laid by the past. We must all work together to clear these traps from our path. We need

---

[1] **kolkhoz:** Soviet agricultural cooperatives. [Ed.]

disputes that help to advance *perestroika* and lead to the consolidation of forces, to cohesion around *perestroika,* and not to disunity. . . .

More light. More initiative. More responsibility. A more rapid mastery of the full profundity of the Marxist-Leninist concept of *perestroika,* of the new political thinking. We can and must revive the Leninist practice of the socialist society — the most humane, the most just. We will firmly and steadily follow the revolutionary principles of *perestroika:* more *glasnost,* more democracy, more socialism.

■ Discussion Questions

1. Why is Andreyeva so critical of Gorbachev's reforms?

2. What arguments do Gorbachev's supporters use to counter her criticisms?

3. According to the *Pravda* article, what are the fundamental features of *glasnost* and *perestroika?*

4. In what ways do these two articles reflect different understandings of Soviet history and its role in shaping the country's future?

■ Comparative Questions _____

1. Based on the first two documents, how did the events of the 1960s turn Western society upside down, and why?

2. How do you think the second, third, and fourth documents represent a broader debate concerning Western dominance over much of the world, which had developed out of a critique of the Vietnam War?

3. How did disagreements over ideology and generational conflict drive the protests of the 1960s and 1970s?

4. What similarities do you see between the message and the medium of the Prague manifesto and those of Gorbachev two decades later? Why did Smrkovský's reforms fail and Gorbachev's succeed?

24

The New Globalism: Opportunities and Dilemmas, 1989 to the Present

A FTER DECADES OF SUPERPOWER rivalry, the cold war virtually came to a halt in 1989 when the Soviet Empire disintegrated. New countries emerged from the Soviet shadow to declare their independence, which radically changed the political map of eastern Europe. However, as the first three documents show, the transition from one-party rule to democracy was not achieved without tensions and complications in Europe and elsewhere in the world. At the same time, the end of superpower rivalry opened the door for a more closely connected, globalized world with its own challenges and opportunities, particularly as people became increasingly aware of industrialization's toll on the environment and human health. The fourth document highlights one enduring response to this challenge, environmental activism. The September 11, 2001, terrorist attacks on the United States starkly revealed how different the world had become since the end of the cold war. The final document warns of new conflicts that may arise from using rigid frameworks to define the post–cold war age.

1.
Zlata Filipović
A Child's Life in Sarajevo
October 6, 1991–June 29, 1992

The end of communist rule in the multiethnic state of Yugoslavia unleashed turmoil and violence unseen in Europe since World War II. Following the rise to power of na-

From Zlata Filipović, *Zlata's Diary: A Child's Life in Sarajevo*. Trans. Christina Pribichevich-Zorić (New York: Penguin, 1995), 3, 6, 7, 9–11, 18, 26–35, 41–43, 46–48, 51–58, 65–66.

tionalist leaders during the 1980s, the country fell into chaos when four of the six republics declared independence beginning in 1991. Serbian president Slobodan Milosevic opposed the independence movements and supported the military efforts of Serb nationals in the breakaway republics of Bosnia and Croatia. One of the deadliest conflicts occurred in a three-way war in Bosnia among Serb, Croat, and Muslim factions. Beginning in 1992, the Bosnian capital of Sarajevo was the focus of a four-year siege by Serb forces in which 12,000 people were killed, including 1,600 children. Zlata Filipović was eleven years old when fighting broke out in Sarajevo. The following entries recorded in her diary during that time provide a child's perspective of life in a war-torn city. In 1993, Zlata and her family were allowed to leave Sarajevo for Paris after the publication of her diary gained her worldwide notoriety.

Sunday, October 6, 1991

I'm watching the American Top 20 on MTV. I don't remember a thing, who's in what place.

I feel great because I've just eaten a "Four Seasons" PIZZA with ham, cheese, ketchup and mushrooms. It was yummy. Daddy bought it for me at Galija's (the pizzeria around the corner). Maybe that's why I didn't remember who took what place — I was too busy enjoying my pizza.

I've finished studying and tomorrow I can go to school BRAVELY, without being afraid of getting a bad grade. I deserve a good grade because I studied all weekend and I didn't even go out to play with my friends in the park. The weather is nice and we usually play "monkey in the middle," talk and go for walks. Basically, we have fun.

Wednesday, October 23, 1991

There's a real war going on in Dubrovnik.[1] It's being badly shelled. People are in shelters, they have no water, no electricity, the phones aren't working. We see horrible pictures on TV. Mommy and Daddy are worried. Is it possible that such a beautiful town is being destroyed? Mommy and Daddy are especially fond of it. It was there, in the Ducal Palace, that they picked up a quill and wrote "YES" to spending the rest of their lives together. Mommy says it's the most beautiful town in the world and it mustn't be destroyed!!!

We're worried about Srdjan (my parents' best friend who lives and works in Dubrovnik, but his family is still in Sarajevo) and his parents. How are they coping with everything that's happening over there? Are they alive? We're trying to talk to him with the help of a ham radio, but it's not working. Bokica (Srdjan's wife) is miserable. Every attempt to get some news ends in failure. Dubrovnik is cut off from the rest of the world.

---

[1]Croation city on Dalmation coast less than 80 miles from Sarajevo.

Thursday, November 14, 1991

Daddy isn't going to the reserves anymore. Hooray!!! . . . Now we'll be able to go to Jahorina and Crnotina on weekends. But, gasoline has been a problem lately. Daddy often spends hours waiting in the line for gasoline, he goes outside of town to get it, and often comes home without getting the job done.

Together with Bokica we sent a package to Srdjan. We learned through the ham radio that they have nothing to eat. They have no water, Srdjan swapped a bottle of whisky for five liters of water. Eggs, apples, potatoes—the people of Dubrovnik can only dream about them.

War in Croatia, war in Dubrovnik, some reservists in Herzegovina. Mommy and Daddy keep watching the news on TV. They're worried. Mommy often cries looking at the terrible pictures on TV. They talk mostly politics with their friends. What is politics? I haven't got a clue. And I'm not really interested. I just finished watching *Midnight Caller* on TV.

Thursday, December 19, 1991

Sarajevo has launched an appeal (on TV) called "Sarajevo Helps the Children of Dubrovnik." In Srdjan's parcel we put a nice New Year's present for him to give to some child in Dubrovnik. We made up a package of sweets, chocolates, vitamins, a doll, some books, pencils, notebooks—whatever we could manage, hoping to bring happiness to some innocent child who has been stopped by the war from going to school, playing, eating what he wants and enjoying his childhood. It's a nice little package. I hope it makes whoever gets it happy. That's the idea. I also wrote a New Year's card saying I hoped the war in Dubrovnik would end soon.

Thursday, March 5, 1992

Oh, God! Things are heating up in Sarajevo. On Sunday (March 1), a small group of armed civilians (as they say on TV) killed a Serbian wedding guest and wounded the priest. On March 2 (Monday) the whole city was full of barricades. There were "1,000" barricades. We didn't even have bread. At 6:00 people got fed up and went out into the streets. The procession set out from the cathedral. It went past the parliament building and made its way through the entire city. Several people were wounded at the Marshal Tito army barracks. People sang and cried "Bosnia, Bosnia," "Sarajevo, Sarajevo," "We'll live together" and "Come outside." Zdravko Grebo[2] said on the radio that history was in the making.

At about 8:00 we heard the bell of a streetcar. The first streetcar had passed through town and life got back to normal. People poured out into the streets hoping that nothing like that would ever happen again. We joined the peace procession. When we got home we had a quiet night's sleep. The next day everything was the same as before. Classes, music school. . . . But in the evening, the news came

---

[2]President of the Soros Foundation in Sarajevo and editor-in-chief of ZID, the independent radio station.

that 3,000 Chetniks [Serbian nationalists] were coming from Pale [resort outside of Sarajevo] to attack Sarajevo, and first, Baščaršija [the old part of town]. Melica said that new barricades had been put up in front of her house and that they wouldn't be sleeping at home tonight. They went to Uncle Nedjad's place. Later there was a real fight on YUTEL TV. Radovan Karadžič [Bosnian Serb leader] and Alija Izetbegovič [President of Bosnia-Herzegovina] phoned in and started arguing. Then Goran Milič[3] got angry and made them agree to meet with some General Kukanjac.[4] Milič is great!!! Bravo!

On March 4 (Wednesday) the barricades were removed, the "kids" [a popular term for politicians] had come to some agreement. Great?!

That day our art teacher brought in a picture for our class-mistress (for March 8, Women's Day). We gave her the present, but she told us to go home. Something was wrong again! There was a panic. The girls started screaming and the boys quietly blinked their eyes. Daddy came home from work early that day too. But everything turned out OK. It's all too much!

Monday, March 30, 1992

Hey, Diary! You know what I think? Since Anne Frank called her diary Kitty, maybe I could give you a name too. What about:

ASFALTINA   PIDŽAMETA
ŠEFIKA   HIKMETA
ŠEVALA   MIMMY

or something else???

I'm thinking, thinking . . .
I've decided! I'm going to call you
MIMMY
All right, then, let's start.

Dear Mimmy,

It's almost half-term. We're all studying for our tests. Tomorrow we're supposed to go to a classical music concert at the Skenderija Hall. Our teacher says we shouldn't go because there will be 10,000 people, pardon me, children, there, and somebody might take us as hostages or plant a bomb in the concert hall. Mommy says I shouldn't go. So I won't.

Hey! You know who won the Yugovision Song Contest?! EXTRA NENA!!!???

I'm afraid to say this next thing. Melica says she heard at the hairdresser's that on Saturday, April 4, 1992, there's going to be BOOM — BOOM, BANG — BANG, CRASH Sarajevo. Translation: they're going to bomb Sarajevo.

Love,
Zlata

---

[3]A well-known newscaster on television; one of the founders of the YUTEL television station before the war.
[4]General of the then Yugoslav Army, who was in Sarajevo when the war broke out.

Sunday, April 5, 1992

Dear Mimmy,

I'm trying to concentrate so I can do my homework (reading), but I simply can't. Something is going on in town. You can hear gunfire from the hills. Columns of people are spreading out from Dobrinja. They're trying to stop something, but they themselves don't know what. You can simply feel that something is coming, something very bad. On TV I see people in front of the B-H parliament building. The radio keeps playing the same song: "Sarajevo, My Love." That's all very nice, but my stomach is still in knots and I can't concentrate on my homework anymore.

Mimmy, I'm afraid of WAR!!!

Zlata

Thursday, April 9, 1992

Dear Mimmy,

I'm not going to school. All the schools in Sarajevo are closed. There's danger hiding in these hills above Sarajevo. But I think things are slowly calming down. The heavy shelling and explosions have stopped. There's occasional gunfire, but it quickly falls silent. Mommy and Daddy aren't going to work. They're buying food in huge quantities. Just in case, I guess. God forbid!

Still, it's very tense. Mommy is beside herself, Daddy tries to calm her down. Mommy has long conversations on the phone. She calls, other people call, the phone is in constant use.

Zlata

Tuesday, April 14, 1992

Dear Mimmy,

People are leaving Sarajevo. The airport, train and bus stations are packed. I saw sad pictures on TV of people parting. Families, friends separating. Some are leaving, others staying. It's so sad. Why? These people and children aren't guilty of anything. Keka and Braco came early this morning. They're in the kitchen with Mommy and Daddy, whispering. Keka and Mommy are crying. I don't think they know what to do—whether to stay or to go. Neither way is good.

Zlata

Saturday, May 2, 1992

Dear Mimmy,

Today was truly, absolutely the worst day ever in Sarajevo. The shooting started around noon. Mommy and I moved into the hall. Daddy was in his office, under our apartment, at the time. We told him on the intercom to run quickly to the downstairs lobby where we'd meet him. We brought Cicko [Zlata's canary] with us. The gunfire was getting worse, and we couldn't get over the wall to the Bobars', so we ran down to our own cellar.

The cellar is ugly, dark, smelly. Mommy, who's terrified of mice, had two fears to cope with. The three of us were in the same corner as the other day. We listened to the pounding shells, the shooting, the thundering noise overhead. We even heard planes. At one moment I realized that this awful cellar was the only place that could save our lives. Suddenly, it started to look almost warm and nice. It was the only way we could defend ourselves against all this terrible shooting. We heard glass shattering in our street. Horrible. I put my fingers in my ears to block out the terrible sounds. I was worried about Cicko. We had left him behind in the lobby. Would he catch cold there? Would something hit him? I was terribly hungry and thirsty. We had left our half-cooked lunch in the kitchen.

When the shooting died down a bit, Daddy ran over to our apartment and brought us back some sandwiches. He said he could smell something burning and that the phones weren't working. He brought our TV set down to the cellar. That's when we learned that the main post office (near us) was on fire and that they had kidnapped our President. At around 8:00 we went back up to our apartment. Almost every window in our street was broken. Ours were all right, thank God. I saw the post office in flames. A terrible sight. The fire-fighters battled with the raging fire. Daddy took a few photos of the post office being devoured by the flames. He said they wouldn't come out because I had been fiddling with something on the camera. I was sorry. The whole apartment smelled of the burning fire. God, and I used to pass by there every day. It had just been done up. It was huge and beautiful, and now it was being swallowed up by the flames. It was disappearing. That's what this neighborhood of mine looks like, my Mimmy. I wonder what it's like in other parts of town? I heard on the radio that it was awful around the Eternal Flame. The place is knee-deep in glass. We're worried about Grandma and Granddad. They live there. Tomorrow, if we can go out, we'll see how they are. A terrible day.

This has been the worst, most awful day in my eleven-year-old life. I hope it will be the only one. Mommy and Daddy are very edgy. I have to go to bed.
Ciao!
Zlata

Wednesday, May 13, 1992
Dear Mimmy,
Life goes on. The past is cruel, and that's exactly why we should forget it.

The present is cruel too and I can't forget it. There's no joking with war. My present reality is the cellar, fear, shells, fire.

Terrible shooting broke out the night before last. We were afraid that we might be hit by shrapnel or a bullet, so we ran over to the Bobars'. We spent all of that night, the next day and the next night in the cellar and in Nedo's apartment. (Nedo is a refugee from Grbavica. He left his parents and came here to his sister's empty apartment.) We saw terrible scenes on TV. The town in ruins, burning, people and children being killed. It's unbelievable.

The phones aren't working, we haven't been able to find out anything about Grandma and Granddad, Melica, how people in other parts of town are doing. On TV we saw the place where Mommy works, Vodoprivreda, all in flames. It's on the aggressor's side of town (Grbavica). Mommy cried. She's depressed. All her years of work and effort — up in flames. It's really horrible. All around Vodoprivreda

there were cars burning, people dying, and nobody could help them. God, why is this happening?
I'M SO MAD I WANT TO SCREAM AND BREAK EVERYTHING!
Your Zlata

Sunday, May 17, 1992

Dear Mimmy,
It's now definite: there's no more school. The war has interrupted our lessons, closed down the schools, sent children to cellars instead of classrooms. They'll give us the grades we got at the end of last term. So I'll get a report card saying I've finished fifth grade.
Ciao!
Zlata

Saturday, May 23, 1992

Dear Mimmy,
I'm not writing to you about me anymore. I'm writing to you about war, death, injuries, shells, sadness and sorrow. Almost all my friends have left. Even if they were here, who knows whether we'd be able to see one another. The phones aren't working, we couldn't even talk to one another. Vanja and Andrej have gone to join Srdjan in Dubrovnik. The war has stopped there. They're lucky. I was so unhappy because of that war in Dubrovnik. I never dreamed it would move to Sarajevo.

Wednesday, May 27, 1992

Dear Mimmy,
SLAUGHTER! MASSACRE! HORROR! CRIME! BLOOD! SCREAMS! TEARS! DESPAIR!
That's what Vaso Miškin Street looks like today. Two shells exploded in the street and one in the market. Mommy was nearby at the time. She ran to Grandma and Granddad's. Daddy and I were beside ourselves because she hadn't come home. I saw some of it on TV but I still can't believe what I actually saw. It's unbelievable. I've got a lump in my throat and a knot in my tummy. HORRIBLE. They're taking the wounded to the hospital. It's a madhouse. We kept going to the window hoping to see Mommy, but she wasn't back. They released a list of the dead and wounded. Daddy and I were tearing our hair out. We didn't know what had happened to her. Was she alive? At 4:00, Daddy decided to go and check the hospital. He got dressed, and I got ready to go to the Bobars', so as not to stay at home alone. I looked out the window one more time and . . . I SAW MOMMY RUNNING ACROSS THE BRIDGE. As she came into the house she started shaking and crying. Through her tears she told us how she had seen dismembered bodies. All the neighbors came because they had been afraid for her. Thank God, Mommy is with us. Thank God.
A HORRIBLE DAY. UNFORGETTABLE.
HORRIBLE! HORRIBLE!
Your Zlata

Saturday, May 30, 1992

Dear Mimmy,

The City Maternity Hospital has burned down. I was born there. Hundreds of thousands of new babies, new residents of Sarajevo, won't have the luck to be born in this maternity hospital now. It was new. The fire devoured everything. The mothers and babies were saved. When the fire broke out two women were giving birth. The babies are alive. God, people get killed here, they die here, they disappear, things go up in flames here, and out of the flames, new lives are born.

Your Zlata

Friday, June 5, 1992

Dear Mimmy,

There's been no electricity for quite some time and we keep thinking about the food in the freezer. There's not much left as it is. It would be a pity for all of it to go bad. There's meat and vegetables and fruit. How can we save it?

Daddy found an old wood-burning stove in the attic. It's so old it looks funny. In the cellar we found some wood, put the stove outside in the yard, lit it and are trying to save the food from the refrigerator. We cooked everything, and joining forces with the Bobars, enjoyed ourselves. There was veal and chicken, squid, cherry strudel, meat and potato pies. All sorts of things. It's a pity, though, that we had to eat everything so quickly. We even overate. WE HAD A MEAT STROKE.

We washed down our refrigerators and freezers. Who knows when we'll be able to cook like this again. Food is becoming a big problem in Sarajevo. There's nothing to buy, and even cigarettes and coffee are becoming a problem for grown-ups. The last reserves are being used up. God, are we going to go hungry to boot???

Zlata

Monday, June 29, 1992

Dear Mimmy,

BOREDOM!!! SHOOTING!!! SHELLING!!! PEOPLE BEING KILLED!!! DESPAIR!!! HUNGER!!! MISERY!!! FEAR!!!

That's my life! The life of an innocent eleven-year-old schoolgirl!! A schoolgirl without a school, without the fun and excitement of school. A child without games, without friends, without the sun, without birds, without nature, without fruit, without chocolate or sweets, with just a little powdered milk. In short, a child without a childhood. A wartime child. I now realize that I am really living through a war, I am witnessing an ugly, disgusting war. I and thousands of other children in this town that is being destroyed, that is crying, weeping, seeking help, but getting none. God, will this ever stop, will I ever be a schoolgirl again, will I ever enjoy my childhood again? I once heard that childhood is the most wonderful time of your life. And it is. I loved it, and now an ugly war is taking it all away from me. Why? I feel sad. I feel like crying. I am crying.

Your Zlata

■ Discussion Questions

1. How are children and their communities affected by war? How does war interfere with daily activities?

2. How does Zlata's tone shift from the earlier entries about the war approaching her city to the later sections describing the siege of Sarajevo?

3. How much do you think Zlata understood about what she calls the "politics" that caused the war?

4. What does Zlata's account reveal about the nature of warfare at the end of the twentieth century?

2.

African National Congress
Introductory Statement to the Truth and Reconciliation Commission
August 19, 1996

In 1995 Nelson Mandela, the first postapartheid president of South Africa, appointed the Truth and Reconciliation Commission (TRC) to help his country make the transition from an oppressive apartheid regime to a democratic multiracial state. The TRC was charged with establishing "as complete a picture as possible of the nature, causes, and extent of gross violations of human rights" committed in South Africa between 1960 and 1994. The commission spent two and a half years evaluating more than twenty-one thousand statements from apartheid victims and perpetrators, and subpoenaed hundreds more, to learn the full extent of the crimes that took place. The TRC's charge was to investigate the crimes in a way that would promote national unity and reconciliation rather than continued bitterness and hatred. The TRC offered amnesty from prosecution for perpetrators who testified about past crimes and provided restitution to victims. In this excerpt, the African National Congress (ANC), a political organization that had lobbied against apartheid since 1912, introduces its statement to the TRC by outlining the need for national reconciliation and the protection of human rights.

INTRODUCTION

As part of the process of the transformation of our country, the ANC had to consider its approach to the difficult but critically important question of what the new South Africa should do with those among our citizens who were involved in gross human rights violations during the struggle for our emancipation.

From African National Congress's Web site: www.anc.org.za/ancdocs/misc/trctoc.html.

The choices we had to make can be stated in a simple and straightforward manner.

We could have decided to hold our own Nuremberg Trials.

We could have decided that all that should be done should be to forgive everything that has happened in the past.

We, however reached the conclusion that neither of these would be the correct decision to take.

In considering the correctness or otherwise of this conclusion, the point needs to be borne in mind that we are in transition from an apartheid to a democratic society.

This is not a single event but a protracted process.

What this speaks to is an unjust cause on one side and a just cause on the other.

Inherent to the system of white minority domination, in this and all other countries where it occurred, was the philosophy and practice of the use of force to ensure the perpetuation of the system.

Force and violence by the dominant against the dominated, the contraposition of power to powerlessness, the attribution of mystical possibilities of retribution to the governors who can visit their wrath on the third and fourth generations of those who hate them, the suspension of all social norms, to enable the state and servants of the state to resort to the unbridled use of violence—all this, and more besides, sustains the continuity of colonial rule.

To maintain its internal integrity, coherence and rationale, this system could not but integrate in its world vision the concept of humans with a right to govern and sub-humans privileged to be governed.

Among other things, this paradigm allows those who enjoy the right to govern the ethical framework which permits them to use maximum force against any sub-human who would dare question his or her duty to accept the sacred obligation to respect the need to be governed.

The simultaneous and interdependent legitimization of the two inherently anti-human concepts of racial superiority and the colonial state as the concentrated expression of the unlimited right to the use of force, of necessity and according to the inherent logic of the system of apartheid, produced the gross violations of human rights by the apartheid state which are the subject of part of the work of the Truth and Reconciliation Commission.

It was as a result of the correct understanding of the nature of the system of apartheid that the United Nations characterized the system itself, and not merely its logical results, as a Crime Against Humanity.

With regard to the narrower context within which the TRC is considering this matter, the theoretical foundation of the enquiry would be the matter we have referred to, the legitimisation of the use of force in general but especially against those who would dare challenge the system.

This has two consequences.

One of these is the elevation of the state organs of repression above all other state structures, their exemption from all norms of common law consistent with limitations on the use of force, the conferring of powers on individuals to mete out violence as they deem fit and the consequent brutalization of such individuals so that the perpetration of violence becomes their second nature.

The second of these consequences is the demonising by the state of those it seeks to destroy and against whom therefore, it permits the maximum use of force. . . .

National Reconciliation

The most important issue in this regard is that the grief of particular individuals, important as it is to the affected individuals and the nation, is relevant also to the extent that it contributes to the achievement of the larger goal of national reconciliation.

National reconciliation will only have meaning if it addresses the historic conflict in our country between black and white.

Through centuries of this conflict, the names of the players have changed continuously, regardless of their color and the causes they served.

What never changed was the character of the conflict, which was between the white colonizing forces and a black liberation movement, based on a social system which elevated the white at the expense of the black.

National reconciliation has to be between black and white.

Without transformation to end the disparities of privilege and deprivation which are the legacy we have inherited from our colonial and apartheid past, but which continue to define the present, national reconciliation is impossible.

Whichever way the TRC interprets its mandate, it cannot avoid the conclusion that the ghost that needs to be laid to rest is — the ending of the domination of the black by the white, in all spheres of social existence.

If our society does not achieve this, racial conflict will continue. The goal of national reconciliation will not be achieved.

Clearly, this objective cannot be achieved by the TRC alone.

It also emphasises the obligation that rests on the Commission to make its own recommendations as to what the larger and varied society from which it is drawn might do, to contribute to the realisation of the goal of national reconciliation.

Protection from Gross Violations of Human Rights

Systematic violations of human rights are a manifestation of a social system, rather than the exceptional faults of particular individuals.

To ensure that our country and people are never again exposed to such systematic violations of human rights as occurred under apartheid, it is necessary that we construct a constitutional, political and socioeconomic order which inherently protects human rights, and has the means to defend itself against any tendency to limit or violate those rights.

The mandate for the construction of such a system of course rests with bodies other than the TRC. As a movement, we are convinced that these institutions are carrying out their mandate.

But we also believe that the TRC has an important role to play in helping to ensure that the specialized institutions established by the apartheid regime to carry out a campaign of repression are completely dismantled.

We refer here not to normal state organs, such as the police, the Defense Force and the intelligence services, but to other clandestine structures established under the National Security Management System, some of which continue to operate as part of the "third force."

The exposure and destruction of these structures is important to ensure that they are stopped from actually or potentially engaging in any acts of destabilization.

This is particularly important in light of the fact that persons who belong to these structures have been trained and motivated as anti-democratic operatives and, in many instances, will not have changed their ideological colors.

It is also important that the nation as a whole should be familiar with this machinery as part of the process of raising the level of national vigilance so that it is difficult for any government in [the] future to create similar structures for use against the people of our country. . . .

CONCLUSION

The ANC is committed to doing everything in its power to help the TRC and the nation to know as much as is possible about the events of the period the TRC is mandated to investigate.

We believe that the TRC should conclude its work as quickly as possible so that we do indeed let bygones be bygones and allow the nation to forgive a past it nevertheless dare not forget.

■ Discussion Questions

1. What do you make of the ANC's emphasis on institutions and ethics rather than individuals? Why do you suppose the ANC concerned itself mainly with these larger structures?

2. What was the ANC's main objective in making this statement to the TRC? What did they hope to achieve through the TRC?

3. What is the advantage in the TRC's granting amnesty to those who agree to tell everything they know about crimes that they or people they knew committed under apartheid? What is the disadvantage of granting amnesty to these persons?

4. At the beginning of this document, the ANC mentions that South Africans could have used a Nuremberg Trial–style system to uncover the truth about crimes committed under apartheid. Why do you think they opted for the TRC-style of investigation, which focused on reconciliation instead of punishment?

3.
Leif Zetterling
Klasskamrater *(Classmates)* Cartoon
January 22, 2001

At the turn of the twenty-first century, when the European Union was gaining strength as a supranational entity that united much of the European continent, it also faced the challenge of amalgamating many diverse countries, cultures, and political traditions into a viable, united body. Although the use of a common currency had been anticipated in 1992 when the European Union decided to adopt the economic and monetary union, enthusiasm for the euro flagged in some member states as the 2002 deadline for its adoption approached. Other thorny debates ensued whenever the question of enlarging the European Union arose, or when smaller member states sensed that their voices were being drowned out by those of the larger, more dominant members. In this political cartoon, Swedish illustrator Leif Zetterling depicts the European Union as a classroom and its national leaders as children. A description of the classmates follows on page 239.

From Leif Zetterling. Courtesy of Leif Zetterling; From Daryl Cagle's Professional Cartoonist Index, http://cagle.slate.msn.com.

The "classmates," from left to right, are Giuliano Amato, prime minister of Italy; Paavo Lipponen, prime minister of Finland (on the floor); Jean-Claude Juncker, prime minister of Luxembourg (balancing something on his nose); Wim Kok, prime minister of the Netherlands (on the floor in striped trousers); Göran Persson, prime minister of Sweden (the largest figure, sitting on the teacher's desk); Gerhard Schröder, chancellor of Germany (holding airplane); José Maria Aznar, prime minister of Spain (in track suit); Poul Nyrup Rasmussen, prime minister of Denmark (holding paper airplane); Jacques Chirac, president of France (with wine glass); Bertie Ahern, prime minister of Ireland (behind Chirac, also with wine glass); Anna Lindh, Swedish minister of foreign affairs (at the chalkboard). (During the Swedish presidency of the European Union, when this cartoon was drawn, Lindh was the chairman for the Council of the European Union. A vocal advocate for Sweden's adoption of the euro, she was brutally assassinated on September 10, 2003, a few days before the Swedes were to vote on the euro.) The rest are Guy Verhofstadt, prime minister of Belgium (in front row with hand raised); Antonio Guterres, prime minister of Portugal; Tony Blair, prime minister of the United Kingdom (holding a baby); and Romano Prodi, former prime minister of Italy, now President of the European Commission (in the doorway).

At the left, the countries excluded from the "classroom," from left to right, are Romania or Turkey—both are applicants to the EU but not yet members (flag is partially obscured and therefore hard to identify); Estonia (became a member 2004); Malta (became a member 2004); and Bulgaria, Slovenia, or Slovakia (difficult to tell which it is in this illustration). Bulgaria has applied for EU membership but has not been accepted as a member; Slovenia and Slovakia became member states in 2004.

■ Discussion Questions

1. What does this cartoon tell you about Leif Zetterling's opinion of the European Union and its leaders?

2. Why do you suppose Zetterling chose to use a classroom setting? What meaning does the setting add to the illustration?

3. Of the ideals listed on the classroom's chalkboard, why do you suppose "Equality" and "Euro" are crossed out? Why were the other words left untouched?

4. What is the advantage of studying a period of time through its political cartoons? What are the challenges a historian faces when trying to understand a cartoon created in a different time period than his or her own?

4.
Petra Kelly
Fighting for Hope
1983

Shifts in the global political map in the 1980s and 1990s went hand in hand with a growing awareness that the health of the earth and its peoples needed to be considered as well. Founded in Western Germany in 1979, the Green Party helped to galvanize environmental activism across Europe due in no small part to Petra Kelly (1947–1992), one of its most influential and outspoken advocates. Kelly was a typical transnational; she had been born in Germany but received some of her childhood education in the United States. When her younger sister died of cancer in 1970, Kelly became an environmentalist and an active member in the German Green Party. Kelly, like many Greens, came to believe that environmentalism involved more than simply eliminating carcinogens in the air. The movement needed to advocate a new lifestyle in general and new forms of political participation. In the excerpt below from her personal memoir, Fighting for Hope, *first published in German in 1983 and in English the following year, Kelly outlines the goals of the Green Party.*

... From very early in our history, there has been radical opposition to the conventions of violence, striving for a profoundly human society, based on solidarity and the renunciation of power. Jesus of Nazareth, Martin Luther King, Cesar Chavez and Mahatma Gandhi are examples of this vision. Non-violence in the Green party represents the same attempt to unite means and ends. For us, the ends do not justify the means. You cannot do away with violence by using violence, or war by waging war, or injustice by resorting to injustice. It follows, then, that the ends are a part of the method of action, and likewise that the method of action is included in the ends....

The Green party must remain a movement for non-violent change, and, at the same time, it must use parliament to make the case for non-violence to the electorate. One of the most important tasks for a parliamentary, extra-parliamentary party is to campaign for the recognition and protection of human rights. Food, health care, work, housing, freedom of religion and belief, freedom of assembly, freedom of expression, humane treatment of prisoners—all these human rights have been formally recognized by the member states of the United Nations, and all of them continue to be abused. These rights derive from a human being's right to life. Abuse of human rights can lead to the outbreak of war. Respect for human rights can help to build peace.

The Greens demand the unconditional abolition of all weapons of mass destruction. This demand is addressed to everybody, immediately and without ex-

---

From Petra Kelly, *Fighting for Hope* (Boston: South End Press, 1984), 19–21. English translation from original text (German, 1983).

ception, regardless of whether or when others make the same move. The destruction of mankind is the most heinous crime against humanity imaginable. There can be no justification for it or for any action which might cause such destruction.

The Greens seek a new life-style for the Western world, as well as in their own personal lives. They would like to see an alternative way of life without exploitation, and they aim for non-violent relationships with others and with themselves. The reaction of the public and politicians to the points contained in the Greens' extra-parliamentary program comes as no surprise. The right preys upon a growing fear of conflict, as the old order is on the verge of collapse. And the left, so fixated on macro-structures, has simply failed to recognize how politics has spilled over into the "private" sphere. An urgent need has arisen, not for material things, but for new relationships between the sexes and between the generations, as well as within them, relationships free from fear and based on mutual support. We should muster some solidarity, some friendship, in the face of our throw-away life-style. More important than material goods, is enhancing the quality of life and living in harmony with the need for the preservation of nature and cyclical renewal. This is one of the most important objectives that the Greens are working for in the new political culture.

However, there can be no future for the Greens if they go in for gaining power in the same way as the established parties. The Greens are ready to work with others if the demand that parliament should speak the language of the people is finally met. So far, parliaments have acted simply as the executive body of the bureaucracy in the ministries, especially where important proposals such as airports or nuclear power stations are concerned. The Greens take a different view of parliament. We believe that parliament must represent the interests of the people, including minorities.

Parliaments have proved themselves incapable of responding to the demands of local action groups. The Greens believe that part of the work of parliament is to conduct hearings and committees of enquiry in public and to make them open to everyone. We aim to democratize parliament as much as possible putting the issues, and the costs of solving them, squarely before the public. We must set ourselves uncompromising programmatic objectives in order to stimulate debate and discussion inside and outside parliament. A place in parliament, together with the success of a non-violent opposition movement on the streets, should, we hope, put us in a position to shake people out of their apathy and quiescence.

We are, and I hope we will remain, half party and half local action group—we shall go on being an anti-party party. The learning process that takes place on the streets, on construction sites, at nuclear bases, must be carried into parliament. . . .

■ Discussion Questions

1. According to Kelly, what principles and goals does the Green Party advocate and why?
2. What does Kelly mean when she describes the Greens as "a parliamentary, extra-parliamentary party," and why is this important to understanding their political strategy?

3. Based on this excerpt, why do you think Kelly entitled her book *Fighting for Hope?* What message does the title convey about environmental activism in general and the Green Party in particular?

5.
Amartya Sen
A World Not Neatly Divided
November 23, 2001

Following the September 11, 2001, terrorist attacks on the United States, some academics, politicians, and journalists framed the event as a "clash of civilizations" between Western democracy and radical Islam. They predicted that this clash would launch a new phase in world politics that would be dominated by cultural conflict. Others anticipated that this conflict would replace the cold war as the framework for international relations and domestic politics. In this New York Times *editorial published shortly after the United States attacked Taliban targets in Afghanistan, Nobel Prize–winning economist Amartya Sen warned that segmenting people into separate camps, such as the "Islamic world" and the "Western world," is a simplistic—and potentially dangerous—view that ignores the diversity of the world's people.*

When people talk about clashing civilizations, as so many politicians and academics do now, they can sometimes miss the central issue. The inadequacy of this thesis begins well before we get to the question of whether civilizations must clash. The basic weakness of the theory lies in its program of categorizing people of the world according to a unique, allegedly commanding system of classification. This is problematic because civilizational categories are crude and inconsistent and also because there are other ways of seeing people (linked to politics, language, literature, class, occupation, or other affiliations).

The befuddling influence of a singular classification also traps those who dispute the thesis of a clash: To talk about "the Islamic world" or "the Western world" is already to adopt an impoverished vision of humanity as unalterably divided. In fact, civilizations are hard to partition in this way, given the diversities within each society as well as the linkages among different countries and cultures. For example, describing India as a "Hindu civilization" misses the fact that India has more Muslims than any other country except Indonesia and possibly Pakistan. It is futile to try to understand Indian art, literature, music, food, or politics without seeing the extensive interactions across barriers of religious communities. These include Hindus and Muslims, Buddhists, Jains, Sikhs, Parsees, Christians (who have been in India since at least the fourth century, well before England's conversion to

From Amartya Sen, "A World Not Neatly Divided," *New York Times* editorial, November 23, 2001, A39.

Christianity), Jews (present since the fall of Jerusalem), and even atheists and agnostics. Sanskrit has a larger atheistic literature than exists in any other classical language. Speaking of India as a Hindu civilization may be comforting to the Hindu fundamentalist, but it is an odd reading of India.

A similar coarseness can be seen in the other categories invoked, like "the Islamic world." Consider Akbar and Aurangzeb, two Muslim emperors of the Mogul dynasty in India. Aurangzeb tried hard to convert Hindus into Muslims and instituted various policies in that direction, of which taxing the non-Muslims was only one example. In contrast, Akbar reveled in his multiethnic court and pluralist laws, and issued official proclamations insisting that no one "should be interfered with on account of religion" and that "anyone is to be allowed to go over to a religion that pleases him."

If a homogeneous view of Islam were to be taken, then only one of these emperors could count as a true Muslim. The Islamic fundamentalist would have no time for Akbar; prime minister Tony Blair, given his insistence that tolerance is a defining characteristic of Islam, would have to consider excommunicating Aurangzeb. I expect both Akbar and Aurangzeb would protest, and so would I. A similar crudity is present in the characterization of what is called "Western civilization." Tolerance and individual freedom have certainly been present in European history. But there is no dearth of diversity here, either. When Akbar was making his pronouncements on religious tolerance in Agra, in the 1590s, the Inquisitions were still going on; in 1600, Giordano Bruno was burned at the stake, for heresy, in Campo dei Fiori in Rome.

Dividing the world into discrete civilizations is not just crude. It propels us into the absurd belief that this partitioning is natural and necessary and must overwhelm all other ways of identifying people. That imperious view goes not only against the sentiment that "we human beings are all much the same," but also against the more plausible understanding that we are diversely different. For example, Bangladesh's split from Pakistan was not connected with religion, but with language and politics.

Each of us has many features in our self-conception. Our religion, important as it may be, cannot be an all-engulfing identity. Even a shared poverty can be a source of solidarity across the borders. The kind of division highlighted by, say, the so-called "antiglobalization" protesters—whose movement is, incidentally, one of the most globalized in the world—tries to unite the underdogs of the world economy and goes firmly against religious, national, or "civilizational" lines of division.

The main hope of harmony lies not in any imagined uniformity, but in the plurality of our identities, which cut across each other and work against sharp divisions into impenetrable civilizational camps. Political leaders who think and act in terms of sectioning off humanity into various "worlds" stand to make the world more flammable—even when their intentions are very different. They also end up, in the case of civilizations defined by religion, lending authority to religious leaders seen as spokesmen for their "worlds." In the process, other voices are muffled and other concerns silenced. The robbing of our plural identities not only reduces us; it impoverishes the world.

■ Discussion Questions

1. Why does Sen object to dividing the world into separate civilizations? What problems does such classification present?

2. What does Sen mean by our "plural identities"?

3. What are the particular dangers of defining separate worlds according to religion?

4. What present-day examples might support Sen's concern about defining civilizations solely along religious lines?

■ Comparative Questions

1. How is Zlata Filipović's experience in a country torn apart by ethnic and religious conflict reflected in Amartya Sen's warning against dividing the world into discrete civilizations?

2. What are the similarities between the end of communism in eastern Europe (Chapter 23) and the end of apartheid in South Africa? What are the differences?

3. Do you see any common ground between Gorbachev's efforts to reshape the Soviet Union, and the European Union's efforts to redefine Europe's role in the twenty-first century?

4. Compare Amartya Sen's vision of finding harmony in the "plurality of our identities" to the Truth and Reconciliation Commission's goals for attaining national unity and reconciliation in South Africa.

5. In what ways does Petra Kelly's memoir offer a response to the realities of late twentieth-century warfare as described by Zlata Filipović?

Acknowledgments (continued)

Chapter 11

The Black Death (Fourteenth Century). From *The Black Death* edited and translated by Rosemary Horrox. Copyright © 1994 by Rosemary Harrox. Reprinted with the permission of Manchester University Press.

Thomas Walsingham. *Peasant Rebels in London* (1381). From *The Peasants' Revolt of 1381*, 2nd edition, R. B. Dobson. Published by Macmillan Press (1983). Courtesy of the publisher.

Giovanni Pico della Mirandola. *Oration on the Dignity of Man* (1496). From *The Italian Renaissance Reader* edited by Julia Conaway Bondanella and Mark Musa. Copyright © 1987 by Julia Conaway Bondanella and Mark Musa. Used by permission of Dutton Signet, a division of Penguin Group (USA) Inc.

Bernardino of Siena. *An Italian Preacher: Sins against Nature* (1380–1444). From *The Preacher's Demons: Bernardino of Siena and the Social Underworld of Early Renaissance Italy* by Franco Mormando. Copyright © 1986. Reprinted by permission of the University of Chicago Press.

Gomes Eanes de Zurara. *Chronicle of the Discovery of Guinea* (c. 1453). From *A Source Book in Geography* edited by George Kish. Copyright © 1978. Reprinted with permission of the University of Harvard Press. Originally published by the Hakluyt Society, #95, 1896, translated by C. R. Beazley and Edgar Prestage.

Chapter 12

Martin Luther. *Freedom of a Christian* (1520). From *Christian Liberty*, edited by Harold J. Grimm. Copyright © 1957 by Harold J. Grimm. Reprinted by permission of Fortress Press.

Saint Ignatius of Loyola. *A New Kind of Catholicism* (1546, 1549, 1553). From *St. Ignatius of Loyola, Personal Writing: Reminiscences, Spiritual Diary, Select Letters, Including the Text of the Spiritual Exercises*. Translated and edited by Joseph A. Munitiz and Philip Endean. Copyright © 1996 Joseph A. Munitiz and Philip Endean. Used by permission of Penguin Books (UK).

Hans Jacob Christoffel von Grimmelshausen. *The Adventures of a Simpleton* (1668–1669). From *The Adventures of a Simplicius Simplicissimus*, translated by George Schulz-Behrend. Published by Camden House (1991). Courtesy of the publisher.

Henry IV. *Edict of Nantes* (1598). From *The Great Pressures and Grievances of the Protestants in Prison*. Edited by Edmund Everand. Reprinted by permission of Faber & Faber, Ltd.

Galileo. *Letter to the Grand Duchess Christina* (1615). From *Discoveries and Opinions of Galileo*, translated by Stillman Drake. Copyright © 1957 by Stillman Drake. Used by permission of Doubleday, a division of Random House, Inc.

The Trial of Suzanne Gaudry (1652). From *Witchcraft in Europe 1100–1700: A Documentary History*, edited by Alan C. Kors and Edward Peters. Copyright © 1972. Reprinted by permission of the University of Pennsylvania Press.

Chapter 13

Madame de Lafayette. *The Princess of Clèves* (1678). From *The Princess of Cleves NCE*, edited by John D. Lyons. Copyright © 1994 by W. W. Norton and Company, Inc. Used by permission of W. W. Norton & Company, Inc.

Chapter 14

Olaudah Equiano. *The Interesting Narrative of the Life of Olaudah Equiano Written by Himself* (1789). From *Equiqno's Travels: His Autobiography*, abridged. Published by Heinemann, 1967. Courtesy of the publisher.

Tsar Peter I. *Letter to His Son, Alexei* (October 22, 1715); and *Alexei's Response* (October 31, 1715). From *Sourcebook of Russian History* by Vermadsky. Copyright © 1972. Reprinted by permission of Yale University Press.

Mary Astell. *Reflections upon Marriage* (1706). From *The First English Feminist: Reflections upon Marriage and Other Writings by Mary Astell* edited by Bridget Hill. Reprinted by permission of the author.

Pietist Spiritual Songbook (1705). From *Pietists: Selected Writings* edited by Peter C. Erb. Copyright © 1983 Paulist Press, Inc. Reprinted by permission of Paulist Press. www.paulistpress.com.

Chapter 15

Marie-Therese Geoffrin and M. d'Alembert. *The Salon of Madame Geoffrin* (1765). From *Historical and Literary Memoirs and Anecdotes,* translated by Robert Bland and Anne Plumptre, 2e. Reprinted in *Western Societies: A Documentary History* edited by Brian Tierney and Joan Scott. McGraw Hill, 1984. Reprinted by permission of the publisher.

Jacques-Louis Menetra. Excerpt from *Journal of My Life* (1764–1802) by Jacques Menetta. Translation copyright © 1986 by Columbia University Press. Reprinted with the permission of the publisher.

Frederick II. *Political Testament* (1752).Excerpted from "The Rise of Prussia" in *Europe in Review,* edited by George Lachmann Mosse, Rondo E. Cameron, Henry Bertram Hill and Michael B. Petrovich. Published by Rand McNally & Company. Copyright © 1957. Reprinted by permission.

Chapter 16

Abbe Sieyes. *What is the Third Estate?* (1789). From *The French Revolution and Human Rights: A Brief Documentary History* translated and edited by Lynn Hunt. Bedford/St. Martin's 1996. Reprinted by permission of the author.

Olympe de Gouges. *Letters on the Trial* (1793). From *Women in Revolutionary Paris 1789–1795: Selected Documents Translated with Notes and Commentary* translated and edited by Darline Gay Levy, Harriet Branson Applewhite, Mary Durham Johnson. Copyright © 1979 by the Board of Trustees of the University of Illinois. Used with permission of the editors and the University of Illinois Press.

Abd al-Rahman al-Jabarti. *Napoleon in Egypt* (1798). From *Napoleon in Egypt: Al-Jabarti's Chronicle of the French Occupation 1798,* translated by Shmuel Moreh. Copyright © 1993 by Shmuel Moreh. Reprinted by permission of E.J. Brill Publishers, The Netherlands.

Napoleon Bonaparte. *Instructions and Letters* (1805–1809). From *The Mind of Napoleon: A Selection from His Written and Spoken Words,* edited and translated by J. Christopher Herold. Published by Columbia University Press, 1955. Reprinted by permission.

Chapter 17

Factory Rules in Berlin (1844). From *Documents of European Economic History,* Volume 1: *The Process of Industrialization 1750–1870* by Sidney Pollard and C. Holmes. Copyright © by St. Martin's Press, Inc. Reprinted by permission of the publisher.

Frederick Engels. *Draft of a Communist Confession of Faith* (1847). From *Collected Works,* vol. 6, 96–103, by Karl Marx and Frederick Engels. Copyright © 1975 International Publishers, Inc. Reprinted by permission of the publisher.

Sándor Petofi. *"National Song"* of Hungary (1848). From *The World's Story, A History of the World in Story, Song, and Art,* Volume VI: *Art, Russia, Austria-Hungary, The Balkan States and Turkey,* edited by Eva March Tappan. Published by Houghton Mifflin, 1914. Reprinted courtesy of the publisher.

Chapter 18

Rudopf von Ihering. *Two Letters* (1866). From *Germany in the Age of Bismark* by Walter Michael Simon. Allen and Unwin, 1968. Reprinted with permission of Taylor & Francis.

Krupa Sattianadan. *Saguna: A Story of a Native Christian Life* (1887–1888). Originally published in *Madras Christian Magazine* (1887, 1888). Later reprinted in *Women Writing in India: 600 B.C. to the Present, Vol. 1,* edited by Susue Tharu and K. Lalita. The Feminist Press, 1991. Courtesy of the publisher.

Edgar Degas. *Notebooks* (1863–1884). From *Impressionism and Post-Impressionism 1874–1904* edited by Linda Nochlin. Copyright © 1966 by Prentice-Hall, Inc. Reprinted by permission of the publisher. All rights reserved.

Chapter 19

Jules Ferry. *Speech before the French National Assembly* (1883). From *Modern Imperialism, Western Overseas Expansion and Its Aftermath 1776–1965,* edited with an introduction by Ralph A. Austen. Copyright © D.C. Heath and Company, 1969. Reprinted with permission by Houghton Mifflin Company.

Sigmund Freud. *Infantile Sexuality* (1905). From *Three Essays on the Theory of Sexuality* by Sigmund Freud. Copyright 1962 by Sigmund Freud Copyrights, Ltd. Reprinted by permission of Basic Books, a member of Perseus Books, LLC.

Chapter 20

Fritz Franke and Siegfried Sassoon. *Two Soldiers' Views of the Horrors of War* (1914–1918). From *A German Student's War Letters,* translated and arranged from the original edition of Dr. Philipp Witkop by A. F. Wedd. Originally published by E. P. Dutton and Company, Inc. (1929).

"Counter Attack." From *Collected Poems* by Siegfried Sassoon. Copyright © 1919, 1920 by E. P. Dutton. Copyright © 1936, 1946, 1947, 1948 by Siegfried Sassoon. Used by permission of Viking Penguin, a division of Penguin Putnam, Inc. By kind permission of George Sassoon.

L. Doriat. *Women on the Home Front* (1917). From *Lines of Fire: Women Writers of World War I* edited by Margaret R. Higonnet. Copyright © 1999 by Margaret R. Higonnet. Used by permission of Plume, a division of Penguin Group (USA) Inc.

Vladimir Ilych Lenin. *Letter to Nikolai Aleksandrovich Rozhkov* (January 29, 1919). From *The Unknown Lenin: From the Secret Archive,* edited and with a new afterward by Richard Pipes. Basic translation of Russian documents by Catherine A. Fitzpatrick. Copyright © 1996 by Richard Pipes. Reprinted by permission of Yale University Press.

Benito Mussolini. *The Doctrine of Fascism* (1932). From *The Social and Political Doctrines of Contemporary Europe* edited and translated by Michael Oakeshott. Copyright © 1939, 1947 by Cambridge University Press. Reprinted with the permission of Cambridge University Press.

Adolf Hitler. *Mein Kampf* (1925). From *Mein Kampf,* translated by Ralph Manheim. Copyright © 1971, 1999. Reprinted by permission of Houghton Mifflin Company All rights reserved.

Chapter 21

Joseph Goebbels. *Nazi Propaganda Pamphlet* (1930). From *Documents of German History* by Louis L. Snyder, Editor. Copyright © 1958 Rutgers University Press. Reprinted with permission of Rutgers University Press.

Isidora Dolores Ibárruru Gómez. *La Pasionaira's Farewell Address* (November 1, 1938). From Dept of English, University of Illinois at Urbana-Champaign. Courtesy of the University of Illinois English Dept.

Sam Bankhalter and Hinda Kibort. *Memories of the Holocaust* (1938–1945). Excerpts from pp. 5–8, 50–55 in *Witnesses to the Holocaust: An Oral History* edited by Rhoda G. Lewin. Excerpts by Sam Bankhalter and Hinda Kibort. Copyright © 1980 by the Jewish Community Relations Council and Anti-Defamation League of Minnesota and the Dakotas. Twayne Publishers. Reprinted by permission of The Gale Group.

Chapter 22

Ho Chi Minh. *Declaration of Independence of the Republic of Vietnam* (1945). From *Conflict in Indo-China and International Repercussions: A Documentary History, 1945–1955*, edited by Allan B. Cole, Prof. of Far Eastern Affairs. Published under the auspices of The Fletcher School of Law and Diplomacy, Tufts University, and the Southeast Asia Program, Cornell University. Courtesy of the publisher.

Simone de Beauvoir. *The Second Sex* (1949). From *The Second Sex* by Simone De Beauvoir, translated by H. M. Parshley. Copyright © 1952 and renewed 1980 by Alfred A. Knopf, a division of Random House, Inc. Used by permission of Alfred A. Knopf, a division of Random House, Inc.

Bela Lipták. *Birth of MEFESZ* (1956). From *A Testament of Revolution* by Bela Liptak. Copyright © 2001 by Bela Liptak. Used by kind permission of Linda Salitros, Texas A & M University Press. All rights reserved.

Chapter 23

Joseph Smrkovský. *What Lies Ahead* (February 9, 1968). From *The Prague Spring 1968: A National Security Archive Document Reader,* edited by Jaromir Navratil. Courtesy of the Central European Press.

Student Voices of Protest (1968). From *Taken' It to the Streets: A Sixties Reader,* edited by Alexander Bloom and W. Breines. Copyright © 1995 by Alexander Bloom and Winifred Brienes. Used by permission of Oxford University Press. Original excerpt published in *1969: A Student Generation in Revolt* by Ronald Fraser et al. Pantheon Books, 1988. Reprinted by permission.

Nick Ut. *Children Fleeing from a Napalm Attack in South Vietnam* (June 8, 1972). Courtesy Wide World Photos.

Glasnost and the Soviet Press (1988). From *Gorbachev and Glasnost: Viewpoints from the Soviet Press,* edited by Isaac J. Tarasulo. Copyright © 1989 by Scholarly Resources Inc. Reproduced with permission of Scholarly Resources Inc. in the format Textbook via Copyright Clearance Center.

Chaper 24

Zlata Filipović. *A Child's Life in Sarajevo* (October 6, 1991–June 29, 1992). From *Zlata's Diary* by Zlata Filipovic. Copyright © 1994 Editions Robert Laffont/Fixot. Used by permission of Viking Penguin, a division of Penguin Group (USA) Inc.

Lief Zetterling. Klassskamrater (Classmates) *Cartoon* (January 22, 2001). © Universal Press Syndicate. Reprinted by permission.

Petra Kelly. *Fighting for Hope* (1983). With Introduction by Heinrich Boll and translation by Marianne Howarth. Copyright © Lamuv Verlag GmbH Martinstrasse 7, 5303 Bornheim-Merten, and Petra Kelly, 1983. Translation copyright © 1984 by Marianne Howarth. Chatto & Windus, The Hogarth Press, 1984. South End Press, 1984. Reprinted with permission of the publisher. All rights reserved.